The BakerStreet Four, Vol. 1

Written by **J. B. DJIAN** and **OLIVIER LEGRAND**

Art by **DAVID ETIEN**

INSIGHT COMICS

San Rafael, California

The Blue Curtain

"It is the unofficial force,
the Baker Street Irregulars."
— Sherlock Holmes

ARTHUR CONAN DOYLE,
The Sign of the Four

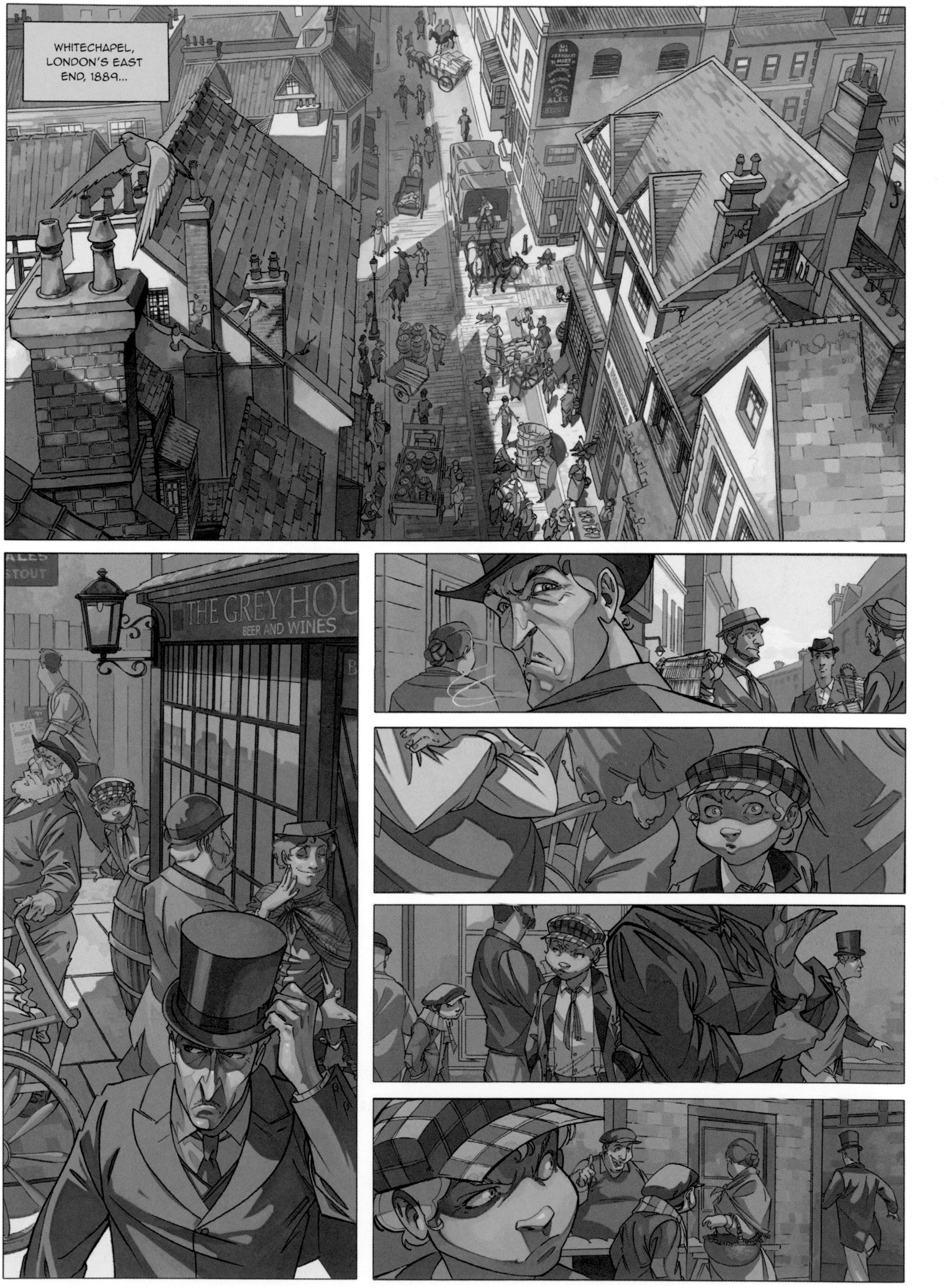
WHITECHAPEL, LONDON'S EAST END, 1889...
ALES
STOUT
THE GREY HOU
BEER AND WINES

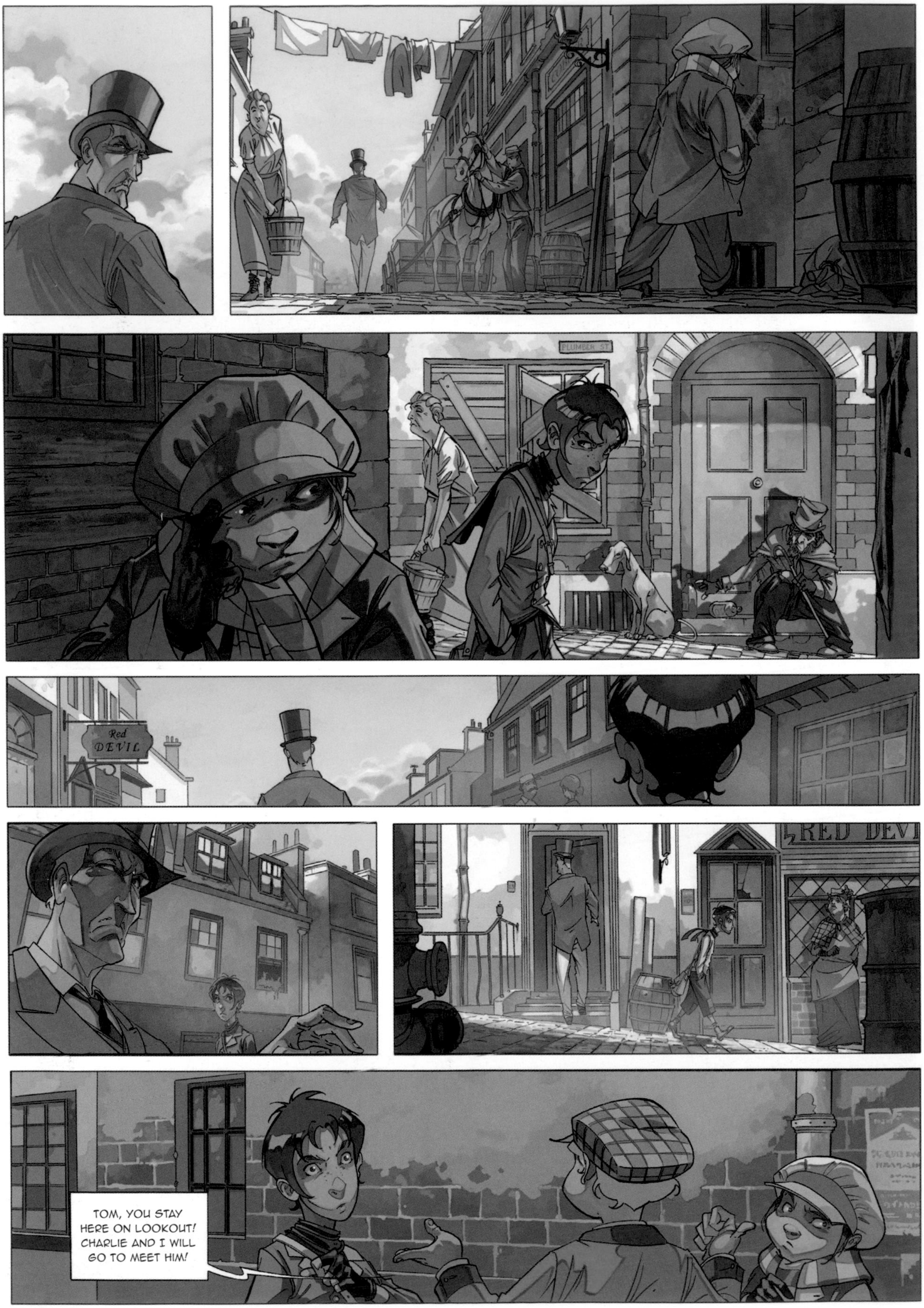
PLUMBER ST
Red DEVIL
TOM, YOU STAY HERE ON LOOKOUT! CHARLIE AND I WILL GO TO MEET HIM!

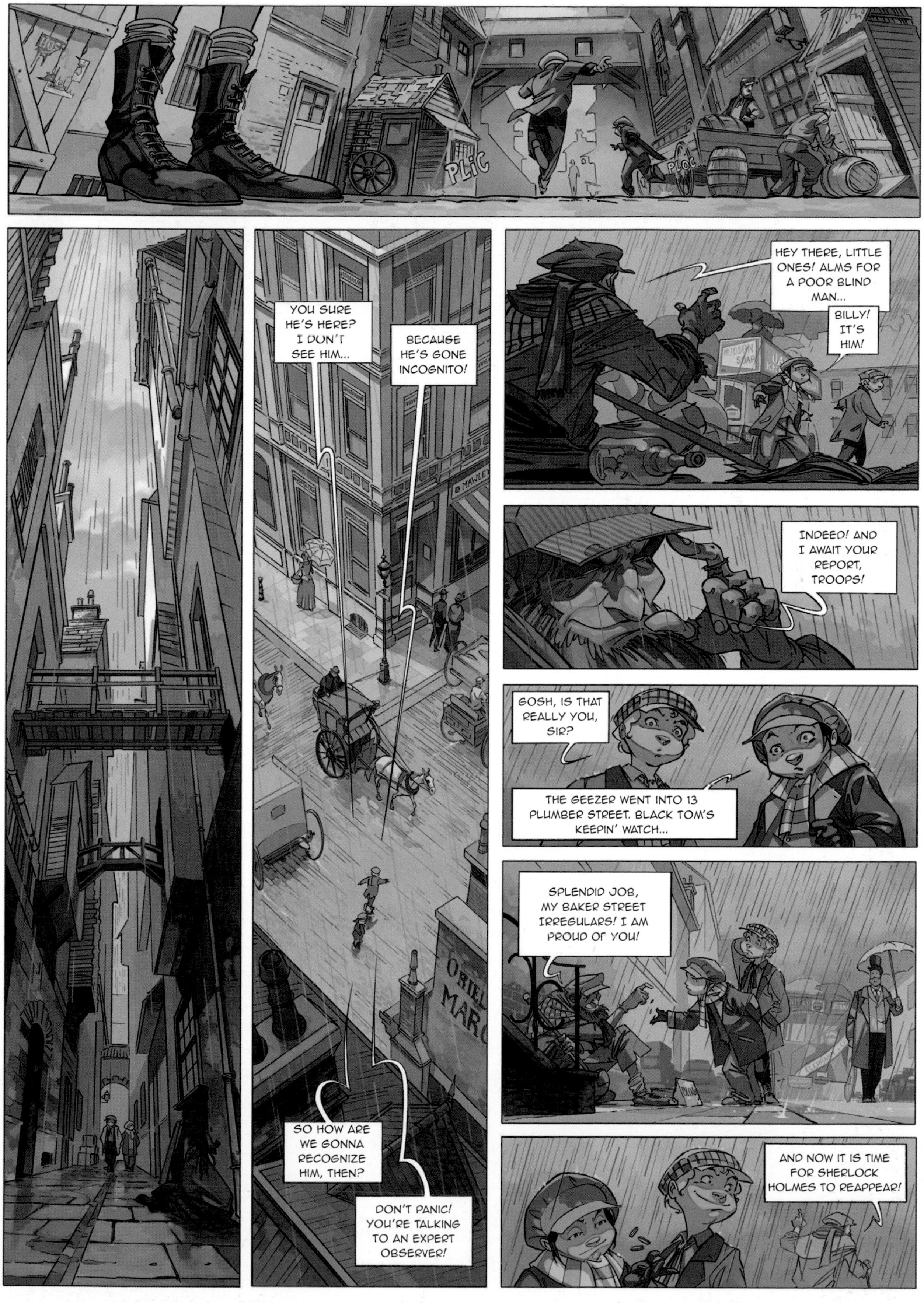
PLIC
PLOC
YOU SURE HE'S HERE? I DON'T SEE HIM...
BECAUSE HE'S GONE INCOGNITO!
SO HOW ARE WE GONNA RECOGNIZE HIM, THEN?
DON'T PANIC! YOU'RE TALKING TO AN EXPERT OBSERVER!
HEY THERE, LITTLE ONES! ALMS FOR A POOR BLIND MAN...
BILLY! IT'S HIM!
INDEED! AND I AWAIT YOUR REPORT, TROOPS!
GOSH, IS THAT REALLY YOU, SIR?
THE GEEZER WENT INTO 13 PLUMBER STREET. BLACK TOM'S KEEPIN' WATCH...
SPLENDID JOB, MY BAKER STREET IRREGULARS! I AM PROUD OF YOU!
AND NOW IT IS TIME FOR SHERLOCK HOLMES TO REAPPEAR!

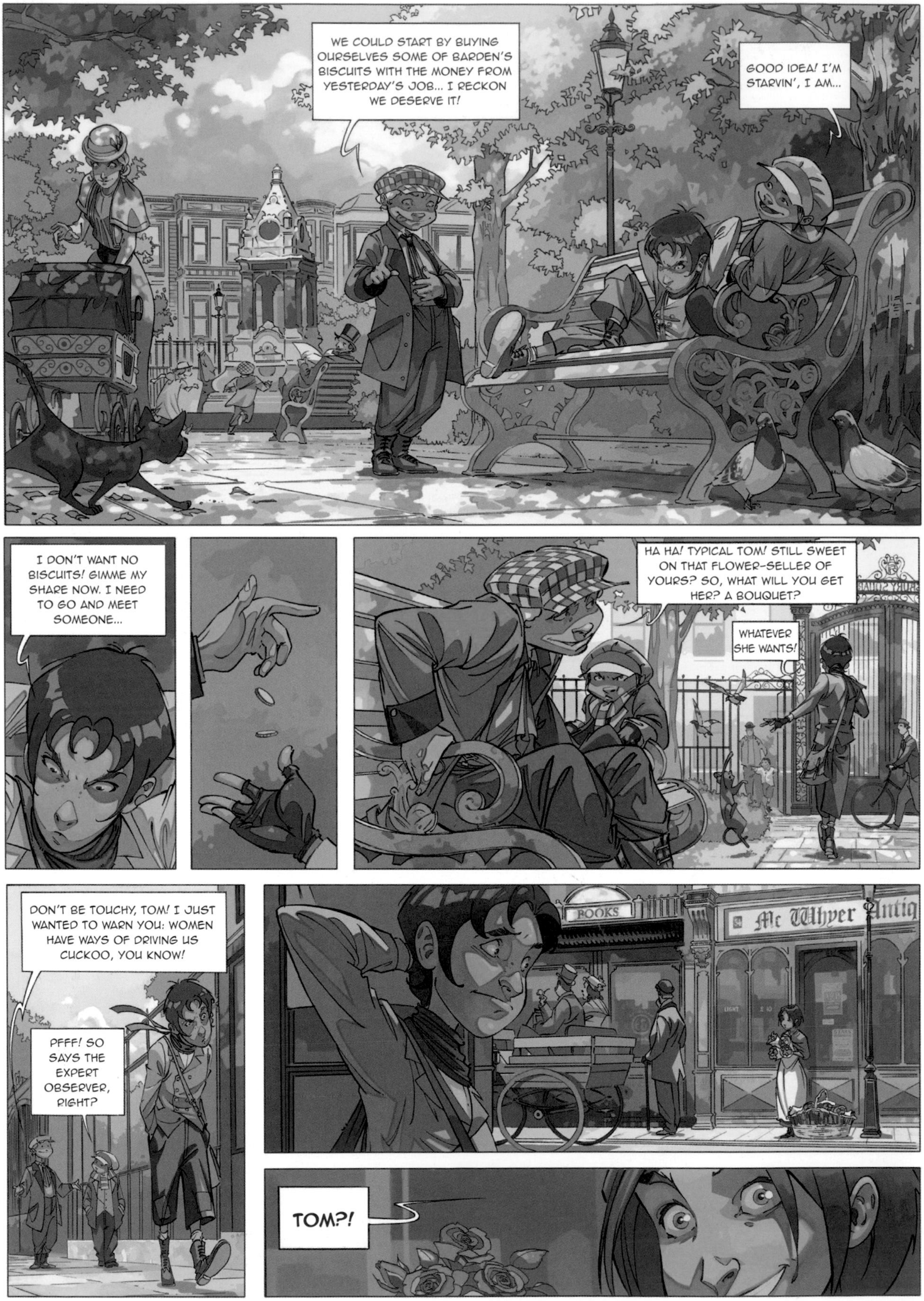
WE COULD START BY BUYING OURSELVES SOME OF BARDEN'S BISCUITS WITH THE MONEY FROM YESTERDAY'S JOB... I RECKON WE DESERVE IT!
GOOD IDEA! I'M STARVIN', I AM...
I DON'T WANT NO BISCUITS! GIMME MY SHARE NOW. I NEED TO GO AND MEET SOMEONE...
HA HA! TYPICAL TOM! STILL SWEET ON THAT FLOWER-SELLER OF YOURS? SO, WHAT WILL YOU GET HER? A BOUQUET?
WHATEVER SHE WANTS!
DON'T BE TOUCHY, TOM! I JUST WANTED TO WARN YOU: WOMEN HAVE WAYS OF DRIVING US CUCKOO, YOU KNOW!
PFFF! SO SAYS THE EXPERT OBSERVER, RIGHT?
BOOKS
Mc Whyer Antiq
TOM?!

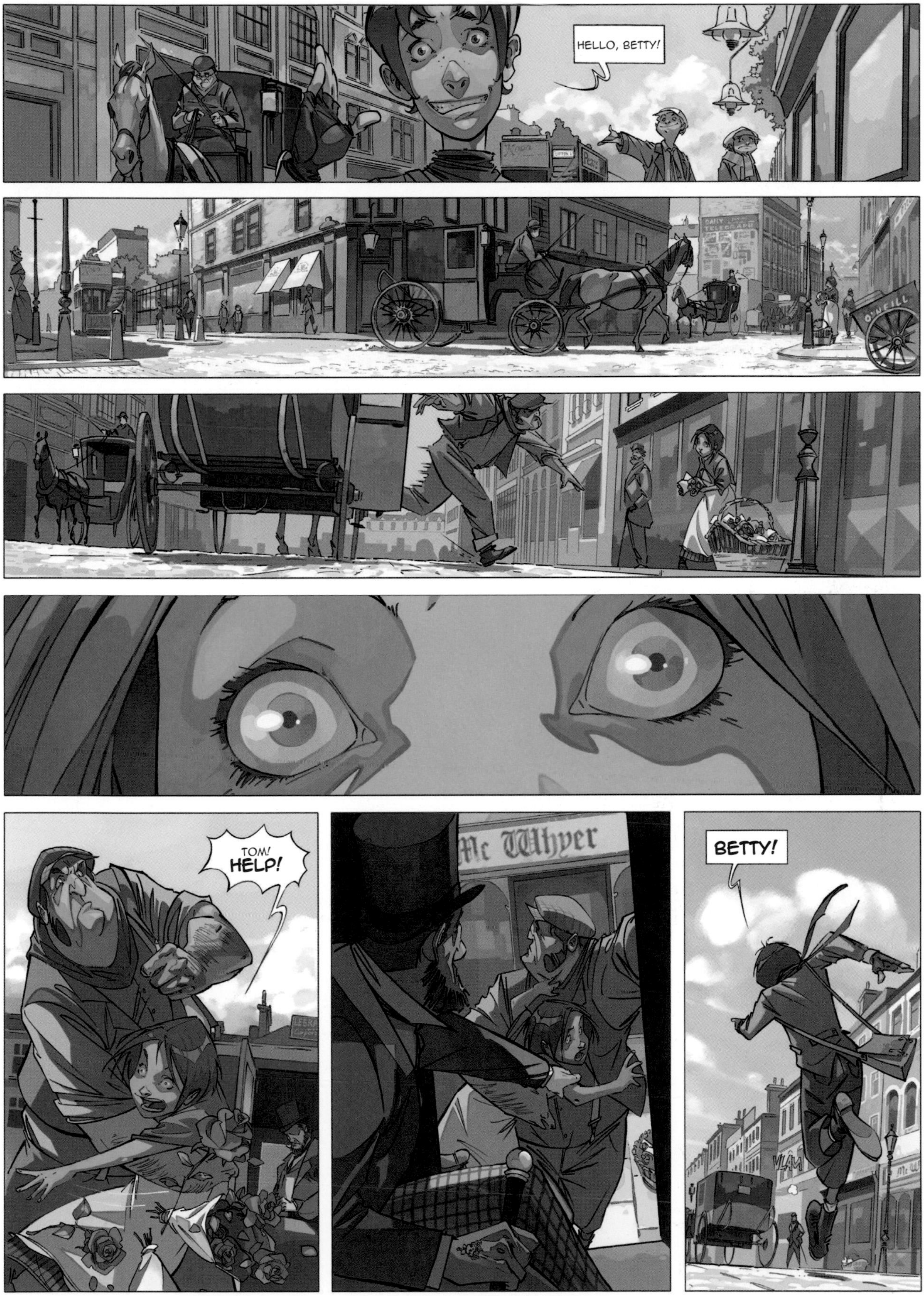
HELLO, BETTY!
TOM! HELP!
Mc Whyer
BETTY!

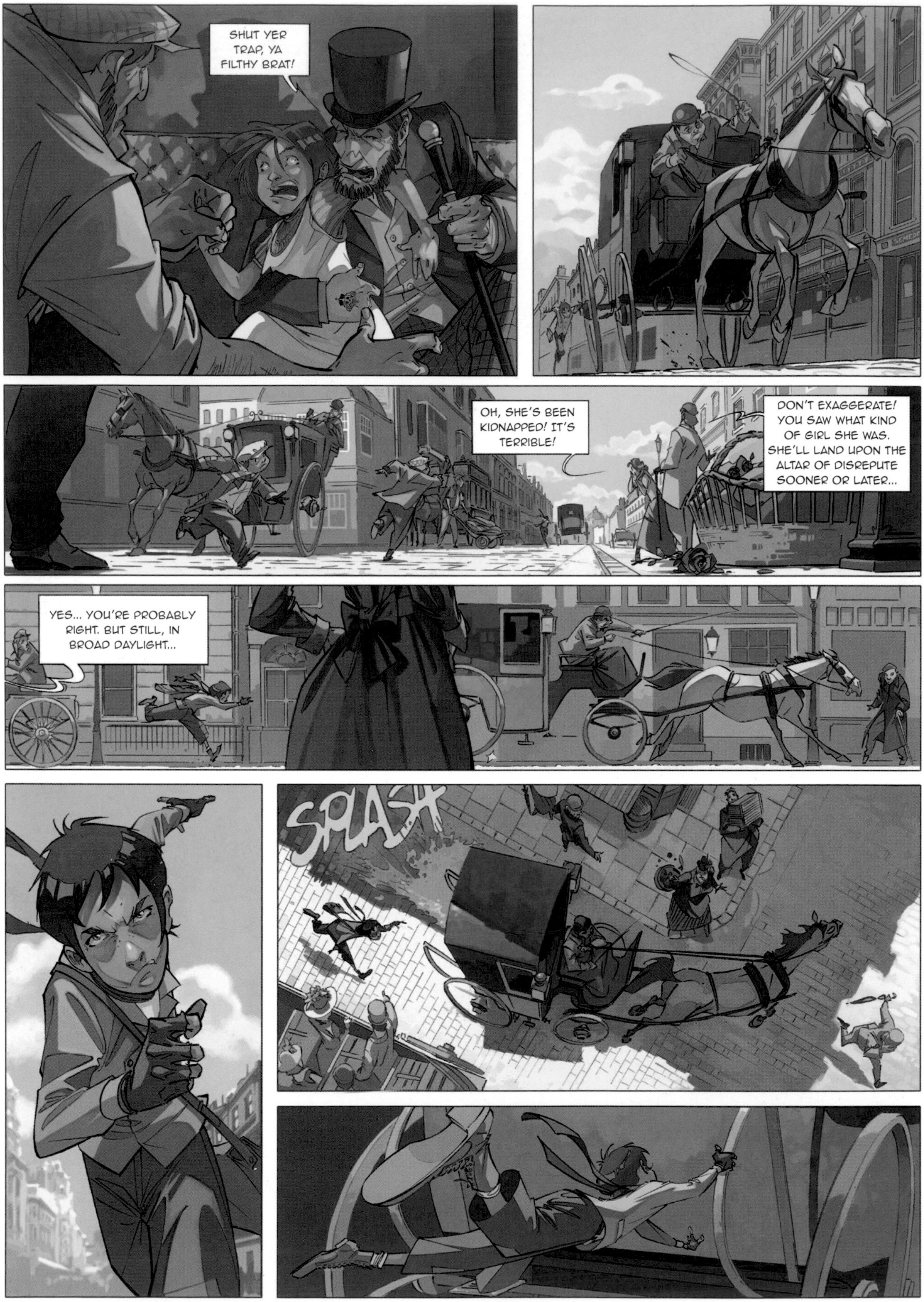
SHUT YER TRAP, YA FILTHY BRAT!
OH, SHE'S BEEN KIDNAPPED! IT'S TERRIBLE!
DON'T EXAGGERATE! YOU SAW WHAT KIND OF GIRL SHE WAS. SHE'LL LAND UPON THE ALTAR OF DISREPUTE SOONER OR LATER...
YES... YOU'RE PROBABLY RIGHT. BUT STILL, IN BROAD DAYLIGHT...
SPLASH

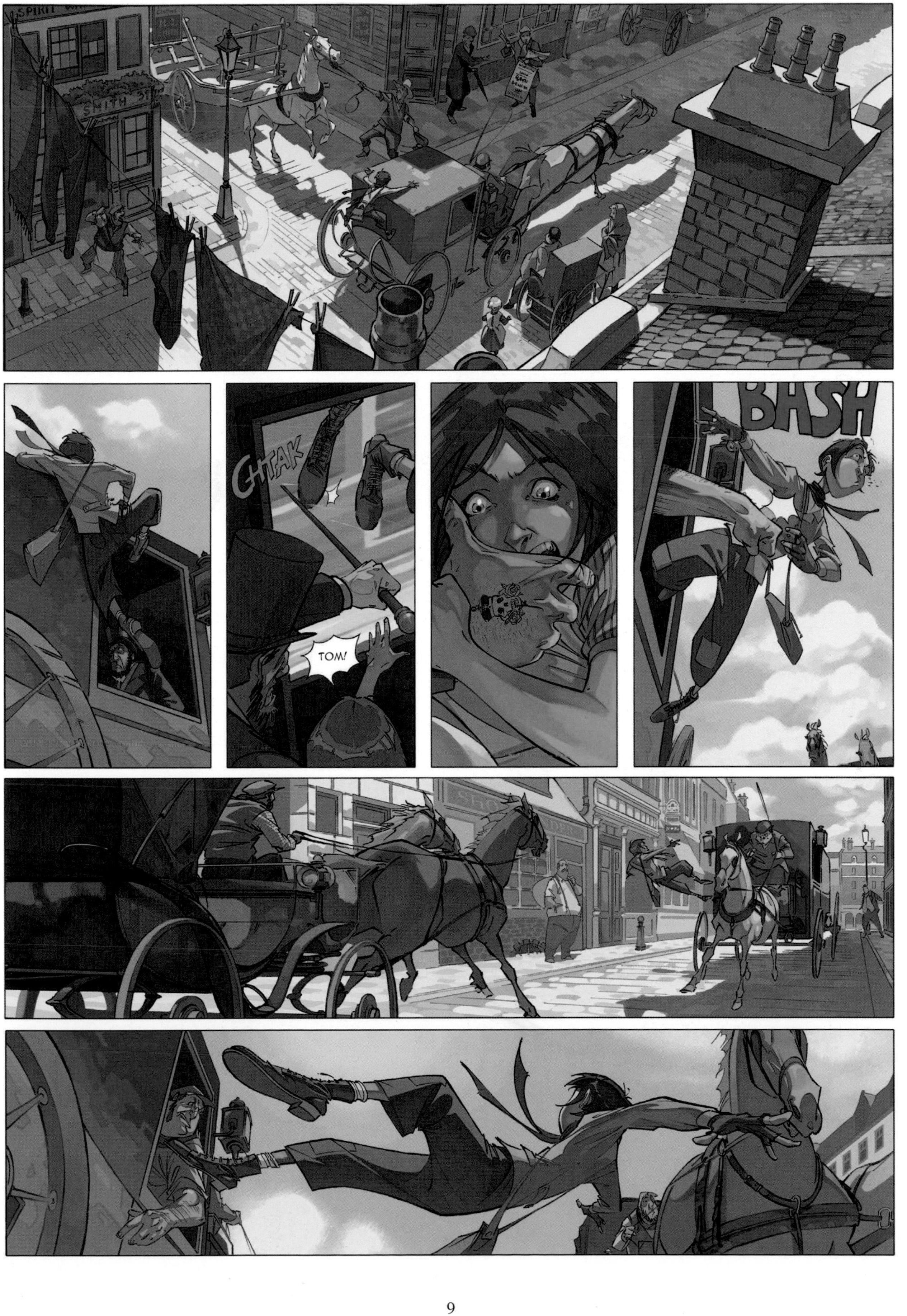
SPIRIT
SMITH 31
CHTAK
TOM!
BASH

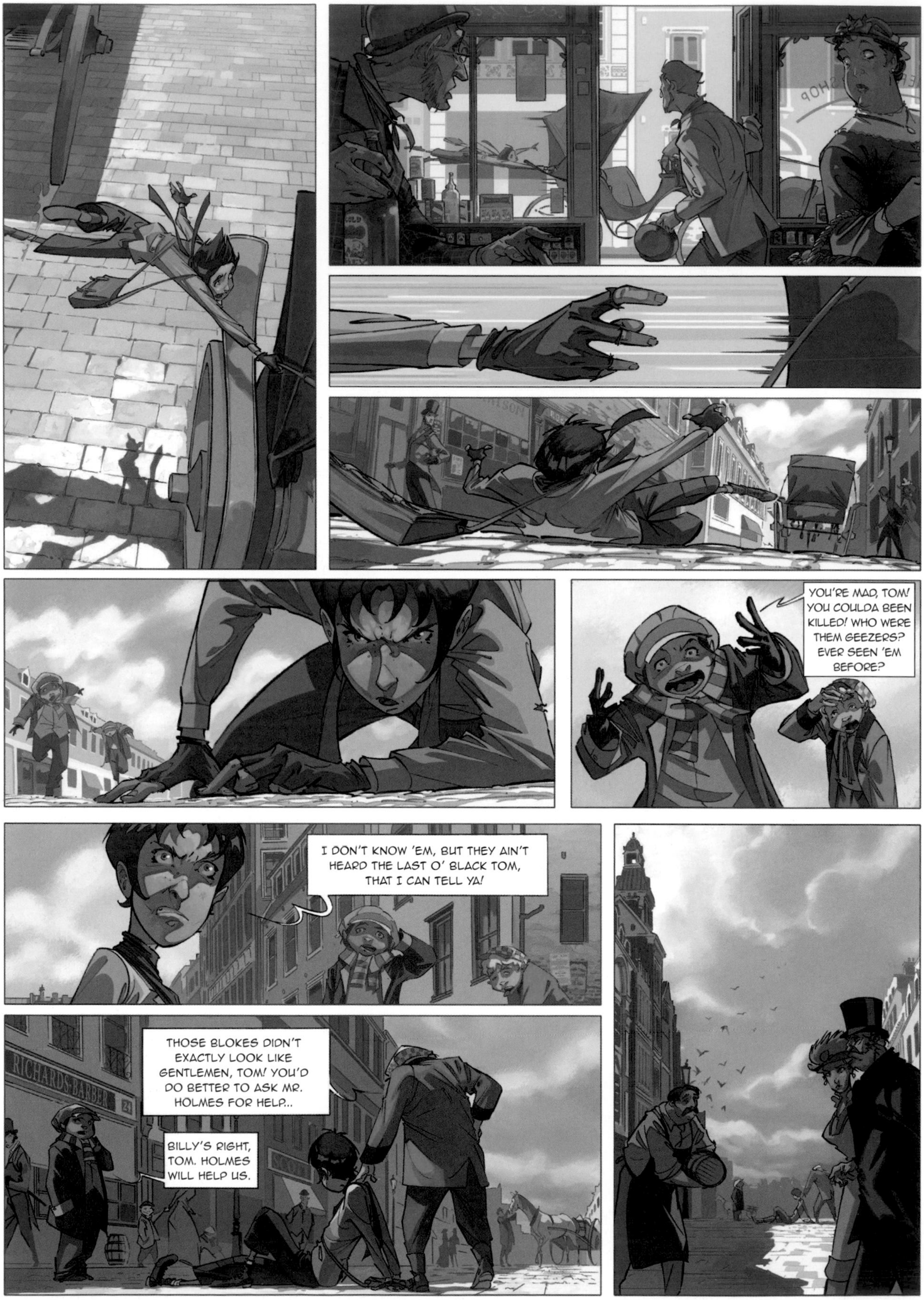
SHOP
YOU'RE MAD, TOM! YOU COULDA BEEN KILLED! WHO WERE THEM GEEZERS? EVER SEEN 'EM BEFORE?
I DON'T KNOW 'EM, BUT THEY AIN'T HEARD THE LAST O' BLACK TOM, THAT I CAN TELL YA!
RICHARDS BARBER
THOSE BLOKES DIDN'T EXACTLY LOOK LIKE GENTLEMEN, TOM! YOU'D DO BETTER TO ASK MR. HOLMES FOR HELP...
BILLY'S RIGHT, TOM. HOLMES WILL HELP US.

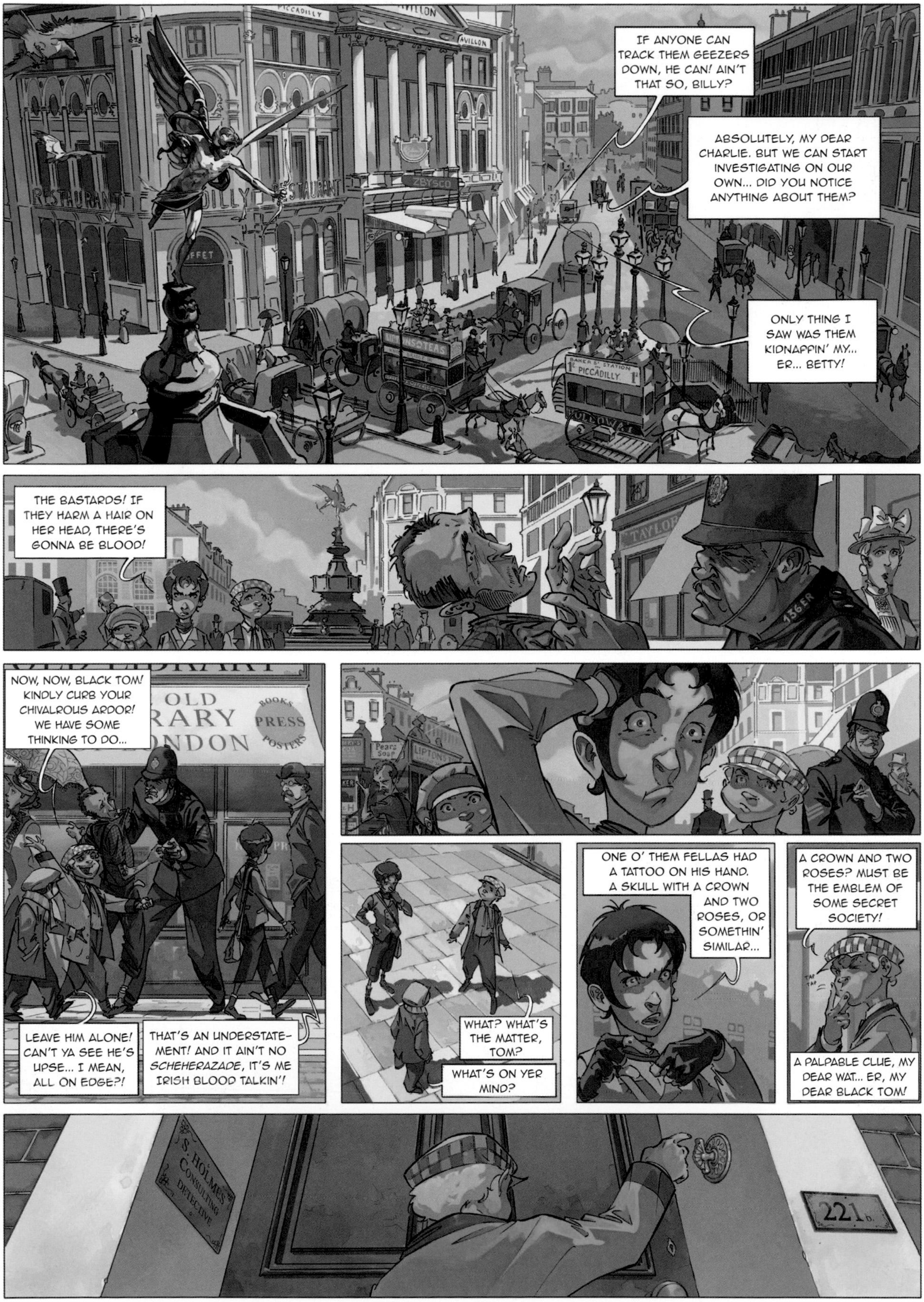
PICCADILLY
IF ANYONE CAN TRACK THEM GEEZERS DOWN, HE CAN! AIN'T THAT SO, BILLY?
ABSOLUTELY, MY DEAR CHARLIE. BUT WE CAN START INVESTIGATING ON OUR OWN... DID YOU NOTICE ANYTHING ABOUT THEM?
ONLY THING I SAW WAS THEM KIDNAPPIN' MY... ER... BETTY!
THE BASTARDS! IF THEY HARM A HAIR ON HER HEAD, THERE'S GONNA BE BLOOD!
NOW, NOW, BLACK TOM! KINDLY CURB YOUR CHIVALROUS ARDOR! WE HAVE SOME THINKING TO DO...
LEAVE HIM ALONE! CAN'T YA SEE HE'S UPSE... I MEAN, ALL ON EDGE?!
THAT'S AN UNDERSTATEMENT! AND IT AIN'T NO *SCHEHERAZADE*, IT'S ME IRISH BLOOD TALKIN'!
WHAT? WHAT'S THE MATTER, TOM?
WHAT'S ON YER MIND?
ONE O' THEM FELLAS HAD A TATTOO ON HIS HAND. A SKULL WITH A CROWN AND TWO ROSES, OR SOMETHIN' SIMILAR...
A CROWN AND TWO ROSES? MUST BE THE EMBLEM OF SOME SECRET SOCIETY!
A PALPABLE CLUE, MY DEAR WAT... ER, MY DEAR BLACK TOM!
S. HOLMES CONSULTING DETECTIVE
221b.

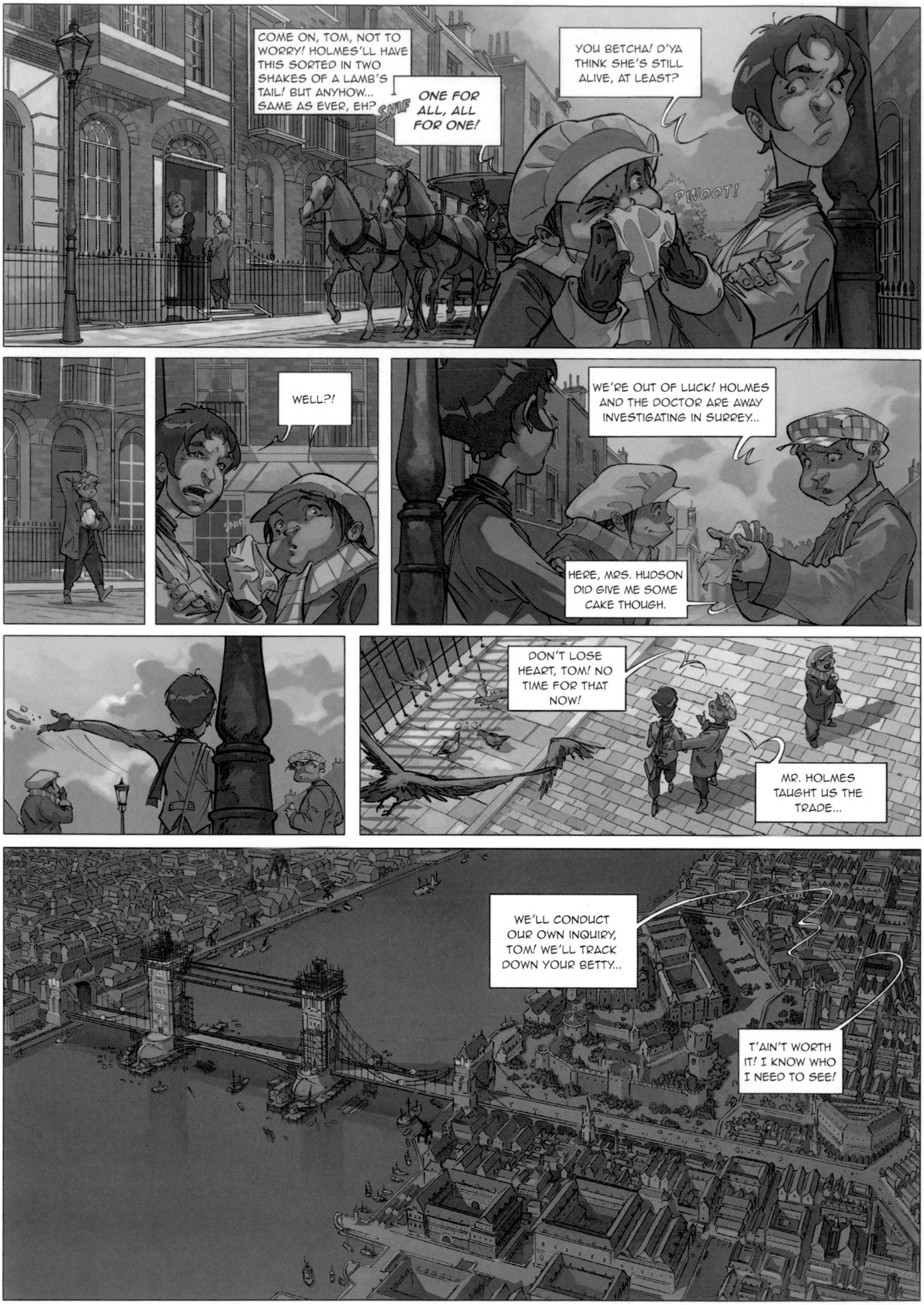

COME ON, TOM, NOT TO WORRY! HOLMES'LL HAVE THIS SORTED IN TWO SHAKES OF A LAMB'S TAIL! BUT ANYHOW... SAME AS EVER, EH?
SNIF
ONE FOR ALL, ALL FOR ONE!
YOU BETCHA! D'YA THINK SHE'S STILL ALIVE, AT LEAST?
PWOOT!
WELL?!
SNIF
WE'RE OUT OF LUCK! HOLMES AND THE DOCTOR ARE AWAY INVESTIGATING IN SURREY...
HERE, MRS. HUDSON DID GIVE ME SOME CAKE THOUGH.
DON'T LOSE HEART, TOM! NO TIME FOR THAT NOW!
MR. HOLMES TAUGHT US THE TRADE...
WE'LL CONDUCT OUR OWN INQUIRY, TOM! WE'LL TRACK DOWN YOUR BETTY...
T'AIN'T WORTH IT! I KNOW WHO I NEED TO SEE!

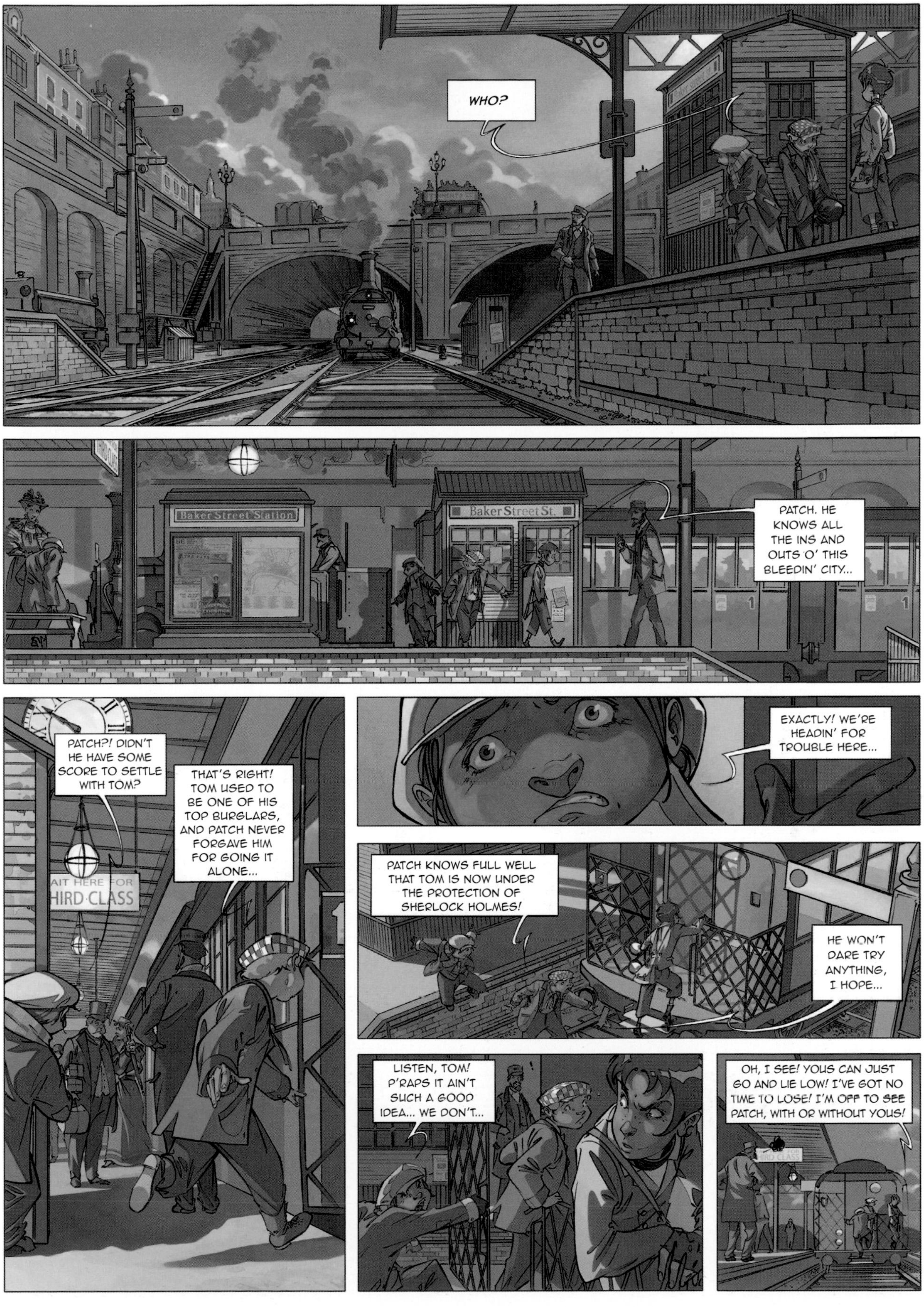
WHO?
Baker Street St.
Baker Street Station
Baker Street St.
PATCH. HE KNOWS ALL THE INS AND OUTS 'O' THIS BLEEDIN' CITY...
PATCH?! DIDN'T HE HAVE SOME SCORE TO SETTLE WITH TOM?
THAT'S RIGHT! TOM USED TO BE ONE OF HIS TOP BURGLARS, AND PATCH NEVER FORGAVE HIM FOR GOING IT ALONE...
AIT HERE FOR
HIRD CLASS
EXACTLY! WE'RE HEADIN' FOR TROUBLE HERE...
PATCH KNOWS FULL WELL THAT TOM IS NOW UNDER THE PROTECTION OF SHERLOCK HOLMES!
HE WON'T DARE TRY ANYTHING, I HOPE...
LISTEN, TOM! P'RAPS IT AIN'T SUCH A GOOD IDEA... WE DON'T...
OH, I SEE! YOUS CAN JUST GO AND LIE LOW! I'VE GOT NO TIME TO LOSE! I'M OFF TO SEE PATCH, WITH OR WITHOUT YOUS!

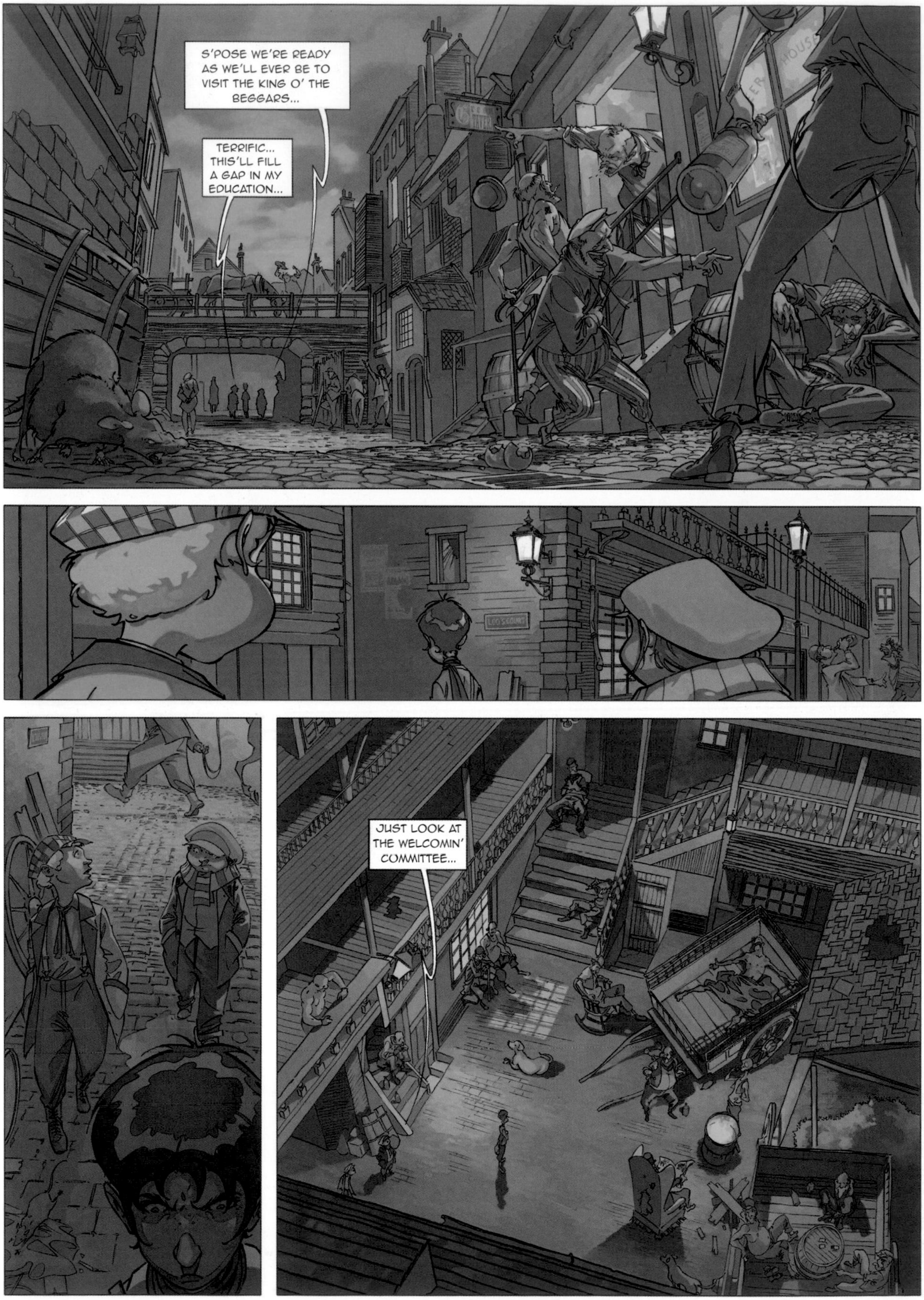
S'POSE WE'RE READY AS WE'LL EVER BE TO VISIT THE KING O' THE BEGGARS...
TERRIFIC... THIS'LL FILL A GAP IN MY EDUCATION...
JUST LOOK AT THE WELCOMIN' COMMITTEE...

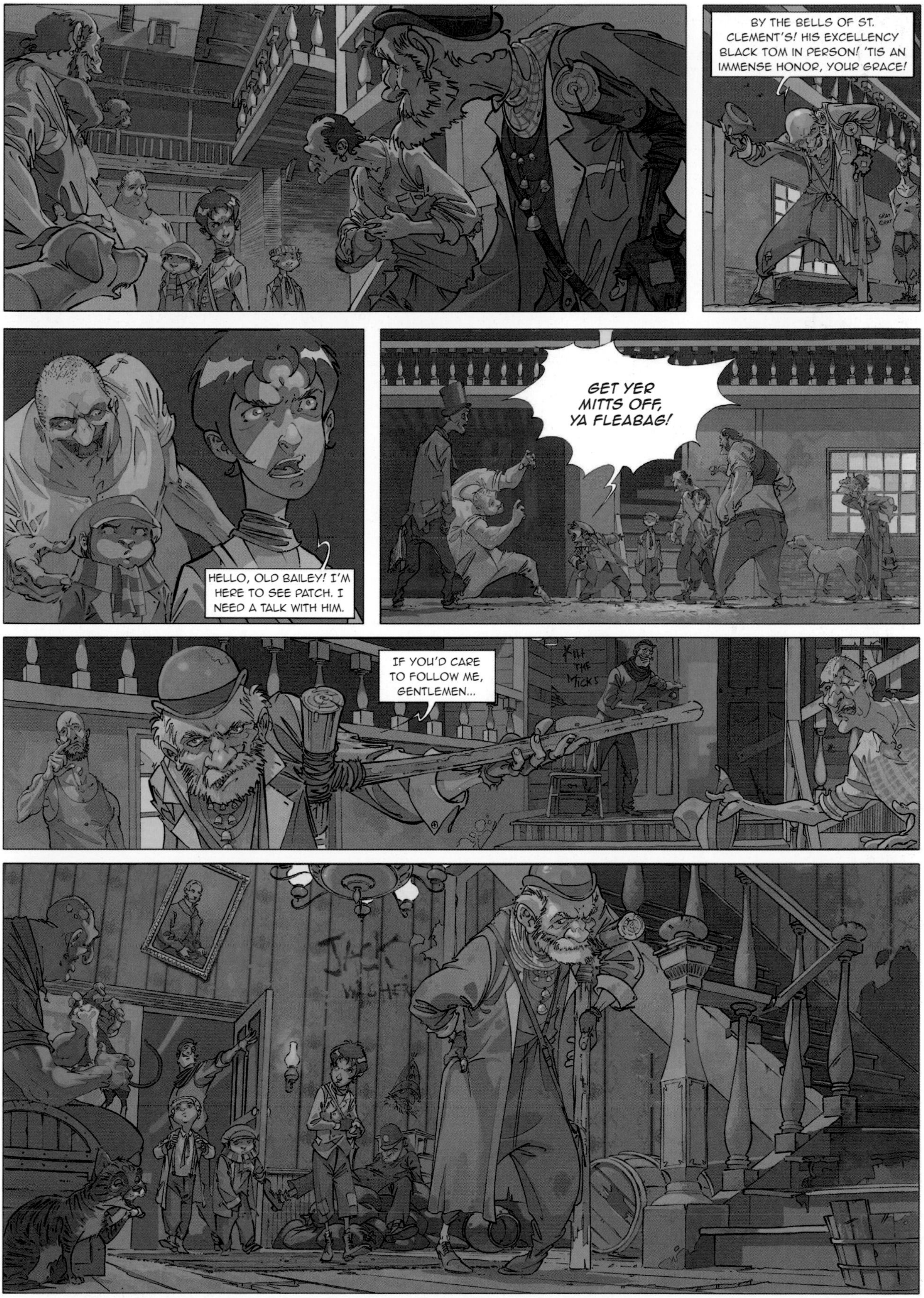
BY THE BELLS OF ST. CLEMENT'S! HIS EXCELLENCY BLACK TOM IN PERSON! 'TIS AN IMMENSE HONOR, YOUR GRACE!
HELLO, OLD BAILEY! I'M HERE TO SEE PATCH. I NEED A TALK WITH HIM.
GET YER MITTS OFF, YA FLEABAG!
IF YOU'D CARE TO FOLLOW ME, GENTLEMEN...
KILL THE MICKS

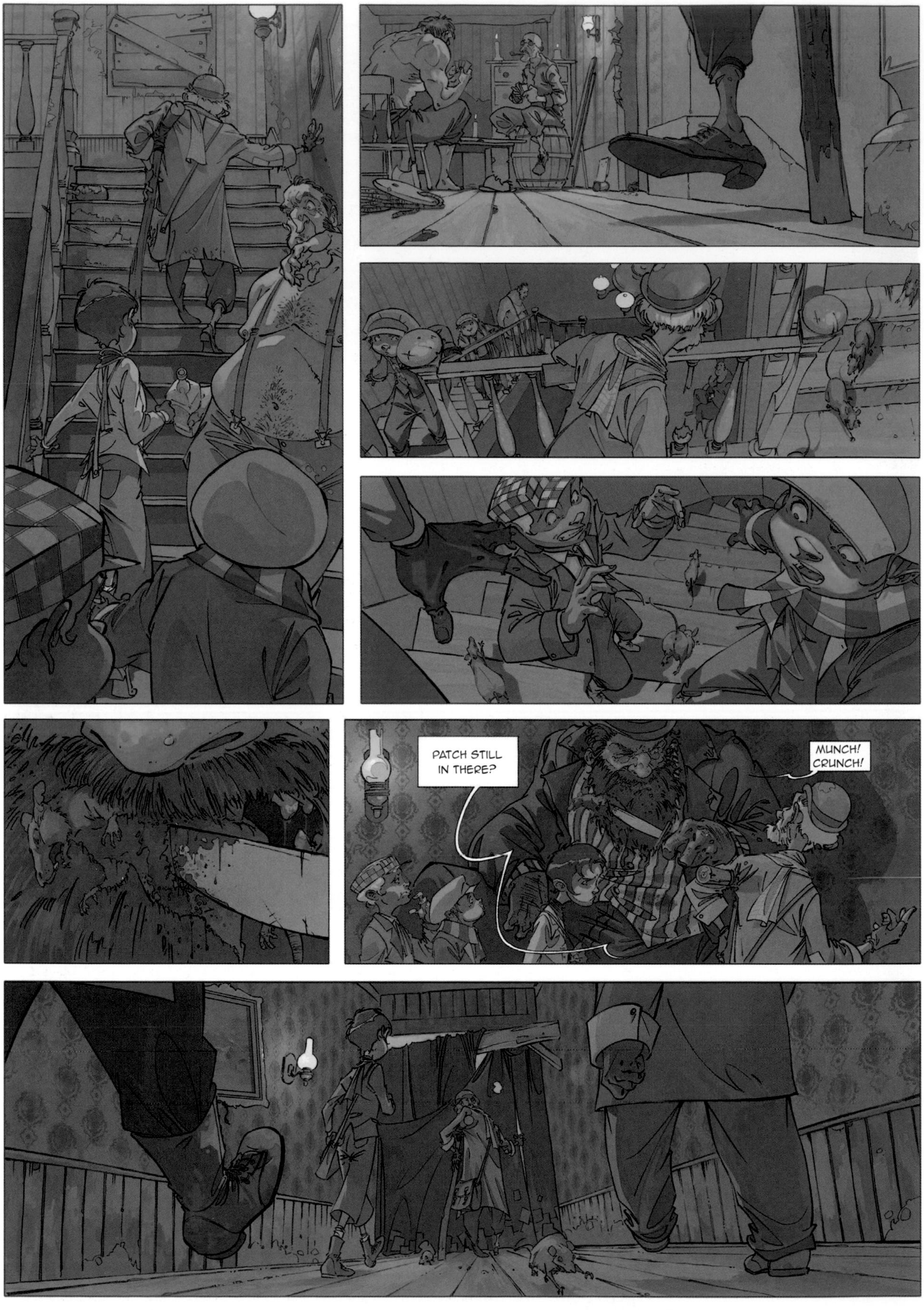
PATCH STILL IN THERE?
MUNCH! CRUNCH!

ZING WOIING ZOUYOUNG

WELL, BLOW ME DOWN! BLACK TOM'S RETURNED AMONGST US! ARE YOU HERE LOOKIN' FOR WORK, SUNSHINE?

...OR IS THIS JUST A COURTESY CALL?

AHA AHA HAHA

NEITHER ONE NOR T'OTHER! I'M HERE TO GET SOME INFORMATION...

YOU HAVE TO SAY "YOUR HIGHNESS" WHEN ADDRESSIN' THE KING, YA IRISH SCUM!

HGM!!

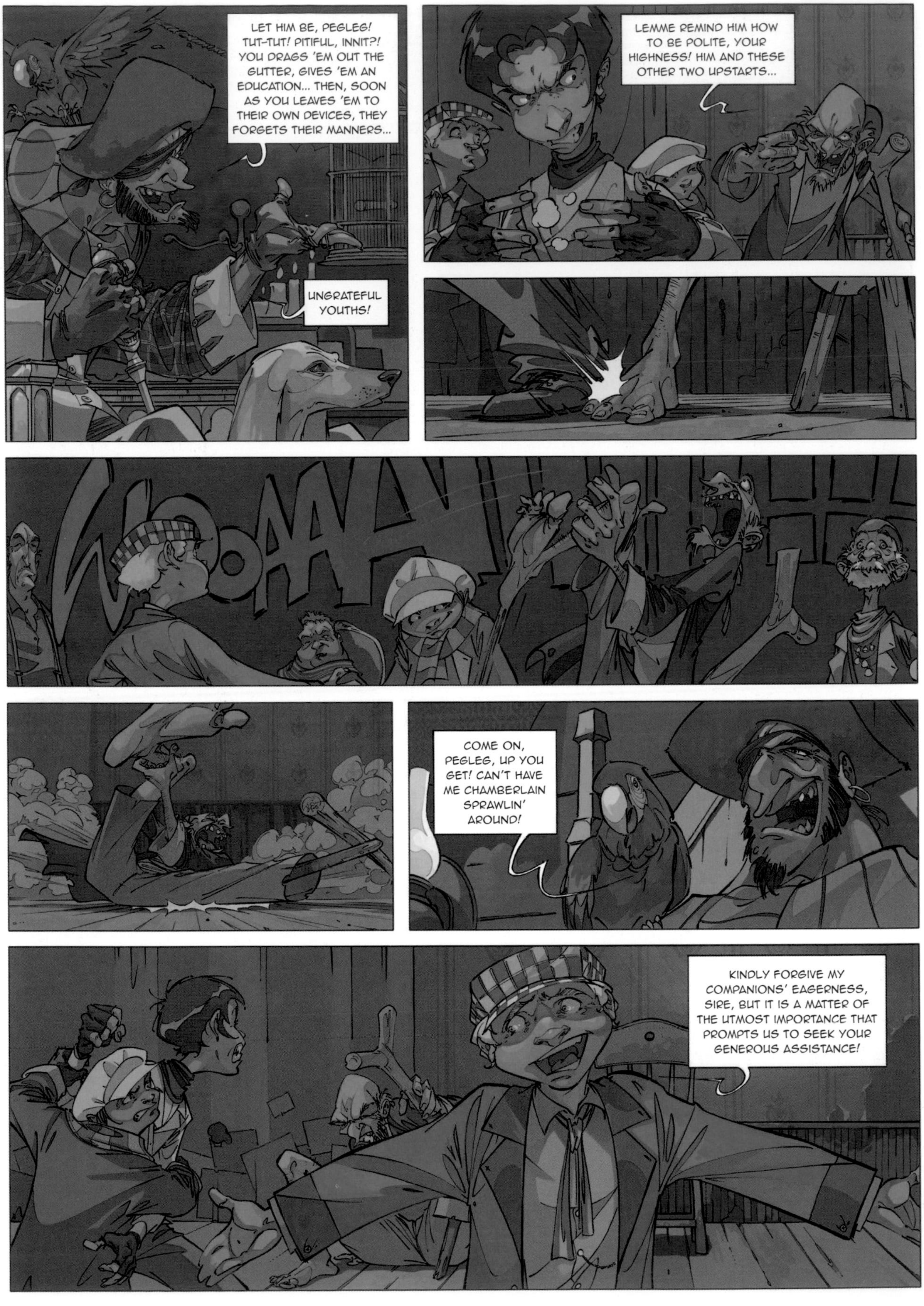
LET HIM BE, PEGLEG! TUT-TUT! PITIFUL, INNIT?! YOU DRAGS 'EM OUT THE GUTTER, GIVES 'EM AN EDUCATION... THEN, SOON AS YOU LEAVES 'EM TO THEIR OWN DEVICES, THEY FORGETS THEIR MANNERS...
UNGRATEFUL YOUTHS!
LEMME REMIND HIM HOW TO BE POLITE, YOUR HIGHNESS! HIM AND THESE OTHER TWO UPSTARTS...
WOAAA
COME ON, PEGLEG, UP YOU GET! CAN'T HAVE ME CHAMBERLAIN SPRAWLIN' AROUND!
KINDLY FORGIVE MY COMPANIONS' EAGERNESS, SIRE, BUT IT IS A MATTER OF THE UTMOST IMPORTANCE THAT PROMPTS US TO SEEK YOUR GENEROUS ASSISTANCE!

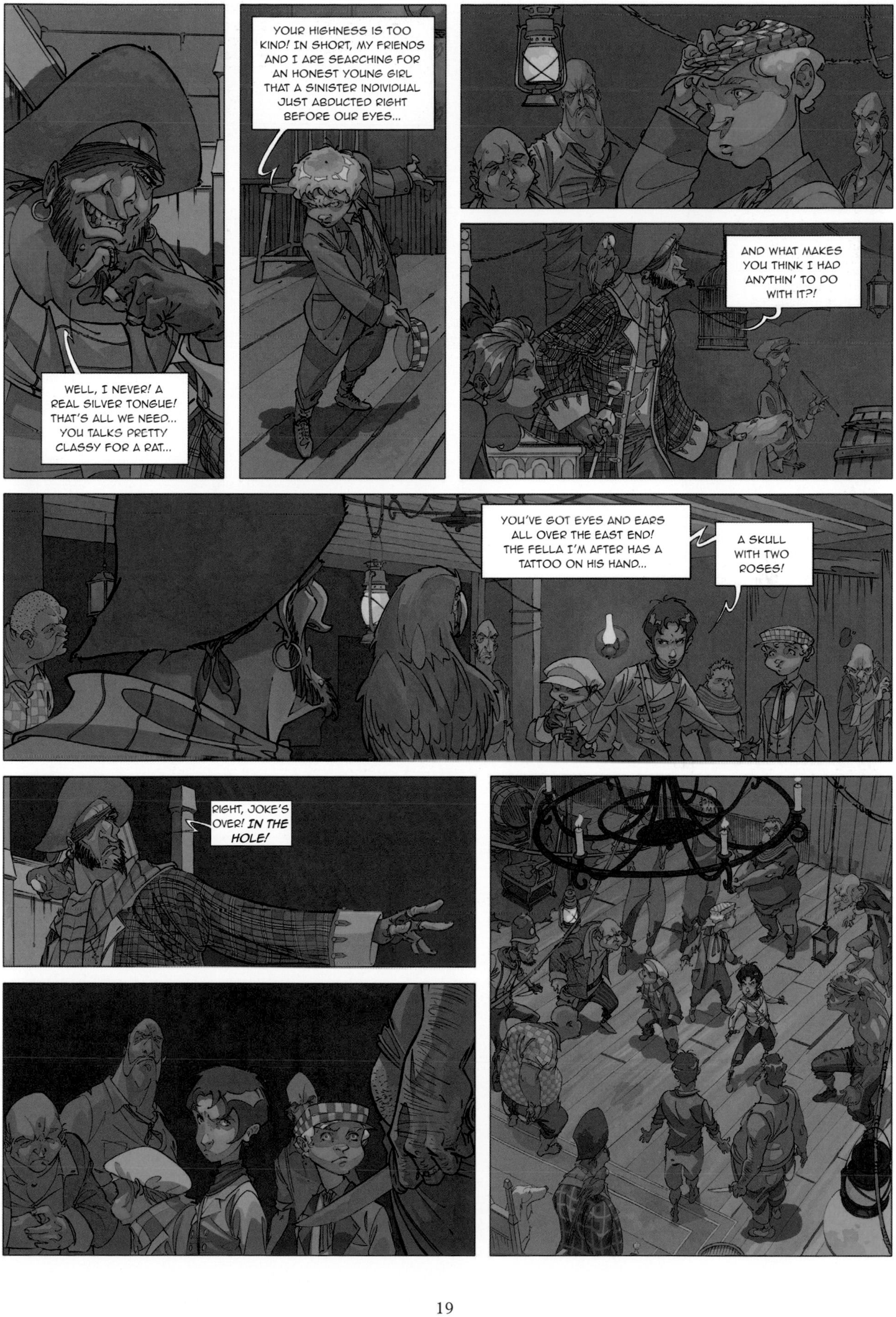
WELL, I NEVER! A REAL SILVER TONGUE! THAT'S ALL WE NEED... YOU TALKS PRETTY CLASSY FOR A RAT...
YOUR HIGHNESS IS TOO KIND! IN SHORT, MY FRIENDS AND I ARE SEARCHING FOR AN HONEST YOUNG GIRL THAT A SINISTER INDIVIDUAL JUST ABDUCTED RIGHT BEFORE OUR EYES...
AND WHAT MAKES YOU THINK I HAD ANYTHIN' TO DO WITH IT?!
YOU'VE GOT EYES AND EARS ALL OVER THE EAST END! THE FELLA I'M AFTER HAS A TATTOO ON HIS HAND...
A SKULL WITH TWO ROSES!
RIGHT, JOKE'S OVER! IN THE HOLE!

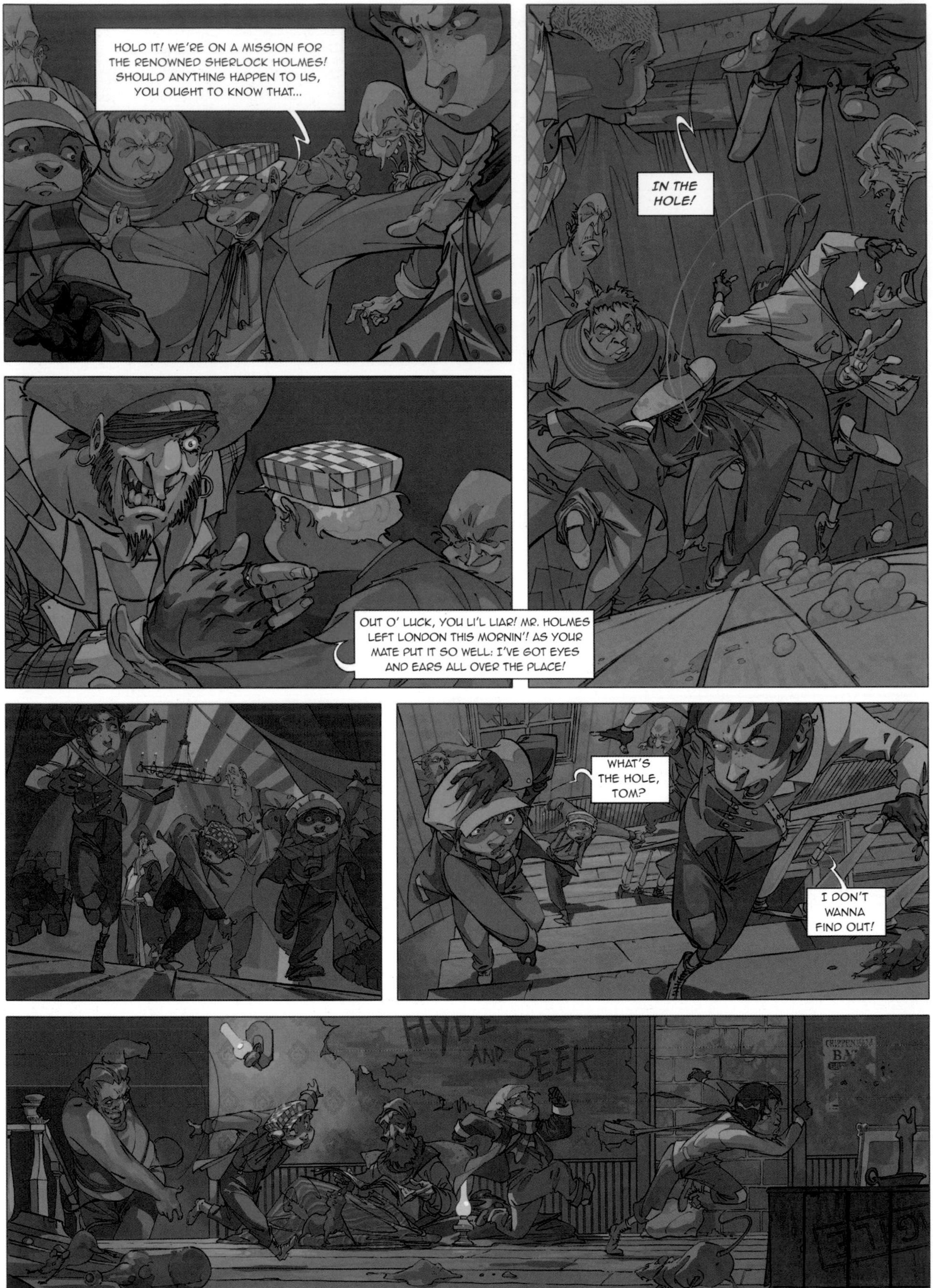
HOLD IT! WE'RE ON A MISSION FOR THE RENOWNED SHERLOCK HOLMES! SHOULD ANYTHING HAPPEN TO US, YOU OUGHT TO KNOW THAT...
OUT O' LUCK, YOU LI'L LIAR! MR. HOLMES LEFT LONDON THIS MORNIN'! AS YOUR MATE PUT IT SO WELL: I'VE GOT EYES AND EARS ALL OVER THE PLACE!
IN THE HOLE!
WHAT'S THE HOLE, TOM?
I DON'T WANNA FIND OUT!
HYDE AND SEEK

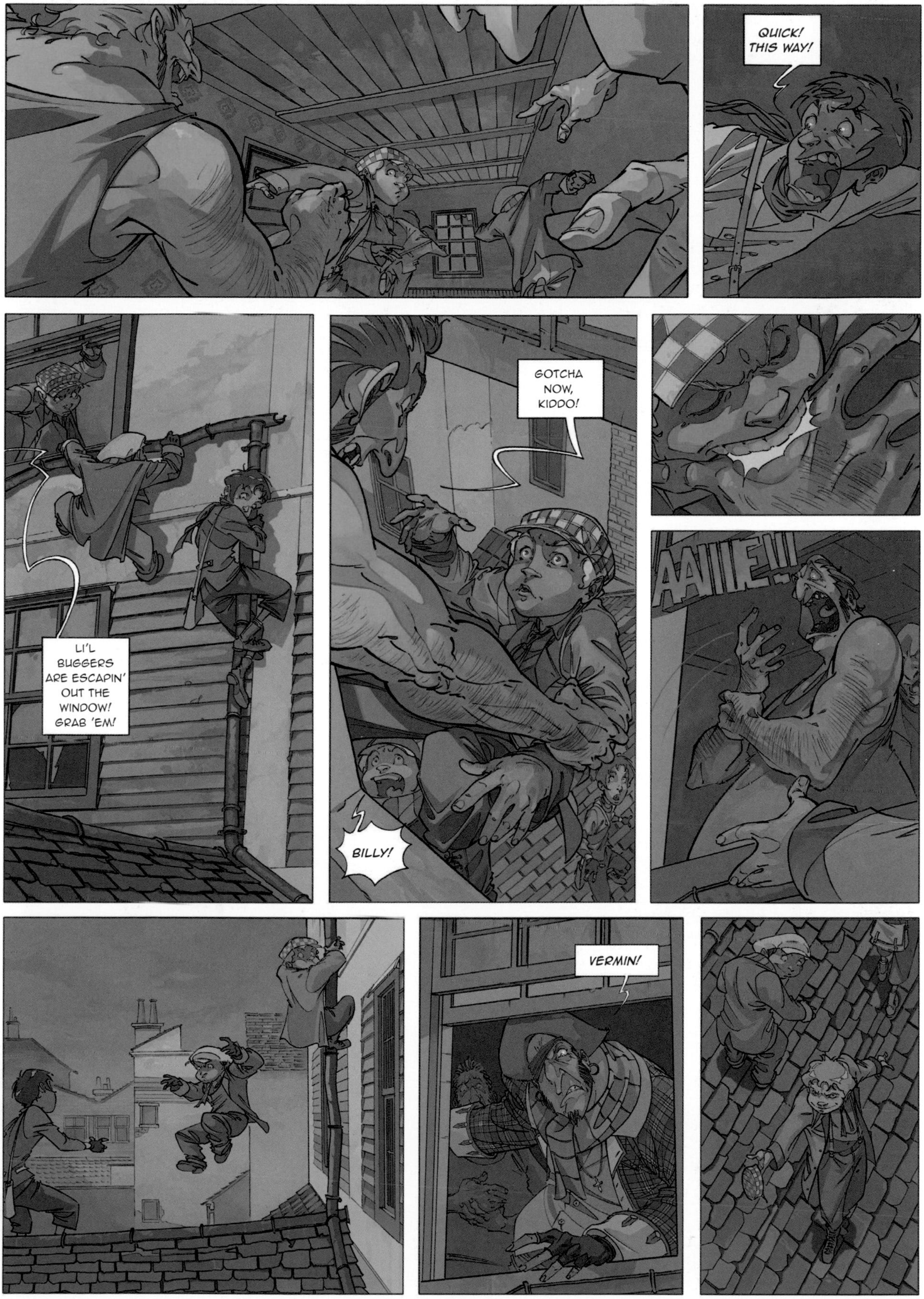
QUICK! THIS WAY!
LI'L BUGGERS ARE ESCAPIN' OUT THE WINDOW! GRAB 'EM!
GOTCHA NOW, KIDDO!
BILLY!
AAIIIE!!
VERMIN!

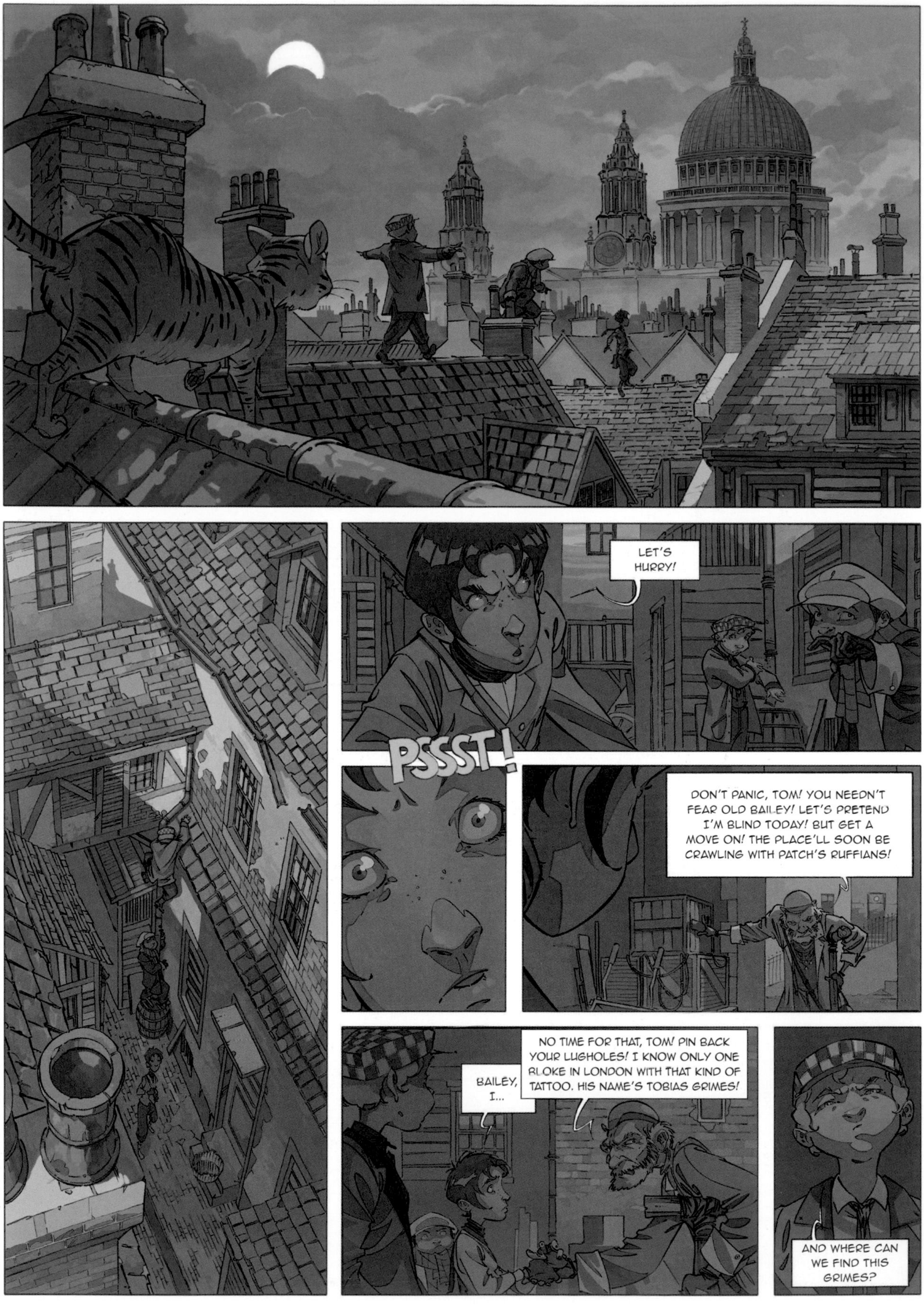
LET'S HURRY!
PSSST!
DON'T PANIC, TOM! YOU NEEDN'T FEAR OLD BAILEY! LET'S PRETEND I'M BLIND TODAY! BUT GET A MOVE ON! THE PLACE'LL SOON BE CRAWLING WITH PATCH'S RUFFIANS!
BAILEY, I...
NO TIME FOR THAT, TOM! PIN BACK YOUR LUGHOLES! I KNOW ONLY ONE BLOKE IN LONDON WITH THAT KIND OF TATTOO. HIS NAME'S TOBIAS GRIMES!
AND WHERE CAN WE FIND THIS GRIMES?

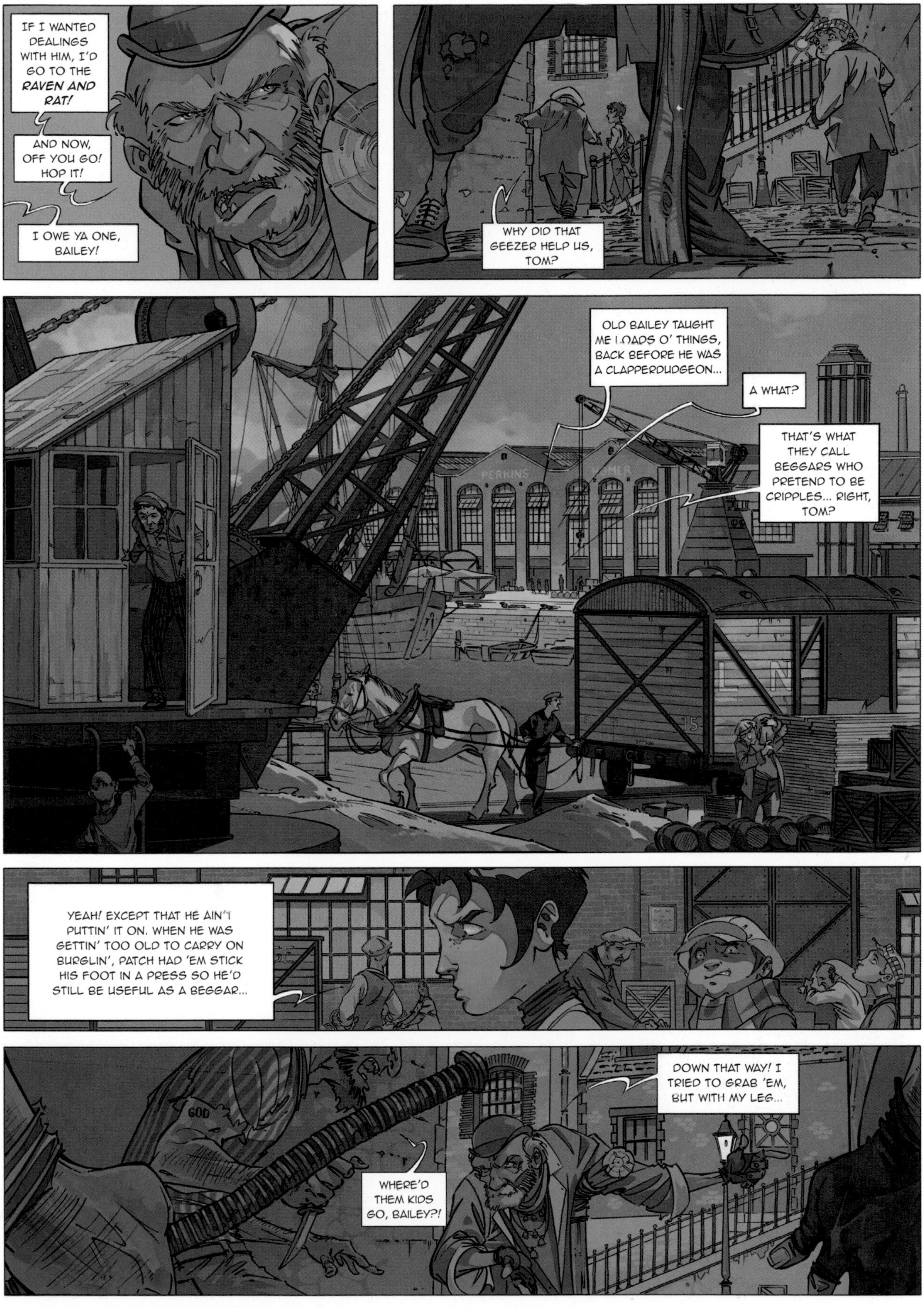
IF I WANTED DEALINGS WITH HIM, I'D GO TO THE RAVEN AND RAT!
AND NOW, OFF YOU GO! HOP IT!
I OWE YA ONE, BAILEY!
WHY DID THAT GEEZER HELP US, TOM?
OLD BAILEY TAUGHT ME LOADS O' THINGS, BACK BEFORE HE WAS A CLAPPERDUDGEON...
A WHAT?
THAT'S WHAT THEY CALL BEGGARS WHO PRETEND TO BE CRIPPLES... RIGHT, TOM?
PERKINS
YEAH! EXCEPT THAT HE AIN'T PUTTIN' IT ON. WHEN HE WAS GETTIN' TOO OLD TO CARRY ON BURGLIN', PATCH HAD 'EM STICK HIS FOOT IN A PRESS SO HE'D STILL BE USEFUL AS A BEGGAR...
DOWN THAT WAY! I TRIED TO GRAB 'EM, BUT WITH MY LEG...
WHERE'D THEM KIDS GO, BAILEY?!

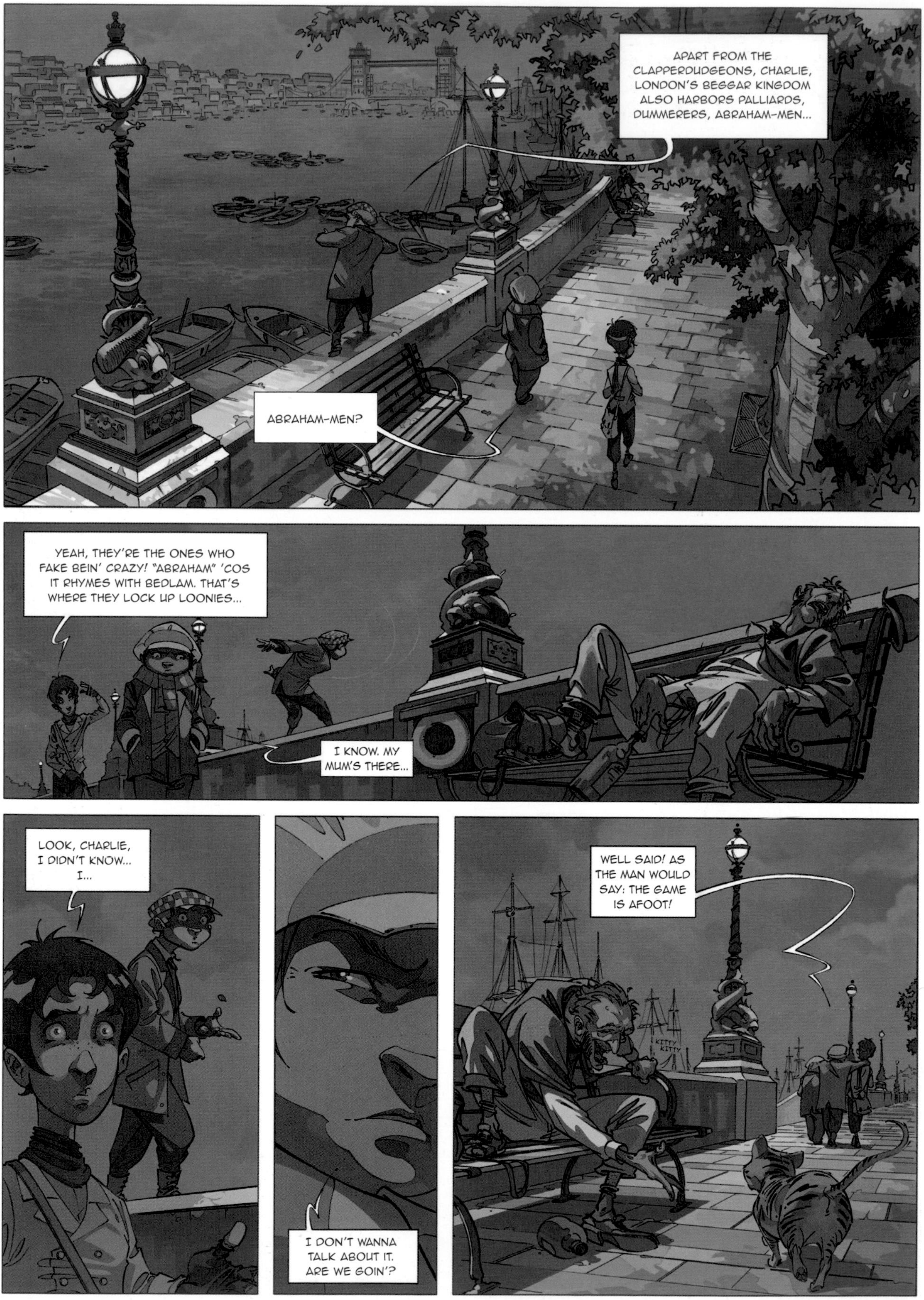
APART FROM THE CLAPPERDUDGEONS, CHARLIE, LONDON'S BEGGAR KINGDOM ALSO HARBORS PALLIARDS, DUMMERERS, ABRAHAM-MEN...
ABRAHAM-MEN?
YEAH, THEY'RE THE ONES WHO FAKE BEIN' CRAZY! "ABRAHAM" 'COS IT RHYMES WITH BEDLAM. THAT'S WHERE THEY LOCK UP LOONIES...
I KNOW. MY MUM'S THERE...
LOOK, CHARLIE, I DIDN'T KNOW... I...
I DON'T WANNA TALK ABOUT IT. ARE WE GOIN'?
WELL SAID! AS THE MAN WOULD SAY: THE GAME IS AFOOT!
KITTY KITTY

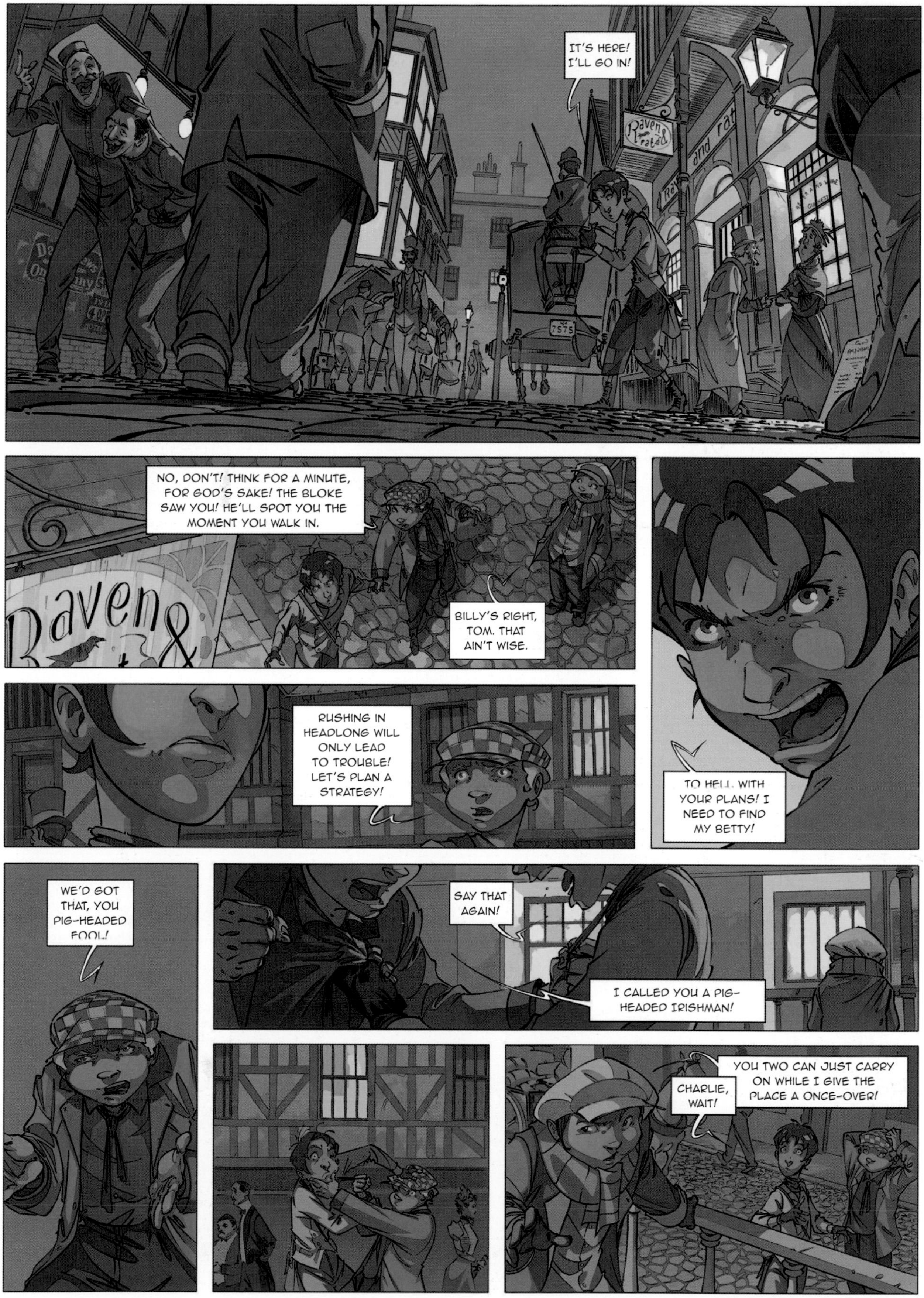
IT'S HERE! I'LL GO IN!
NO, DON'T! THINK FOR A MINUTE, FOR GOD'S SAKE! THE BLOKE SAW YOU! HE'LL SPOT YOU THE MOMENT YOU WALK IN.
BILLY'S RIGHT, TOM. THAT AIN'T WISE.
TO HELL WITH YOUR PLANS! I NEED TO FIND MY BETTY!
RUSHING IN HEADLONG WILL ONLY LEAD TO TROUBLE! LET'S PLAN A STRATEGY!
WE'D GOT THAT, YOU PIG-HEADED FOOL!
SAY THAT AGAIN!
I CALLED YOU A PIG-HEADED IRISHMAN!
CHARLIE, WAIT!
YOU TWO CAN JUST CARRY ON WHILE I GIVE THE PLACE A ONCE-OVER!

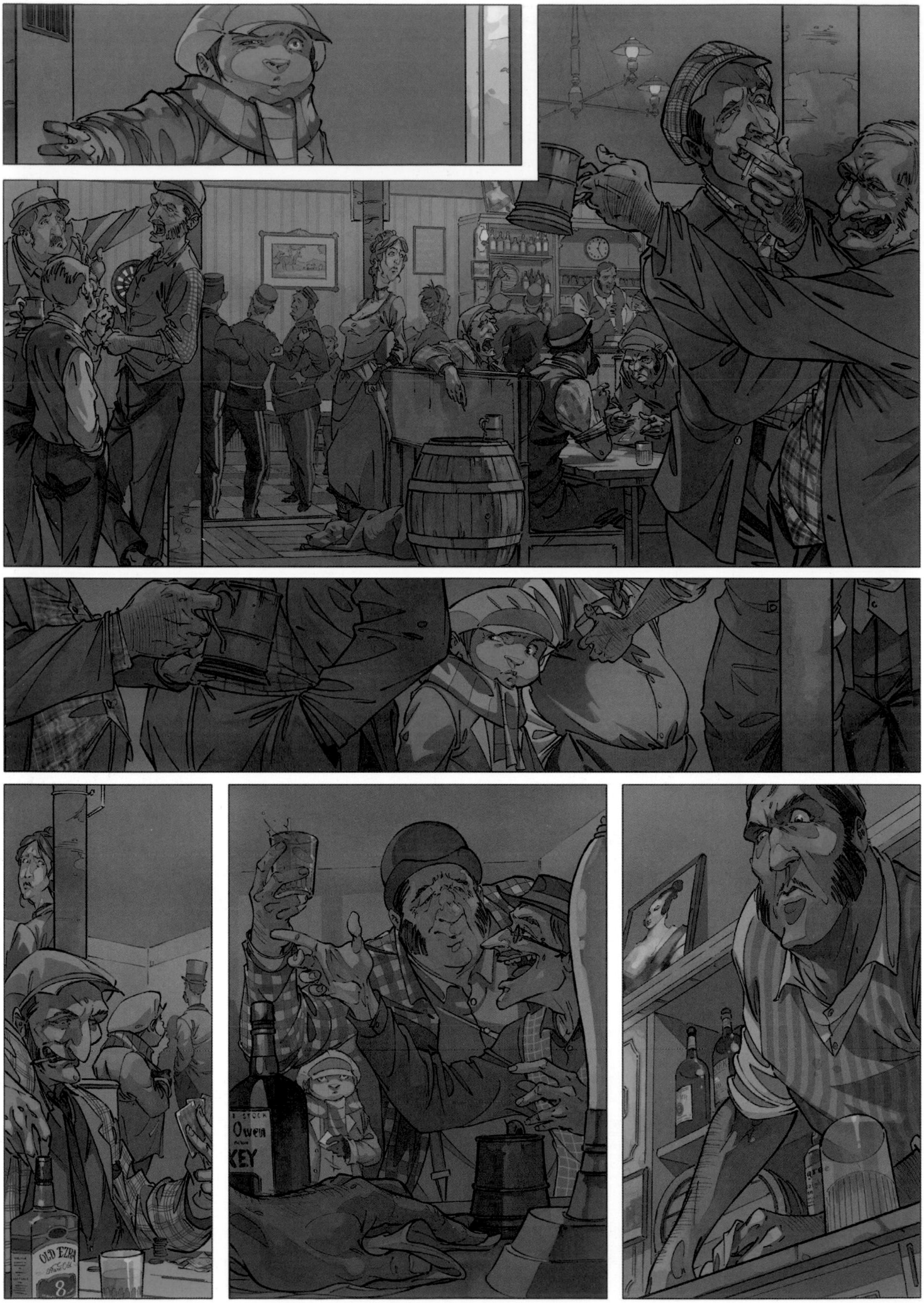
Owen
KEY
OLD EZRA
8

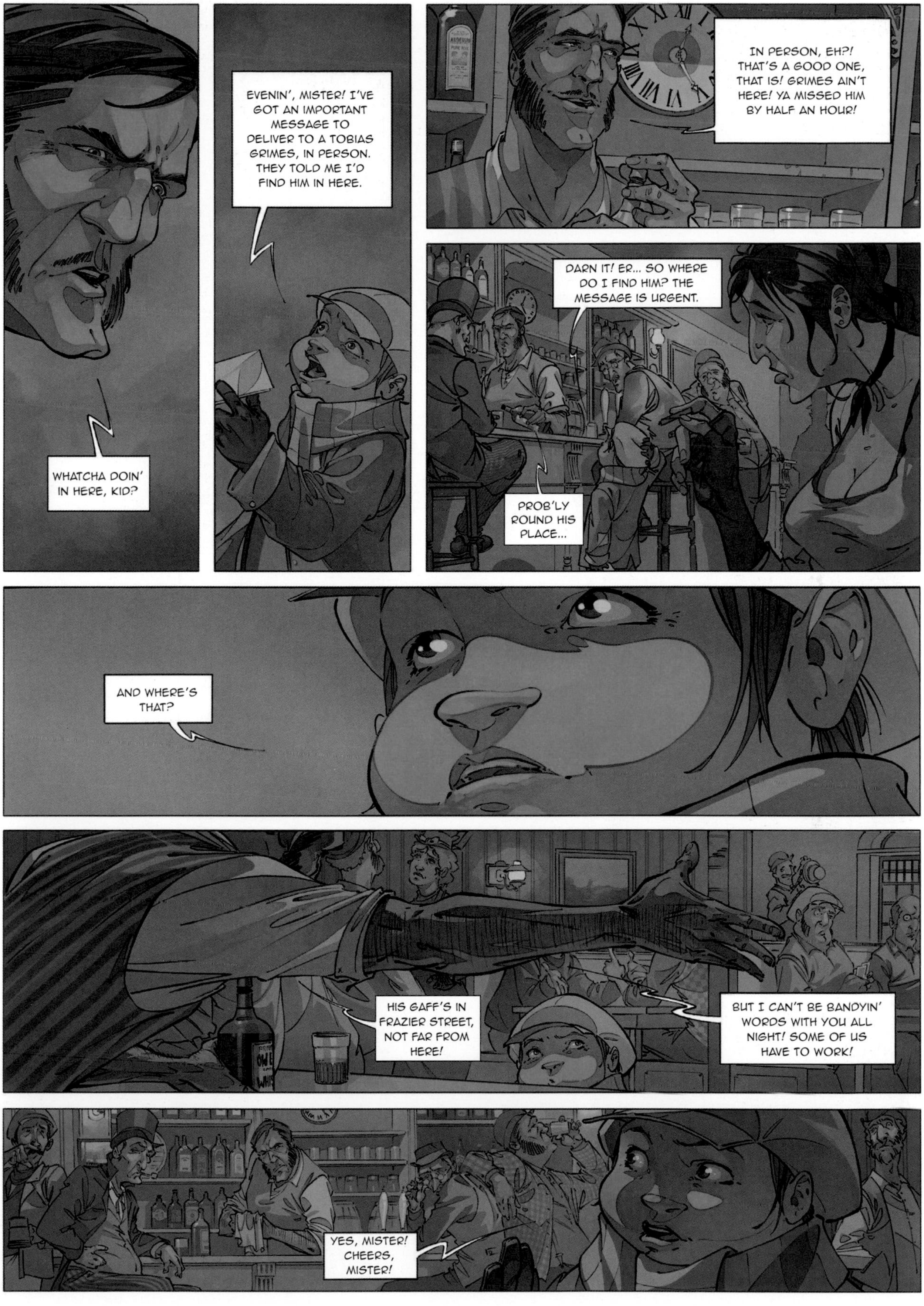
WHATCHA DOIN' IN HERE, KID?
EVENIN', MISTER! I'VE GOT AN IMPORTANT MESSAGE TO DELIVER TO A TOBIAS GRIMES, IN PERSON. THEY TOLD ME I'D FIND HIM IN HERE.
IN PERSON, EH?! THAT'S A GOOD ONE, THAT IS! GRIMES AIN'T HERE! YA MISSED HIM BY HALF AN HOUR!
DARN IT! ER... SO WHERE DO I FIND HIM? THE MESSAGE IS URGENT.
PROB'LY ROUND HIS PLACE...
AND WHERE'S THAT?
HIS GAFF'S IN FRAZIER STREET, NOT FAR FROM HERE!
BUT I CAN'T BE BANDYIN' WORDS WITH YOU ALL NIGHT! SOME OF US HAVE TO WORK!
YES, MISTER! CHEERS, MISTER!

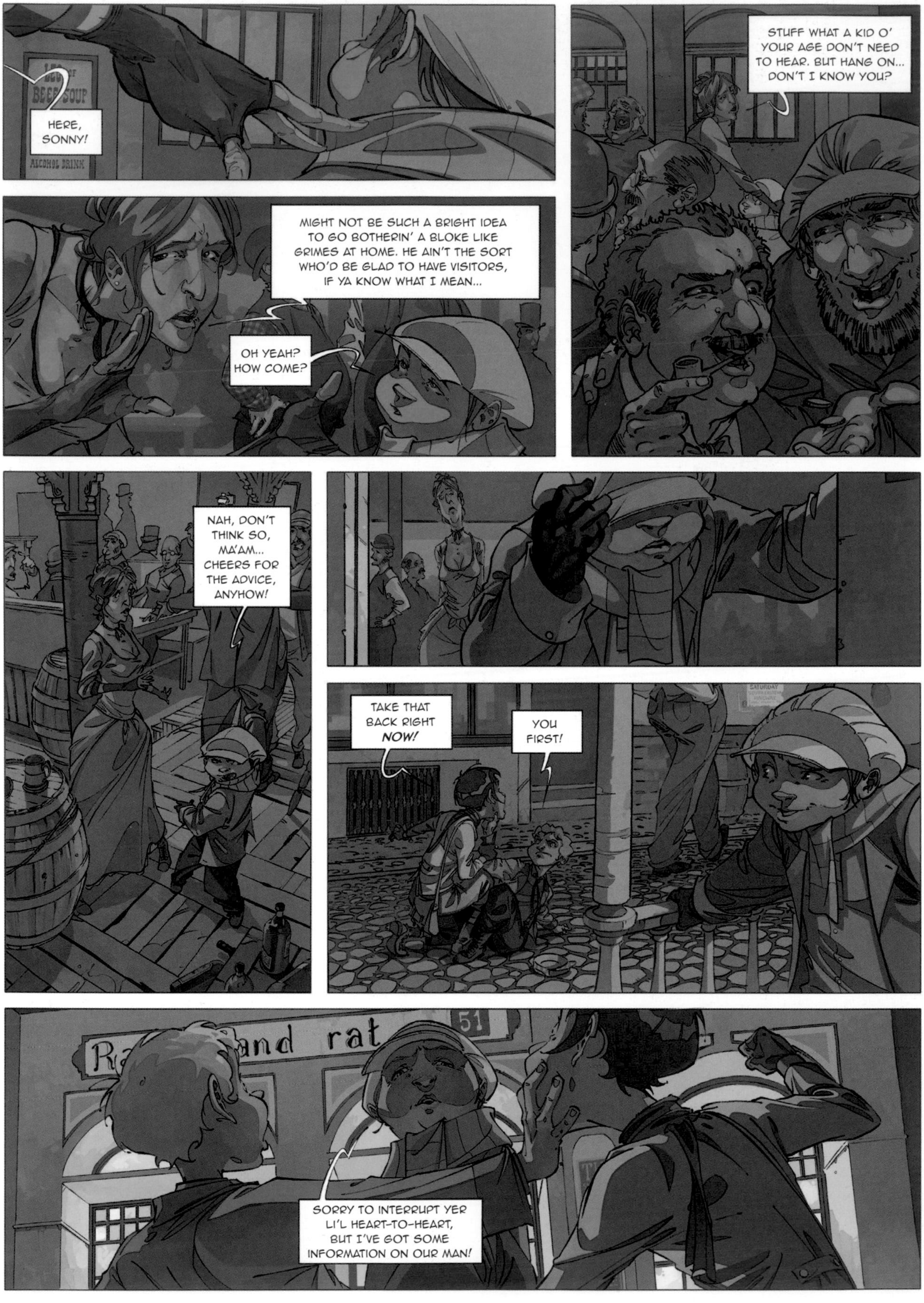
BEEF SOUP
ALCOHOL DRINK
HERE, SONNY!
STUFF WHAT A KID O' YOUR AGE DON'T NEED TO HEAR. BUT HANG ON... DON'T I KNOW YOU?
MIGHT NOT BE SUCH A BRIGHT IDEA TO GO BOTHERIN' A BLOKE LIKE GRIMES AT HOME. HE AIN'T THE SORT WHO'D BE GLAD TO HAVE VISITORS, IF YA KNOW WHAT I MEAN...
OH YEAH? HOW COME?
NAH, DON'T THINK SO, MA'AM... CHEERS FOR THE ADVICE, ANYHOW!
TAKE THAT BACK RIGHT *NOW!*
YOU FIRST!
51
and rat
SORRY TO INTERRUPT YER LI'L HEART-TO-HEART, BUT I'VE GOT SOME INFORMATION ON OUR MAN!

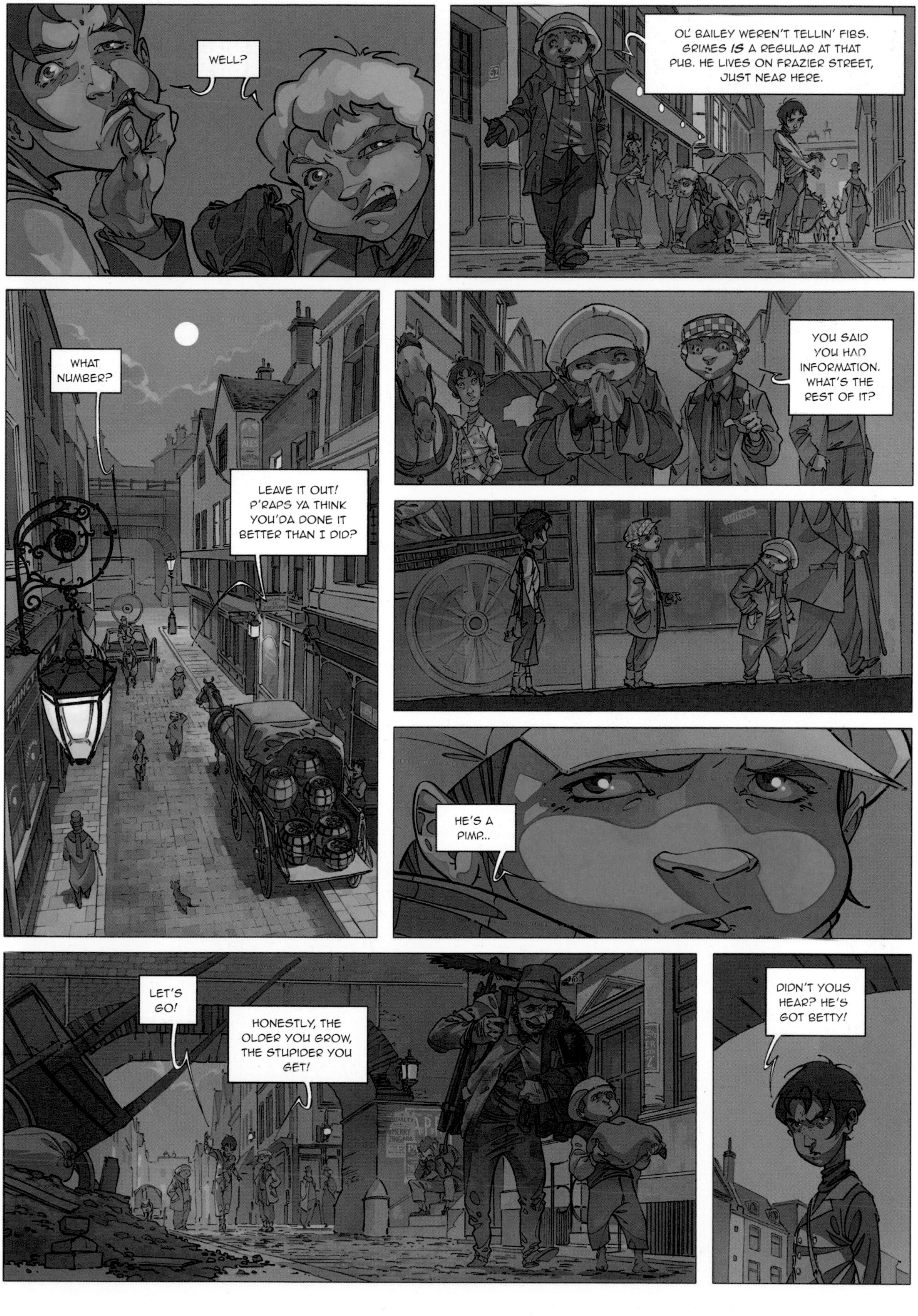
WELL?
OL' BAILEY WEREN'T TELLIN' FIBS. GRIMES IS A REGULAR AT THAT PUB. HE LIVES ON FRAZIER STREET, JUST NEAR HERE.
WHAT NUMBER?
LEAVE IT OUT! P'RAPS YA THINK YOU'DA DONE IT BETTER THAN I DID?
YOU SAID YOU HAD INFORMATION. WHAT'S THE REST OF IT?
HE'S A PIMP...
LET'S GO!
HONESTLY, THE OLDER YOU GROW, THE STUPIDER YOU GET!
DIDN'T YOUS HEAR? HE'S GOT BETTY!

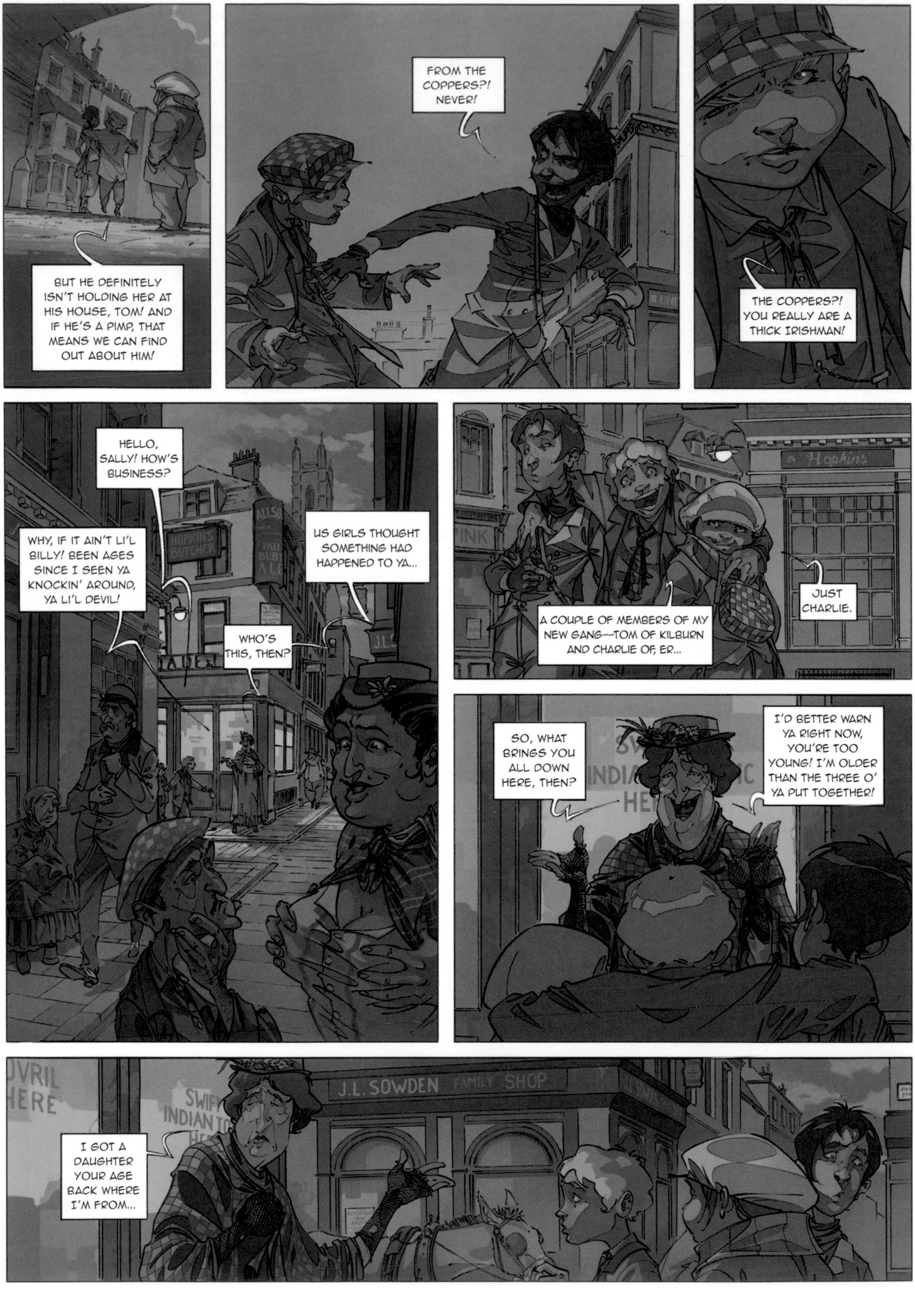
BUT HE DEFINITELY ISN'T HOLDING HER AT HIS HOUSE, TOM! AND IF HE'S A PIMP, THAT MEANS WE CAN FIND OUT ABOUT HIM!
FROM THE COPPERS?! NEVER!
THE COPPERS?! YOU REALLY ARE A THICK IRISHMAN!
HELLO, SALLY! HOW'S BUSINESS?
WHY, IF IT AIN'T LI'L BILLY! BEEN AGES SINCE I SEEN YA KNOCKIN' AROUND, YA LI'L DEVIL!
US GIRLS THOUGHT SOMETHING HAD HAPPENED TO YA...
WHO'S THIS, THEN?
HOPKINS BUTCHER
Hopkins
A COUPLE OF MEMBERS OF MY NEW GANG--TOM OF KILBURN AND CHARLIE OF, ER...
JUST CHARLIE.
SO, WHAT BRINGS YOU ALL DOWN HERE, THEN?
I'D BETTER WARN YA RIGHT NOW, YOU'RE TOO YOUNG! I'M OLDER THAN THE THREE O' YA PUT TOGETHER!
J.L. SOWDEN FAMILY SHOP
I GOT A DAUGHTER YOUR AGE BACK WHERE I'M FROM...

YOU'VE MISCONSTRUED OUR INTENTIONS, SAL! ACTUALLY, I CAME HERE MERELY TO REQUEST SOME INFORMATION.

YOU WHAT?

WHAT DO YOU KNOW OF ONE TOBIAS GRIMES?

AIN'T NONE O' YOUR CONCERN! AND IF YA TAKE MY ADVICE, YOU OUGHTA STEER WELL CLEAR OF HIM! YOU HEAR ME, BILLY?

I HEAR YOU, SALLY, AND I'M MUCH OBLIGED THAT YOU CARE ABOUT MY SAFETY!

BUT WHY DON'T WE CARRY ON OUR CHAT OVER A GLASS OF GIN?

YOU'RE A REAL GENT, YOU ARE, BILLY FLETCHER!

LET'S GO TO *THE THREE HOUNDS!* I'LL TREAT YA!

HE USED TO SERVE IN HER MAJESTY'S ARMY, OVER IN INDIA, I THINK. HE'S A HEARTLESS BRUTE. NOT REALLY THE GENTEEL TYPE, IF YA GET MY MEANIN'...

ANYTHING ELSE ABOUT HIM?

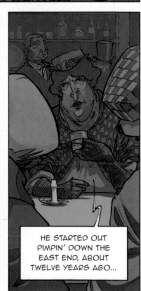

HE STARTED OUT PIMPIN' DOWN THE EAST END, ABOUT TWELVE YEARS AGO...

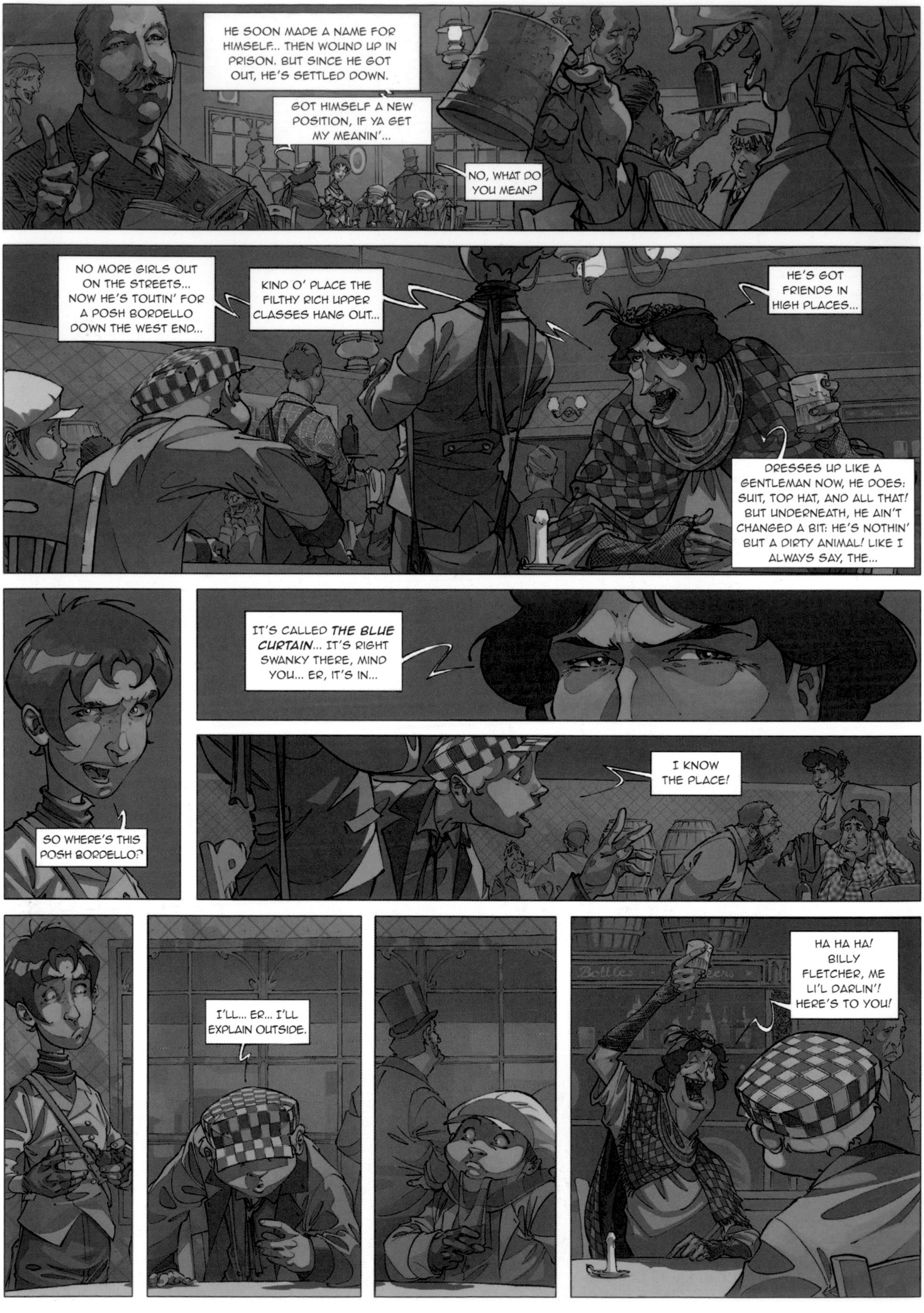
HE SOON MADE A NAME FOR HIMSELF... THEN WOUND UP IN PRISON. BUT SINCE HE GOT OUT, HE'S SETTLED DOWN.
GOT HIMSELF A NEW POSITION, IF YA GET MY MEANIN'...
NO, WHAT DO YOU MEAN?
NO MORE GIRLS OUT ON THE STREETS... NOW HE'S TOUTIN' FOR A POSH BORDELLO DOWN THE WEST END...
KIND O' PLACE THE FILTHY RICH UPPER CLASSES HANG OUT...
HE'S GOT FRIENDS IN HIGH PLACES...
DRESSES UP LIKE A GENTLEMAN NOW, HE DOES: SUIT, TOP HAT, AND ALL THAT! BUT UNDERNEATH, HE AIN'T CHANGED A BIT: HE'S NOTHIN' BUT A DIRTY ANIMAL! LIKE I ALWAYS SAY, THE...
SO WHERE'S THIS POSH BORDELLO?
IT'S CALLED *THE BLUE CURTAIN*... IT'S RIGHT SWANKY THERE, MIND YOU... ER, IT'S IN...
I KNOW THE PLACE!
I'LL... ER... I'LL EXPLAIN OUTSIDE.
HA HA HA! BILLY FLETCHER, ME LI'L DARLIN'! HERE'S TO YOU!

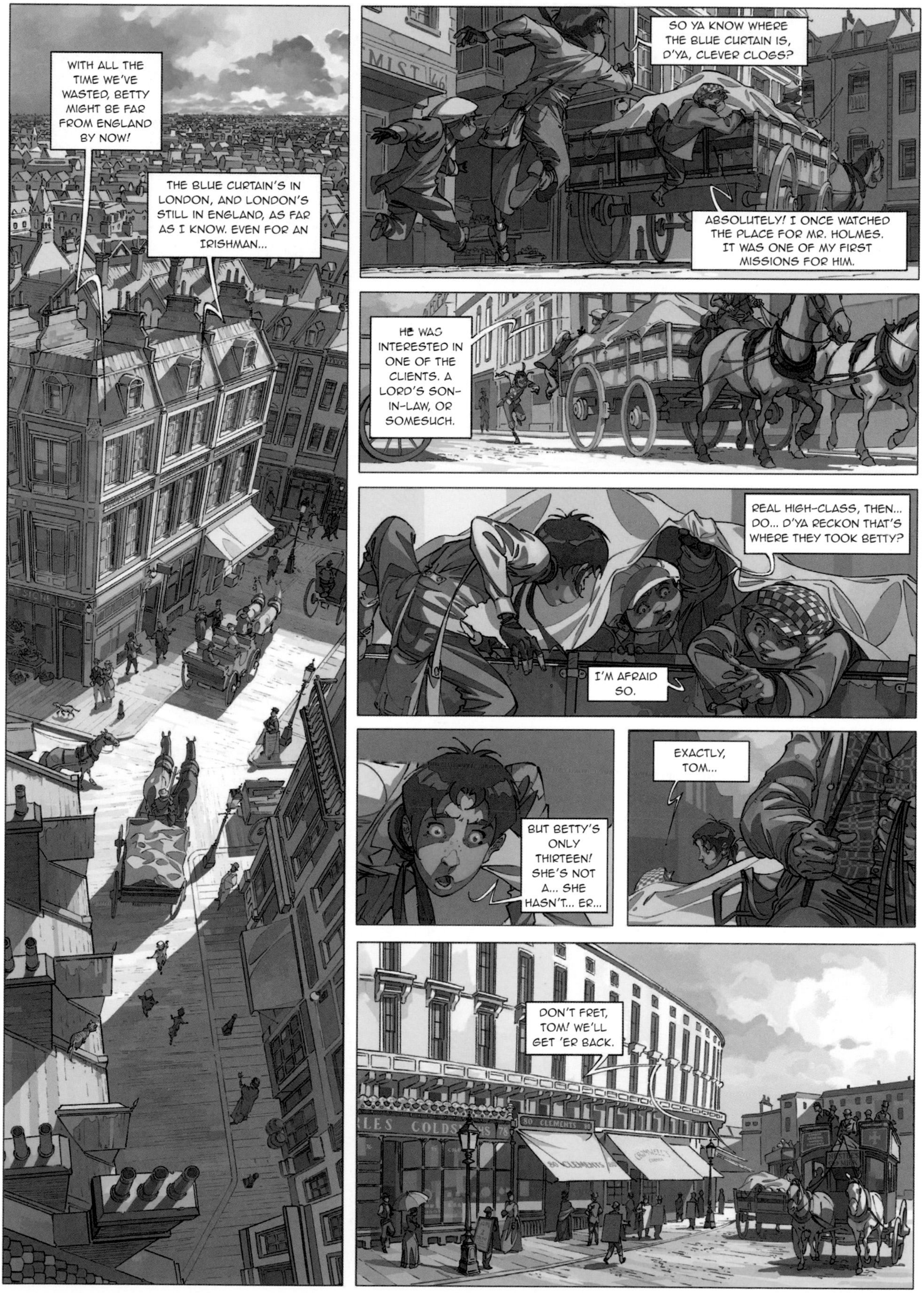
WITH ALL THE TIME WE'VE WASTED, BETTY MIGHT BE FAR FROM ENGLAND BY NOW!
THE BLUE CURTAIN'S IN LONDON, AND LONDON'S STILL IN ENGLAND, AS FAR AS I KNOW. EVEN FOR AN IRISHMAN...
SO YA KNOW WHERE THE BLUE CURTAIN IS, D'YA, CLEVER CLOGS?
ABSOLUTELY! I ONCE WATCHED THE PLACE FOR MR. HOLMES. IT WAS ONE OF MY FIRST MISSIONS FOR HIM.
HE WAS INTERESTED IN ONE OF THE CLIENTS. A LORD'S SON-IN-LAW, OR SOMESUCH.
REAL HIGH-CLASS, THEN... DO... D'YA RECKON THAT'S WHERE THEY TOOK BETTY?
I'M AFRAID SO.
BUT BETTY'S ONLY THIRTEEN! SHE'S NOT A... SHE HASN'T... ER...
EXACTLY, TOM...
DON'T FRET, TOM! WE'LL GET 'ER BACK.

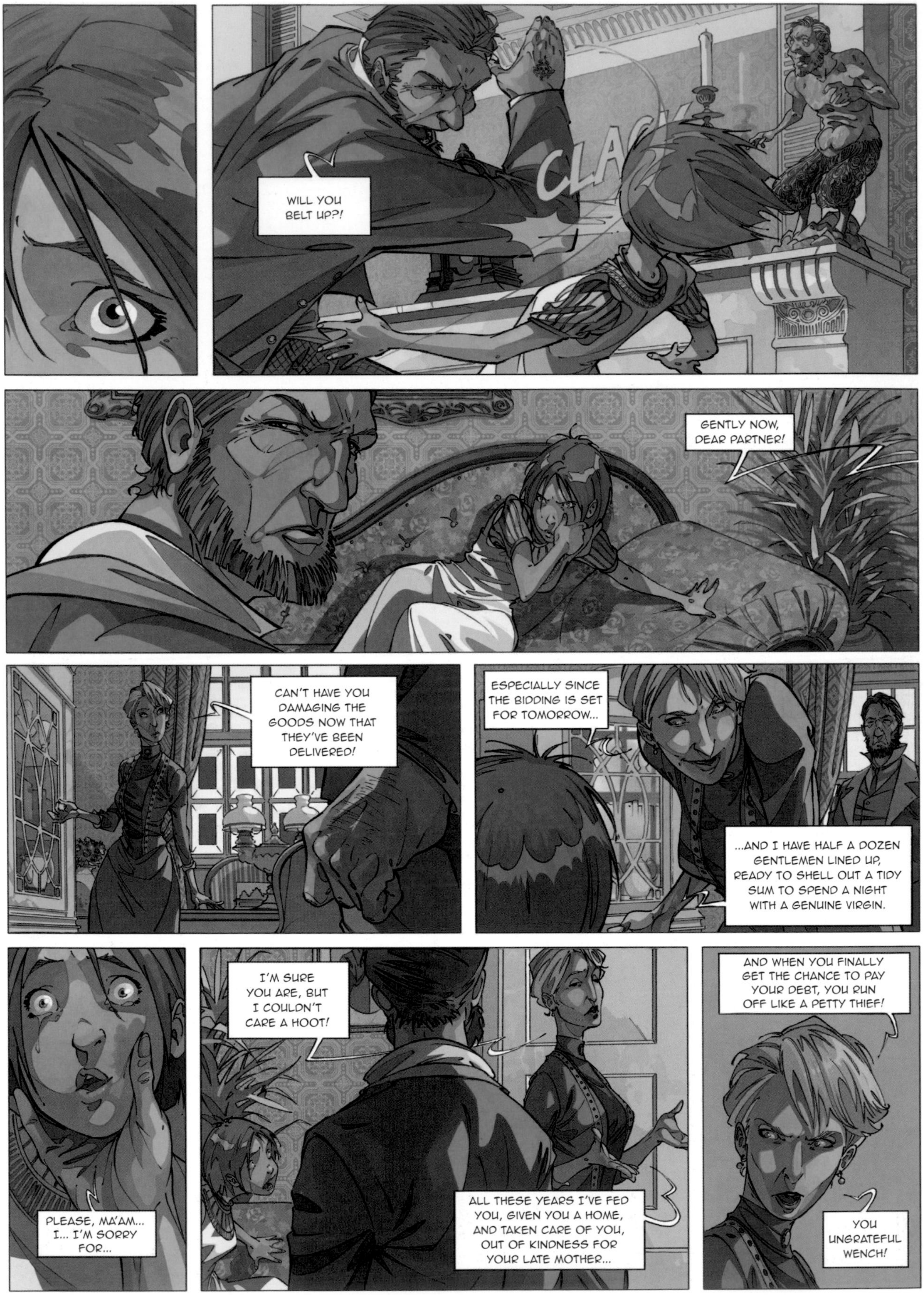
CLACK
WILL YOU BELT UP?!
GENTLY NOW, DEAR PARTNER!
CAN'T HAVE YOU DAMAGING THE GOODS NOW THAT THEY'VE BEEN DELIVERED!
ESPECIALLY SINCE THE BIDDING IS SET FOR TOMORROW...
...AND I HAVE HALF A DOZEN GENTLEMEN LINED UP, READY TO SHELL OUT A TIDY SUM TO SPEND A NIGHT WITH A GENUINE VIRGIN.
PLEASE, MA'AM... I... I'M SORRY FOR...
I'M SURE YOU ARE, BUT I COULDN'T CARE A HOOT!
ALL THESE YEARS I'VE FED YOU, GIVEN YOU A HOME, AND TAKEN CARE OF YOU, OUT OF KINDNESS FOR YOUR LATE MOTHER...
AND WHEN YOU FINALLY GET THE CHANCE TO PAY YOUR DEBT, YOU RUN OFF LIKE A PETTY THIEF!
YOU UNGRATEFUL WENCH!

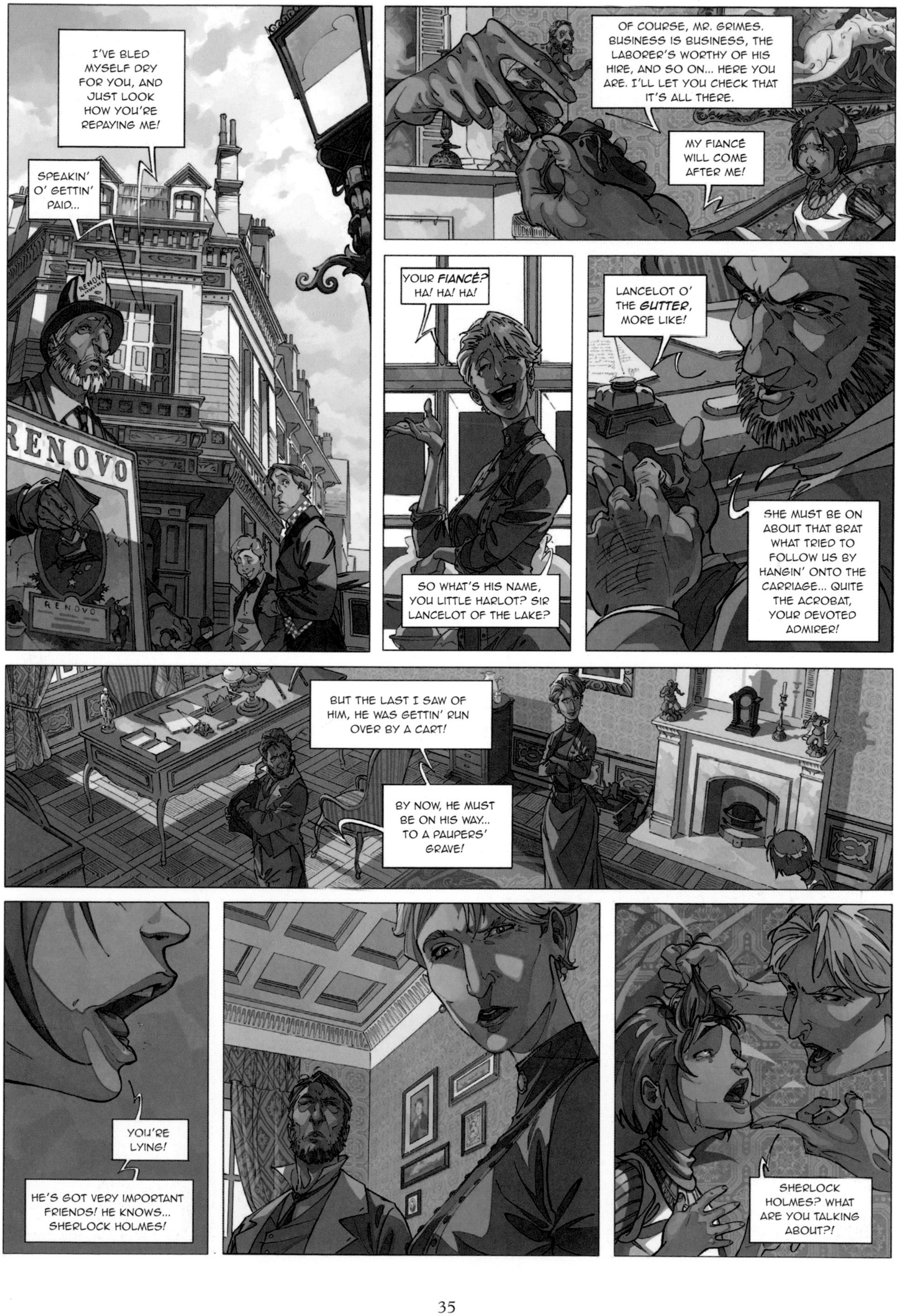

I'VE BLED MYSELF DRY FOR YOU, AND JUST LOOK HOW YOU'RE REPAYING ME!
SPEAKIN' O' GETTIN' PAID...
RENOVO
RENOVO
OF COURSE, MR. GRIMES. BUSINESS IS BUSINESS, THE LABORER'S WORTHY OF HIS HIRE, AND SO ON... HERE YOU ARE. I'LL LET YOU CHECK THAT IT'S ALL THERE.
MY FIANCÉ WILL COME AFTER ME!
YOUR FIANCÉ? HA! HA! HA!
SO WHAT'S HIS NAME, YOU LITTLE HARLOT? SIR LANCELOT OF THE LAKE?
LANCELOT O' THE GUTTER, MORE LIKE!
SHE MUST BE ON ABOUT THAT BRAT WHAT TRIED TO FOLLOW US BY HANGIN' ONTO THE CARRIAGE... QUITE THE ACROBAT, YOUR DEVOTED ADMIRER!
BUT THE LAST I SAW OF HIM, HE WAS GETTIN' RUN OVER BY A CART!
BY NOW, HE MUST BE ON HIS WAY... TO A PAUPERS' GRAVE!
YOU'RE LYING!
HE'S GOT VERY IMPORTANT FRIENDS! HE KNOWS... SHERLOCK HOLMES!
SHERLOCK HOLMES? WHAT ARE YOU TALKING ABOUT?!

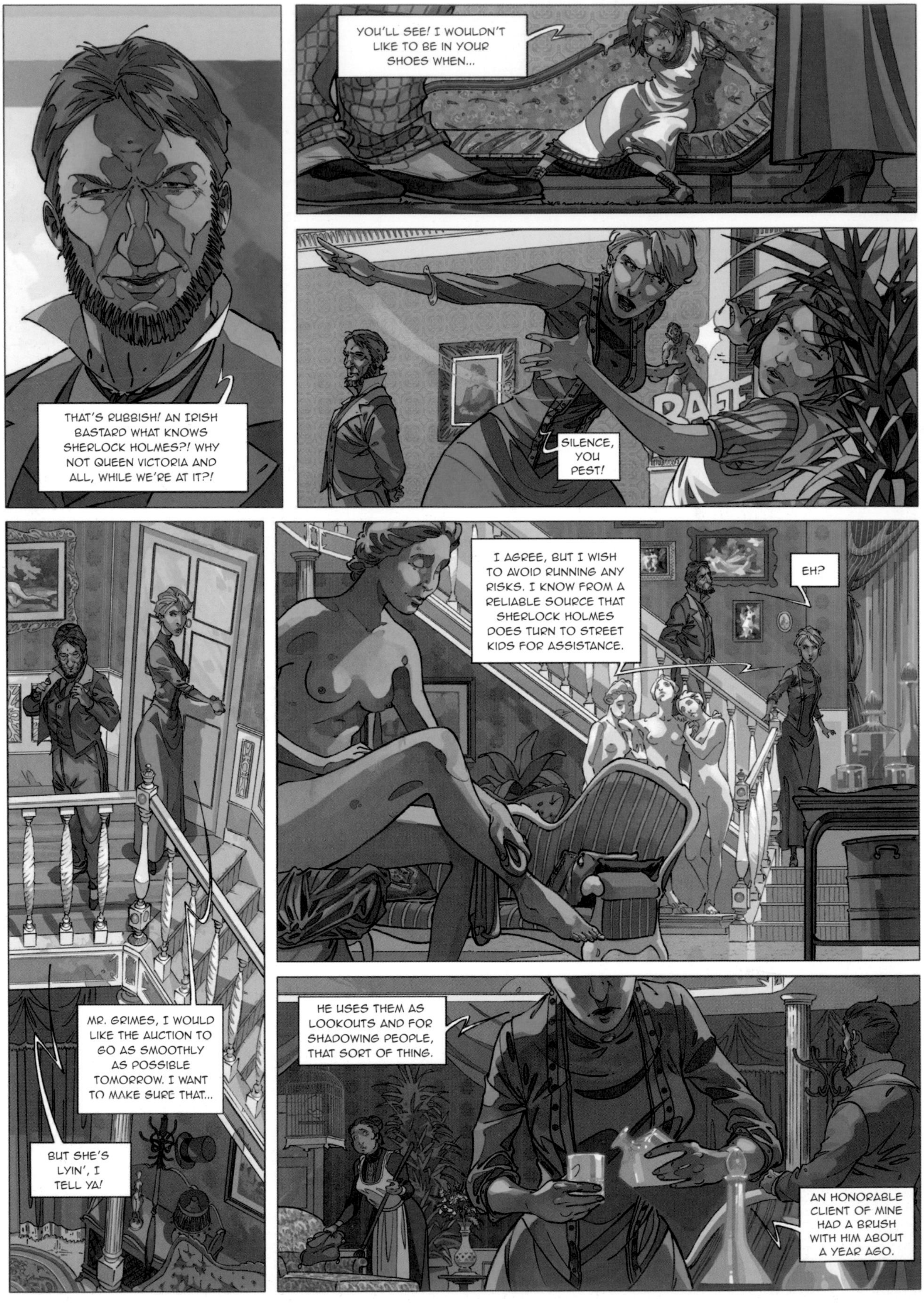

YOU'LL SEE! I WOULDN'T LIKE TO BE IN YOUR SHOES WHEN...
THAT'S RUBBISH! AN IRISH BASTARD WHAT KNOWS SHERLOCK HOLMES?! WHY NOT QUEEN VICTORIA AND ALL, WHILE WE'RE AT IT?!
SILENCE, YOU PEST!
MR. GRIMES, I WOULD LIKE THE AUCTION TO GO AS SMOOTHLY AS POSSIBLE TOMORROW. I WANT TO MAKE SURE THAT...
BUT SHE'S LYIN', I TELL YA!
I AGREE, BUT I WISH TO AVOID RUNNING ANY RISKS. I KNOW FROM A RELIABLE SOURCE THAT SHERLOCK HOLMES DOES TURN TO STREET KIDS FOR ASSISTANCE.
EH?
HE USES THEM AS LOOKOUTS AND FOR SHADOWING PEOPLE, THAT SORT OF THING.
AN HONORABLE CLIENT OF MINE HAD A BRUSH WITH HIM ABOUT A YEAR AGO.

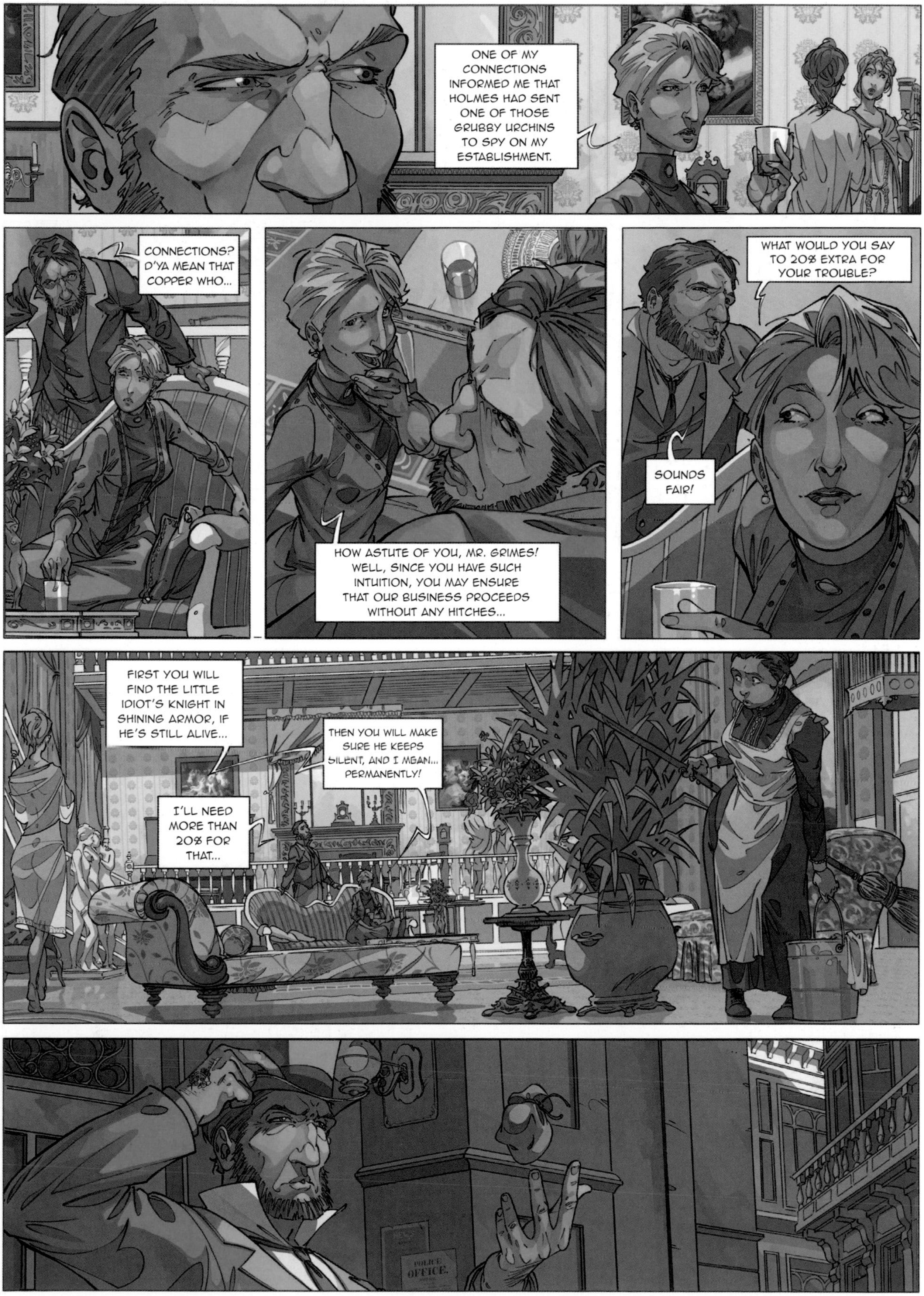
ONE OF MY CONNECTIONS INFORMED ME THAT HOLMES HAD SENT ONE OF THOSE GRUBBY URCHINS TO SPY ON MY ESTABLISHMENT.
CONNECTIONS? D'YA MEAN THAT COPPER WHO...
HOW ASTUTE OF YOU, MR. GRIMES! WELL, SINCE YOU HAVE SUCH INTUITION, YOU MAY ENSURE THAT OUR BUSINESS PROCEEDS WITHOUT ANY HITCHES...
WHAT WOULD YOU SAY TO 20% EXTRA FOR YOUR TROUBLE?
SOUNDS FAIR!
FIRST YOU WILL FIND THE LITTLE IDIOT'S KNIGHT IN SHINING ARMOR, IF HE'S STILL ALIVE...
THEN YOU WILL MAKE SURE HE KEEPS SILENT, AND I MEAN... PERMANENTLY!
I'LL NEED MORE THAN 20% FOR THAT...
POLICE OFFICE.

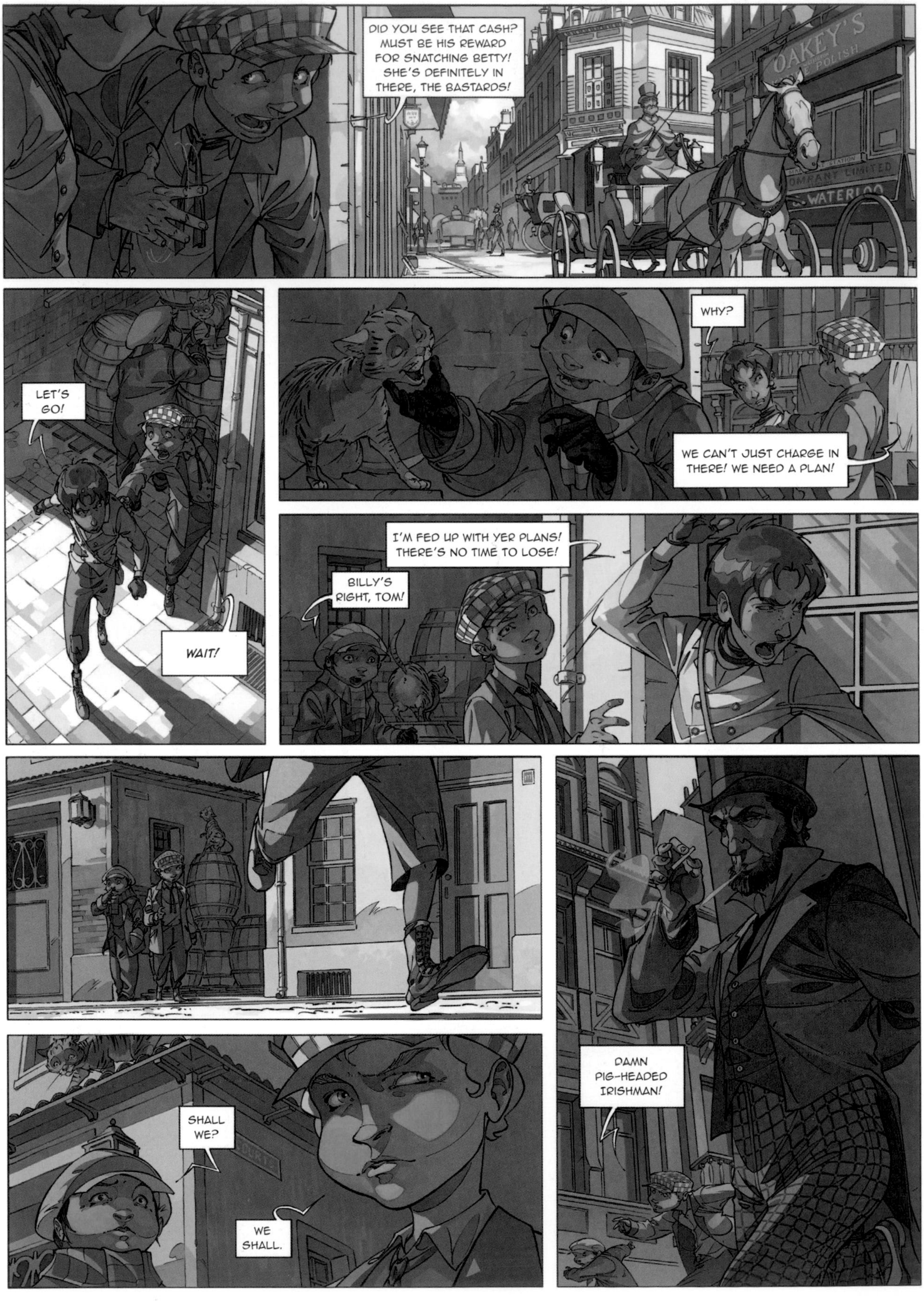
DID YOU SEE THAT CASH? MUST BE HIS REWARD FOR SNATCHING BETTY! SHE'S DEFINITELY IN THERE, THE BASTARDS!
OAKEY'S
WATERLOO
LET'S GO!
WAIT!
WHY?
WE CAN'T JUST CHARGE IN THERE! WE NEED A PLAN!
I'M FED UP WITH YER PLANS! THERE'S NO TIME TO LOSE!
BILLY'S RIGHT, TOM!
SHALL WE?
WE SHALL.
DAMN PIG-HEADED IRISHMAN!

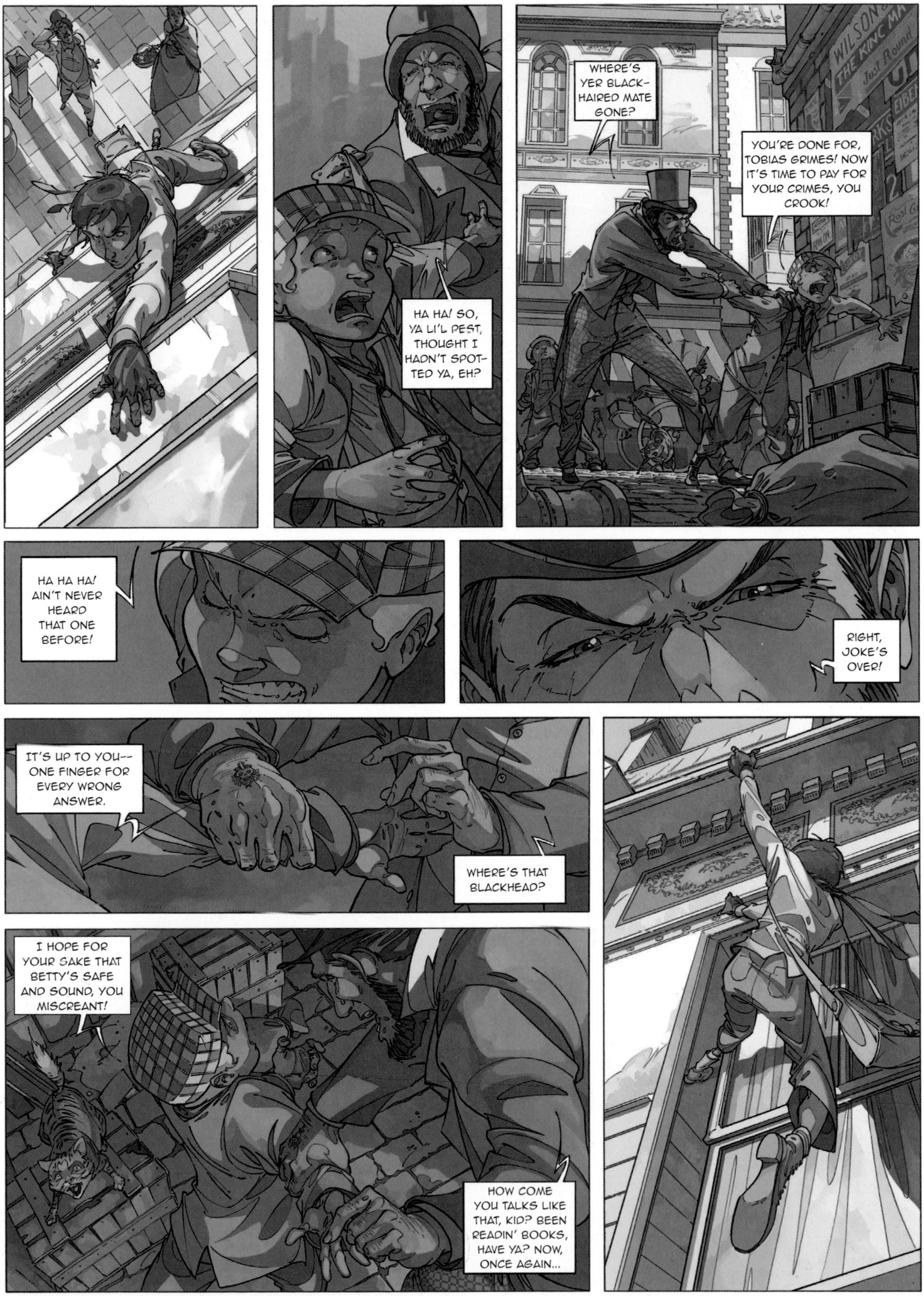
HA HA! SO, YA LI'L PEST, THOUGHT I HADN'T SPOTTED YA, EH?
WHERE'S YER BLACK-HAIRED MATE GONE?
YOU'RE DONE FOR, TOBIAS GRIMES! NOW IT'S TIME TO PAY FOR YOUR CRIMES, YOU CROOK!
WILSON
THE KING MA
Just Round
HA HA HA! AIN'T NEVER HEARD THAT ONE BEFORE!
RIGHT, JOKE'S OVER!
IT'S UP TO YOU-- ONE FINGER FOR EVERY WRONG ANSWER.
WHERE'S THAT BLACKHEAD?
I HOPE FOR YOUR SAKE THAT BETTY'S SAFE AND SOUND, YOU MISCREANT!
HOW COME YOU TALKS LIKE THAT, KID? BEEN READIN' BOOKS, HAVE YA? NOW, ONCE AGAIN...

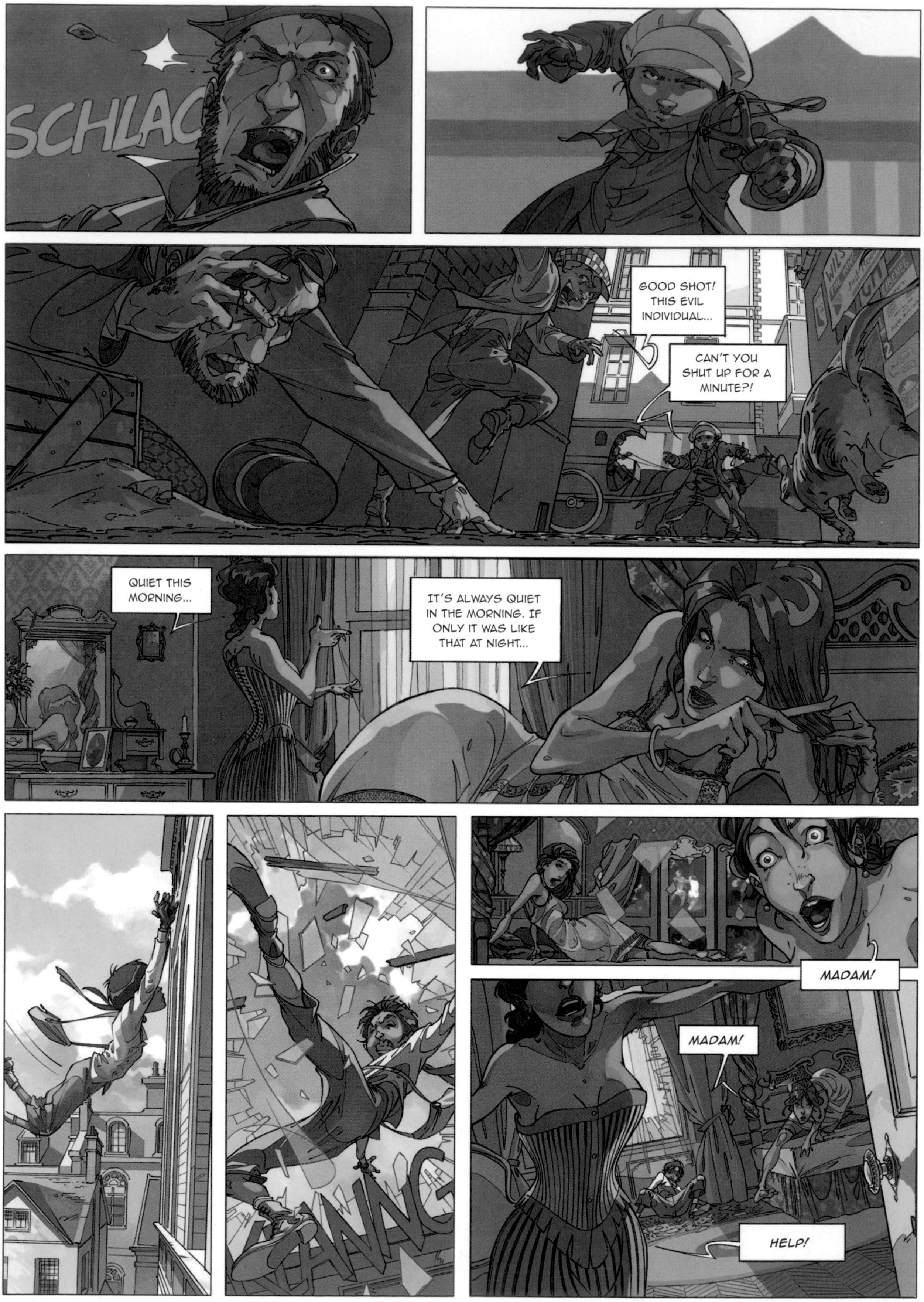
SCHLAC
GOOD SHOT! THIS EVIL INDIVIDUAL...
CAN'T YOU SHUT UP FOR A MINUTE?!
QUIET THIS MORNING...
IT'S ALWAYS QUIET IN THE MORNING. IF ONLY IT WAS LIKE THAT AT NIGHT...
MADAM!
MADAM!
HELP!

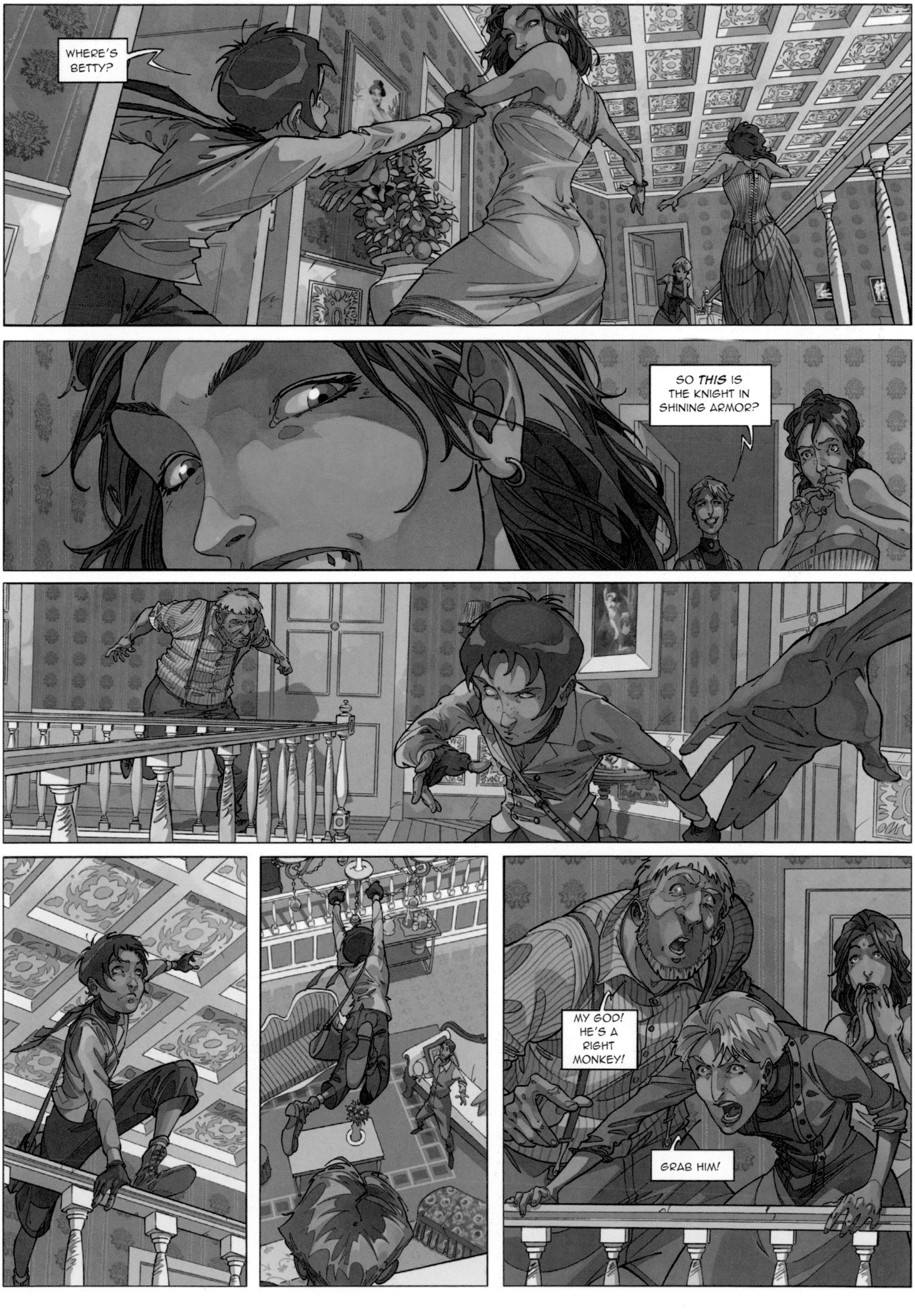
WHERE'S BETTY?
SO THIS IS THE KNIGHT IN SHINING ARMOR?
MY GOD! HE'S A RIGHT MONKEY!
GRAB HIM!

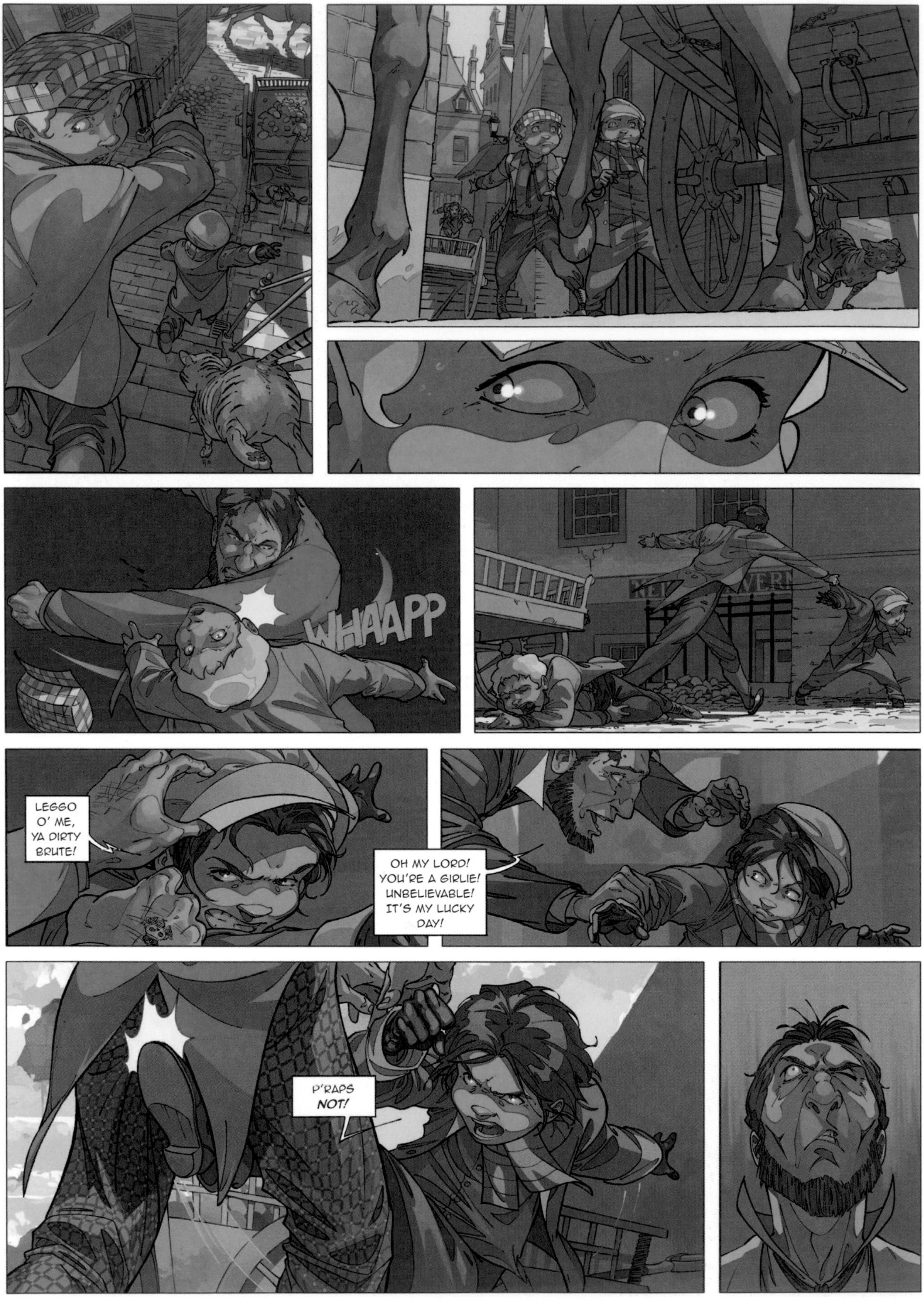
WHAAPP
LEGGO O' ME, YA DIRTY BRUTE!
OH MY LORD! YOU'RE A GIRLIE! UNBELIEVABLE! IT'S MY LUCKY DAY!
P'RAPS NOT!

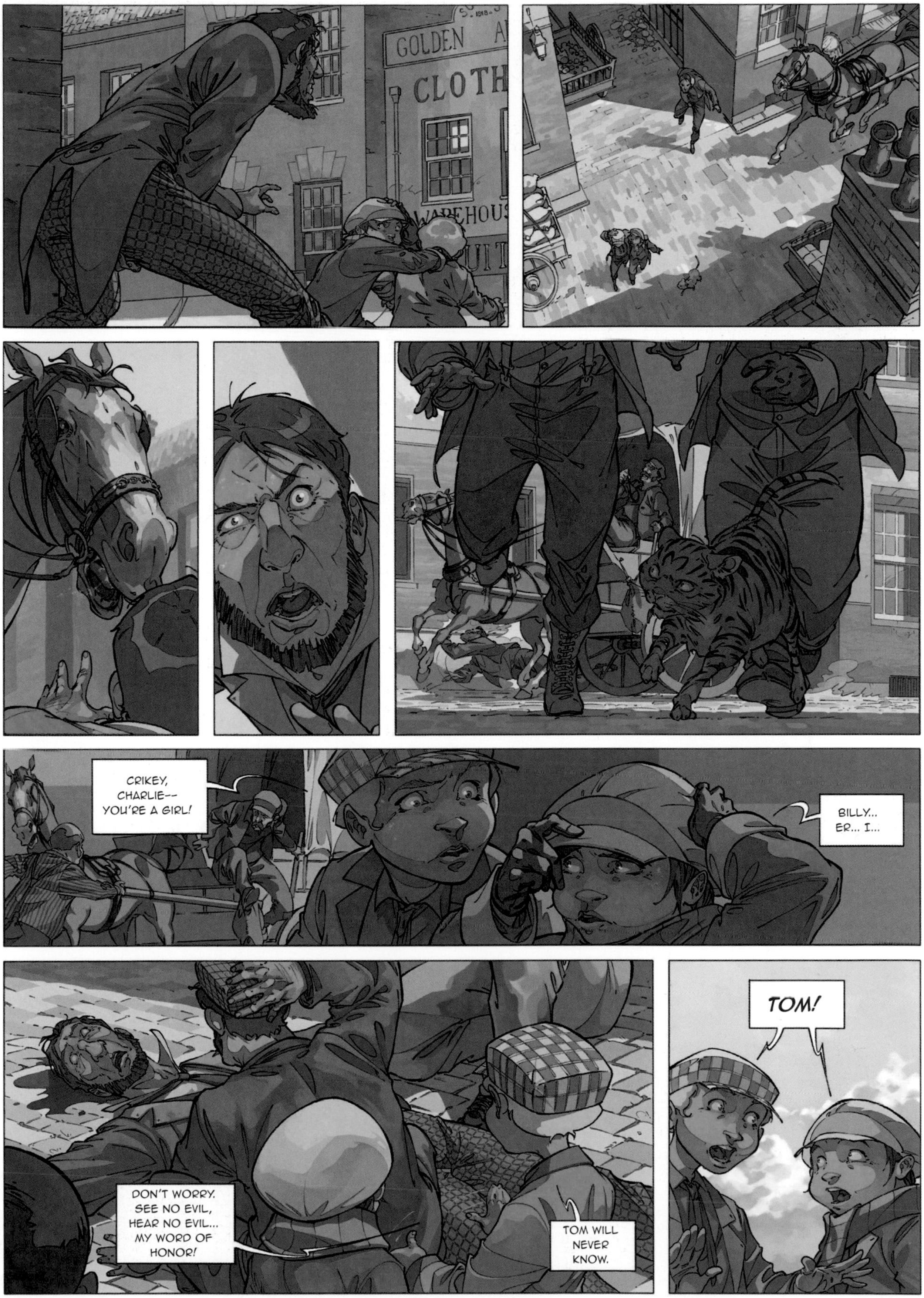
GOLDEN
CLOTH
WAREHOUS
CRIKEY, CHARLIE-- YOU'RE A GIRL!
BILLY... ER... I...
DON'T WORRY. SEE NO EVIL, HEAR NO EVIL... MY WORD OF HONOR!
TOM WILL NEVER KNOW.
TOM!

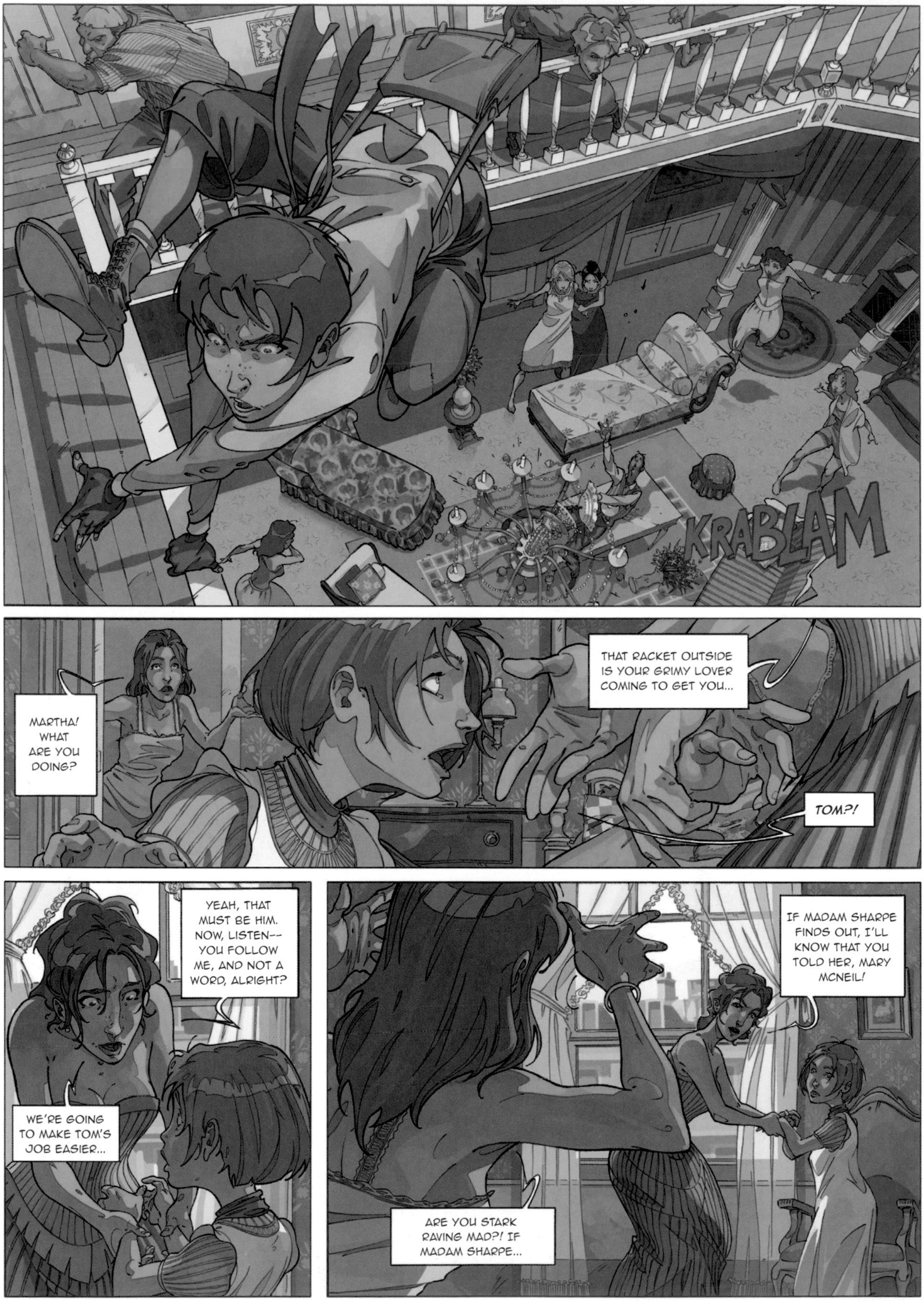
KRABLAM
MARTHA! WHAT ARE YOU DOING?
THAT RACKET OUTSIDE IS YOUR GRIMY LOVER COMING TO GET YOU...
TOM?!
YEAH, THAT MUST BE HIM. NOW, LISTEN-- YOU FOLLOW ME, AND NOT A WORD, ALRIGHT?
WE'RE GOING TO MAKE TOM'S JOB EASIER...
ARE YOU STARK RAVING MAD?! IF MADAM SHARPE...
IF MADAM SHARPE FINDS OUT, I'LL KNOW THAT YOU TOLD HER, MARY MCNEIL!

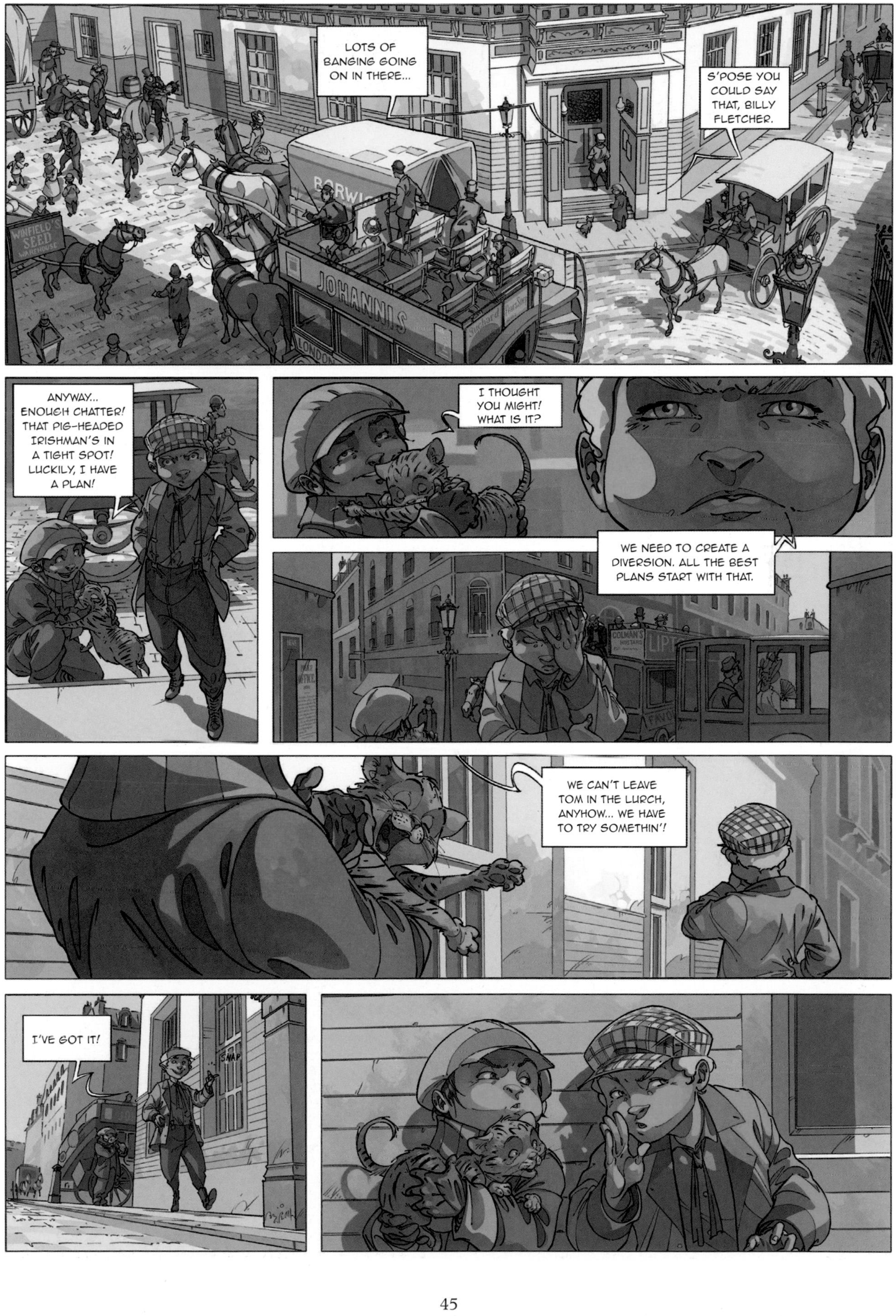

LOTS OF BANGING GOING ON IN THERE...
S'POSE YOU COULD SAY THAT, BILLY FLETCHER.
WINFIELD'S SEED WAREHOUSE
JOHANNIS
ANYWAY... ENOUGH CHATTER! THAT PIG-HEADED IRISHMAN'S IN A TIGHT SPOT! LUCKILY, I HAVE A PLAN!
I THOUGHT YOU MIGHT! WHAT IS IT?
WE NEED TO CREATE A DIVERSION. ALL THE BEST PLANS START WITH THAT.
COLMAN'S MUSTARD
WE CAN'T LEAVE TOM IN THE LURCH, ANYHOW... WE HAVE TO TRY SOMETHIN'!
I'VE GOT IT!
SNAP

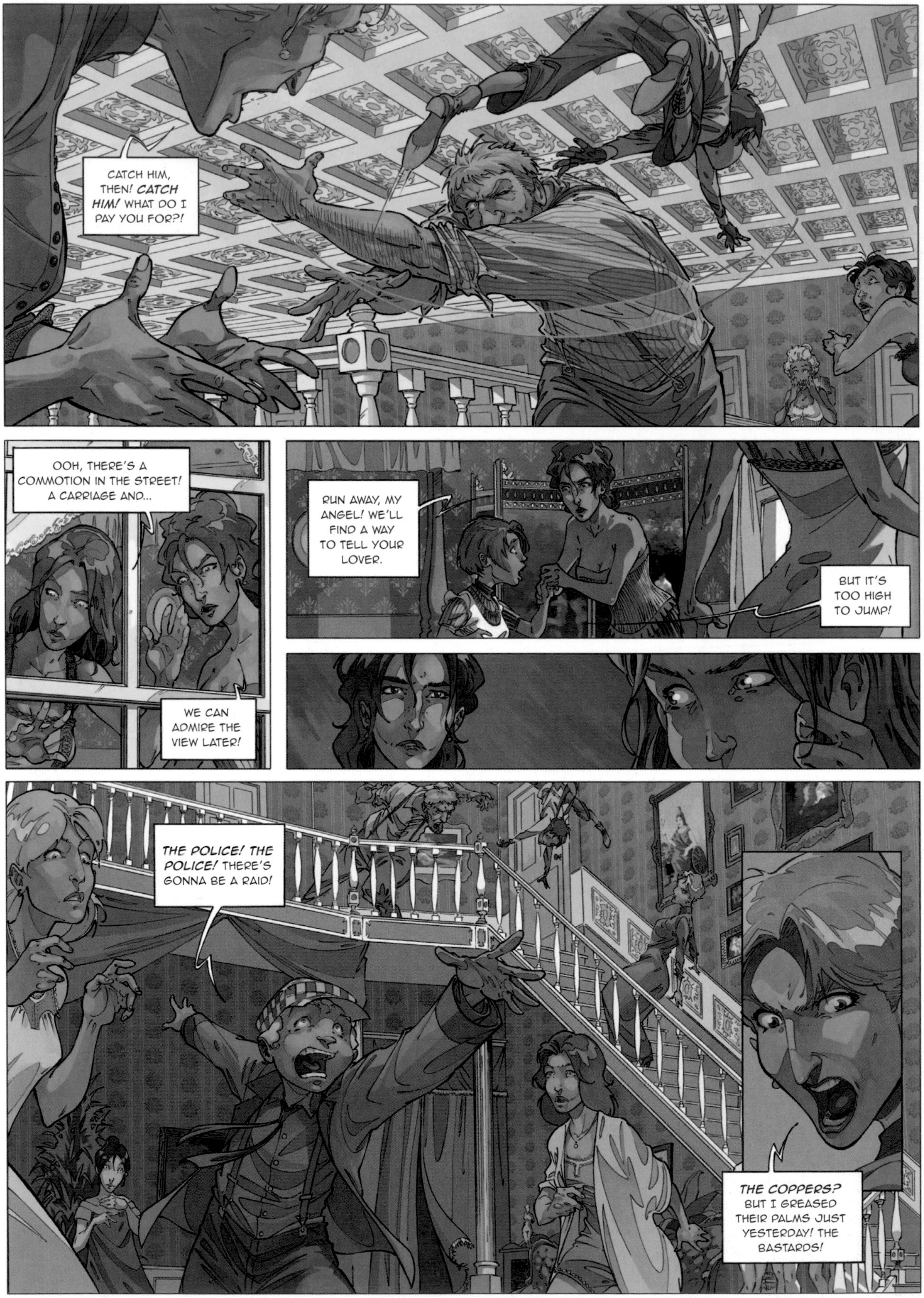
CATCH HIM, THEN! CATCH HIM! WHAT DO I PAY YOU FOR?!
OOH, THERE'S A COMMOTION IN THE STREET! A CARRIAGE AND...
WE CAN ADMIRE THE VIEW LATER!
RUN AWAY, MY ANGEL! WE'LL FIND A WAY TO TELL YOUR LOVER.
BUT IT'S TOO HIGH TO JUMP!
THE POLICE! THE POLICE! THERE'S GONNA BE A RAID!
THE COPPERS? BUT I GREASED THEIR PALMS JUST YESTERDAY! THE BASTARDS!

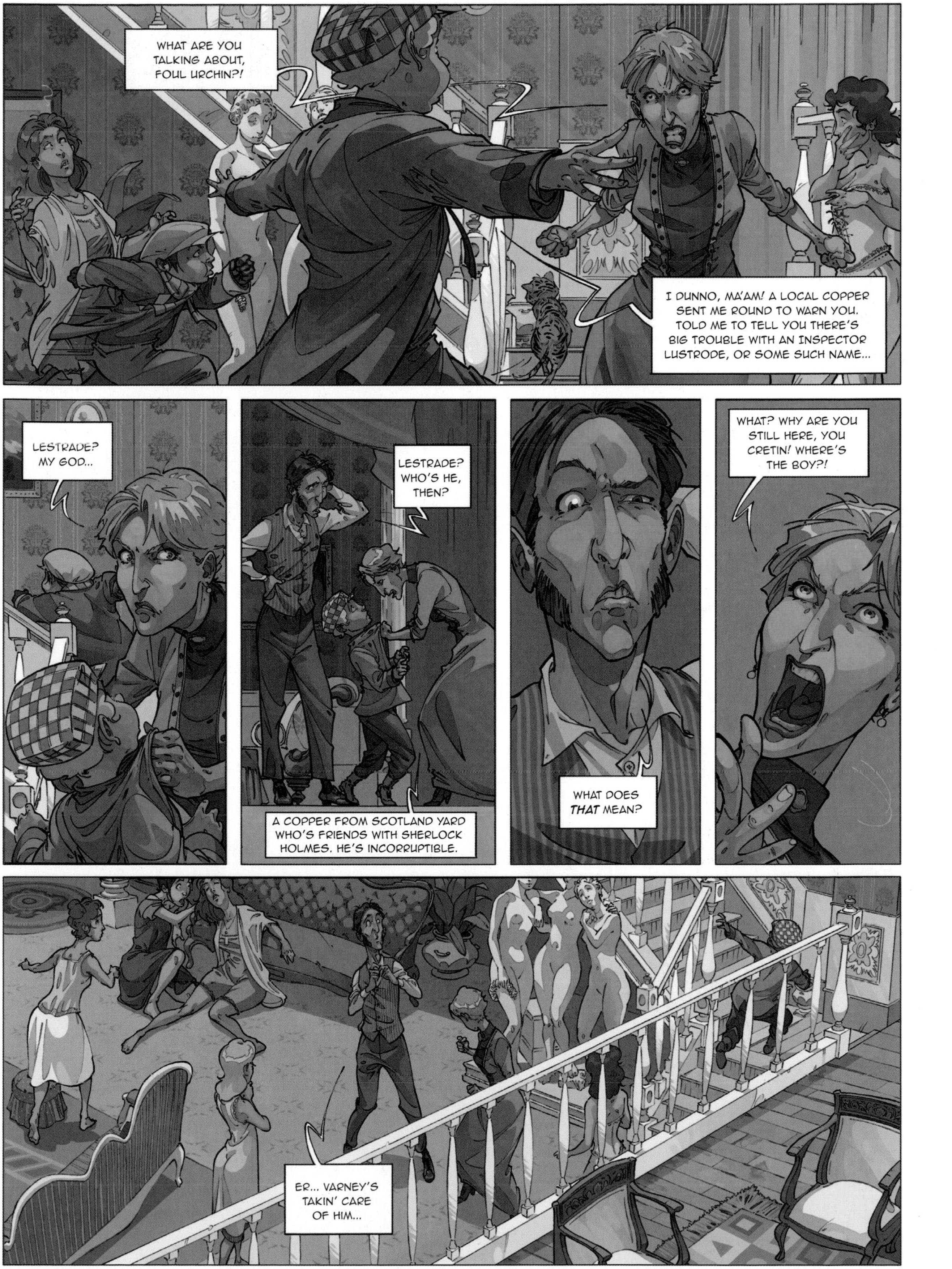
WHAT ARE YOU TALKING ABOUT, FOUL URCHIN?!
I DUNNO, MA'AM! A LOCAL COPPER SENT ME ROUND TO WARN YOU. TOLD ME TO TELL YOU THERE'S BIG TROUBLE WITH AN INSPECTOR LUSTRODE, OR SOME SUCH NAME...
LESTRADE? MY GOD...
LESTRADE? WHO'S HE, THEN?
A COPPER FROM SCOTLAND YARD WHO'S FRIENDS WITH SHERLOCK HOLMES. HE'S INCORRUPTIBLE.
WHAT DOES *THAT* MEAN?
WHAT? WHY ARE YOU STILL HERE, YOU CRETIN! WHERE'S THE BOY?!
ER... VARNEY'S TAKIN' CARE OF HIM...

CORNERED LIKE A RAT, YOU IRISH SCUM!

YOU'LL REGRET MAKIN' ME RUN--

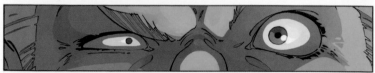

WOUAIH!

MAOUW!?

CAT-TOSSING? SIMPLE BUT EFFECTIVE...

AHRGH

BEST I COULD COME UP WITH!

TOM! WE NEED TO GET GOIN'!

NOT WITHOUT BETTY!

MAOUW!!

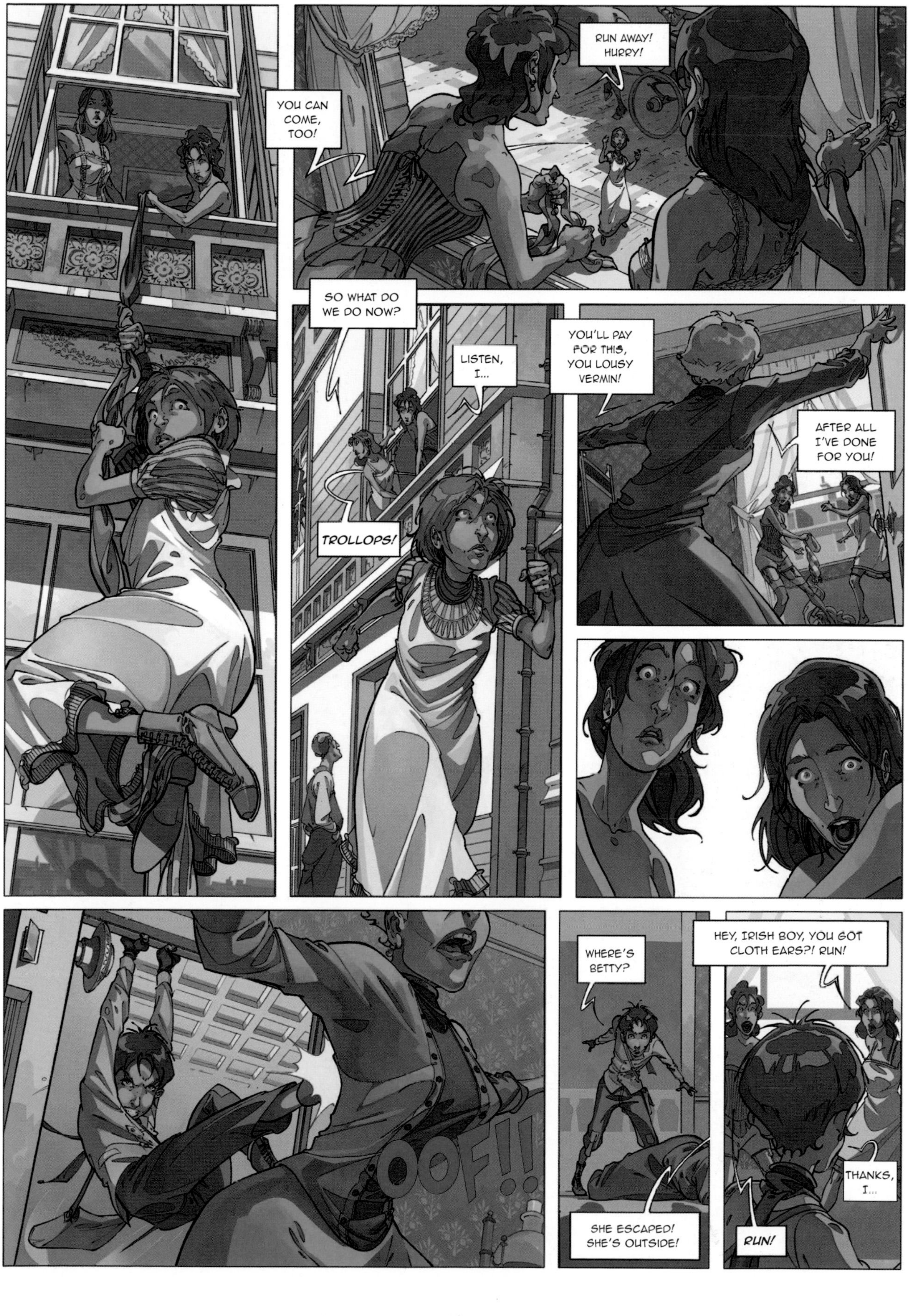
YOU CAN COME, TOO!
RUN AWAY! HURRY!
SO WHAT DO WE DO NOW?
LISTEN, I...
TROLLOPS!
YOU'LL PAY FOR THIS, YOU LOUSY VERMIN!
AFTER ALL I'VE DONE FOR YOU!
OOF!!
WHERE'S BETTY?
SHE ESCAPED! SHE'S OUTSIDE!
HEY, IRISH BOY, YOU GOT CLOTH EARS?! RUN!
THANKS, I...
RUN!

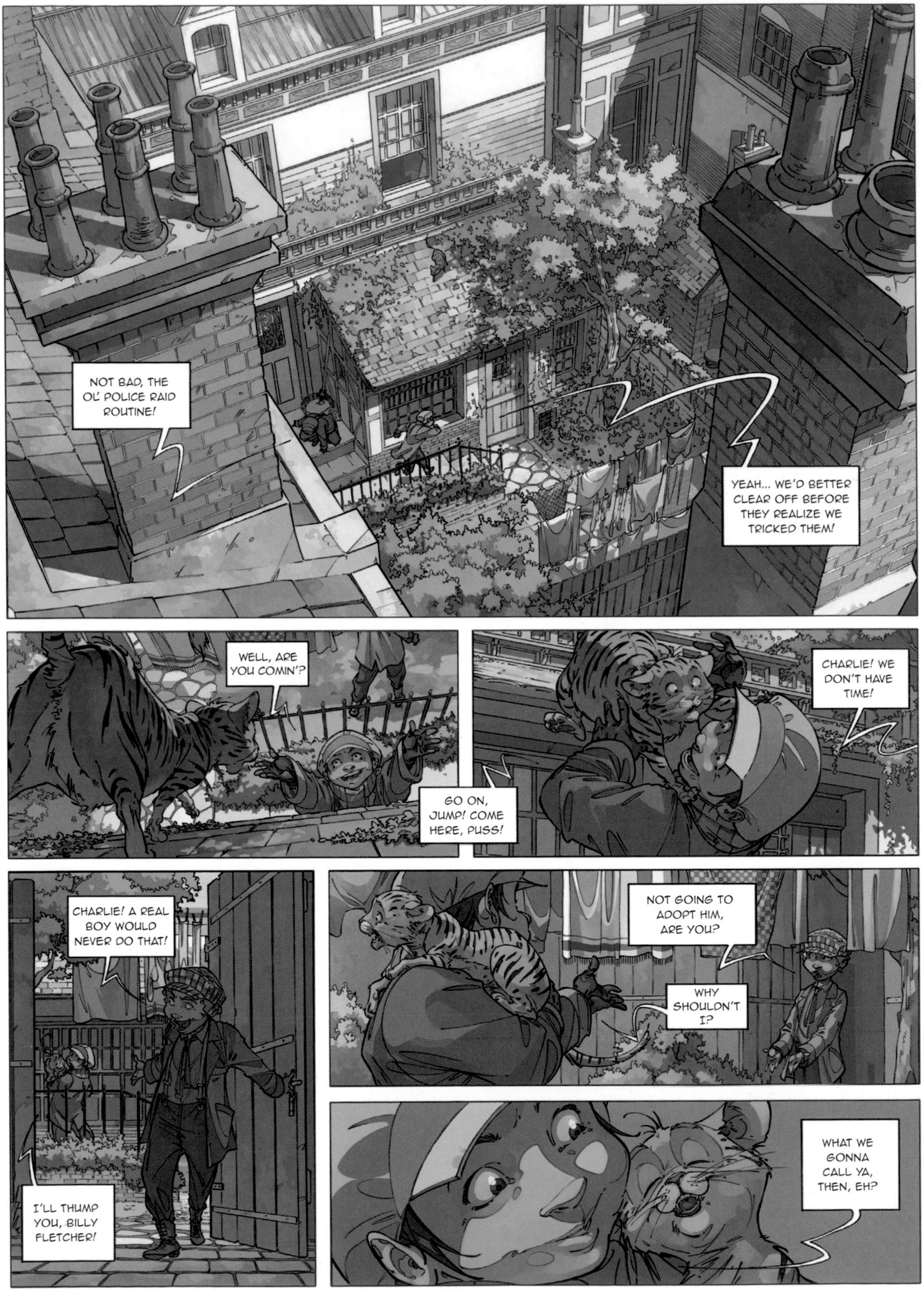
NOT BAD, THE OL' POLICE RAID ROUTINE!
YEAH... WE'D BETTER CLEAR OFF BEFORE THEY REALIZE WE TRICKED THEM!
WELL, ARE YOU COMIN'?
GO ON, JUMP! COME HERE, PUSS!
CHARLIE! WE DON'T HAVE TIME!
CHARLIE! A REAL BOY WOULD NEVER DO THAT!
I'LL THUMP YOU, BILLY FLETCHER!
NOT GOING TO ADOPT HIM, ARE YOU?
WHY SHOULDN'T I?
WHAT WE GONNA CALL YA, THEN, EH?

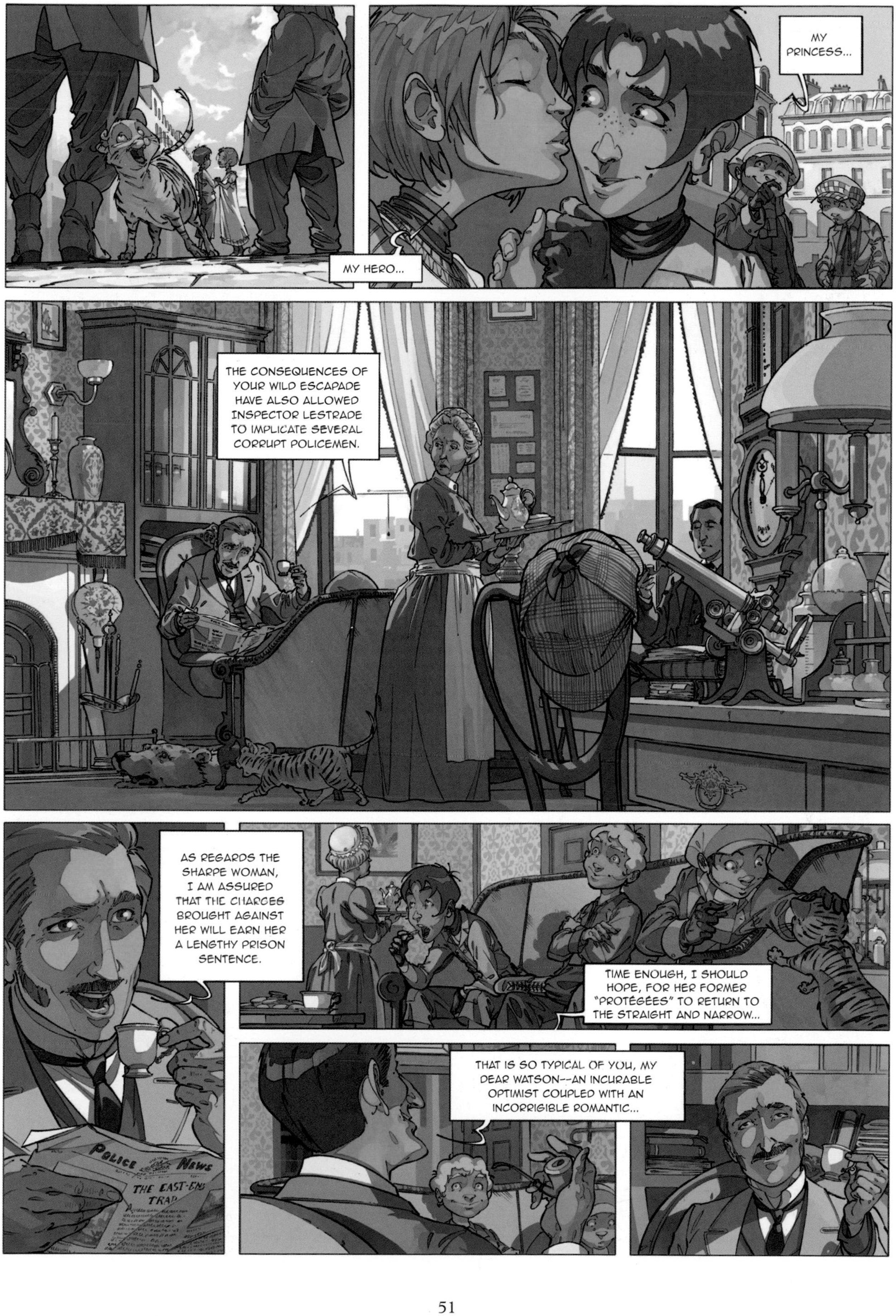
MY PRINCESS...
MY HERO...
THE CONSEQUENCES OF YOUR WILD ESCAPADE HAVE ALSO ALLOWED INSPECTOR LESTRADE TO IMPLICATE SEVERAL CORRUPT POLICEMEN.
AS REGARDS THE SHARPE WOMAN, I AM ASSURED THAT THE CHARGES BROUGHT AGAINST HER WILL EARN HER A LENGTHY PRISON SENTENCE.
TIME ENOUGH, I SHOULD HOPE, FOR HER FORMER "PROTÉGÉES" TO RETURN TO THE STRAIGHT AND NARROW...
POLICE NEWS
THE EAST-END TRAP
THAT IS SO TYPICAL OF YOU, MY DEAR WATSON--AN INCURABLE OPTIMIST COUPLED WITH AN INCORRIGIBLE ROMANTIC...

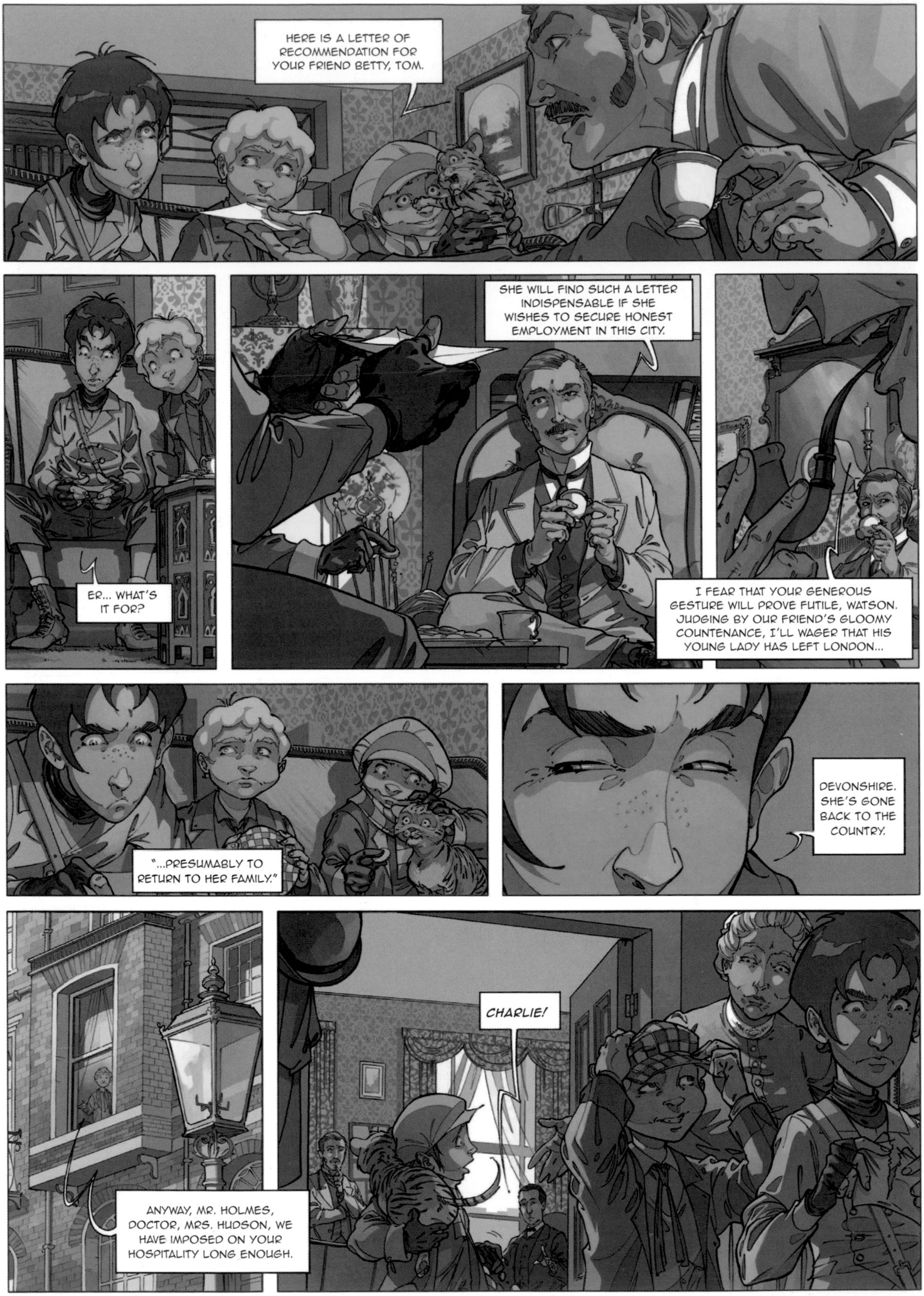
HERE IS A LETTER OF RECOMMENDATION FOR YOUR FRIEND BETTY, TOM.
ER... WHAT'S IT FOR?
SHE WILL FIND SUCH A LETTER INDISPENSABLE IF SHE WISHES TO SECURE HONEST EMPLOYMENT IN THIS CITY.
I FEAR THAT YOUR GENEROUS GESTURE WILL PROVE FUTILE, WATSON. JUDGING BY OUR FRIEND'S GLOOMY COUNTENANCE, I'LL WAGER THAT HIS YOUNG LADY HAS LEFT LONDON...
"...PRESUMABLY TO RETURN TO HER FAMILY."
DEVONSHIRE. SHE'S GONE BACK TO THE COUNTRY.
ANYWAY, MR. HOLMES, DOCTOR, MRS. HUDSON, WE HAVE IMPOSED ON YOUR HOSPITALITY LONG ENOUGH.
CHARLIE!

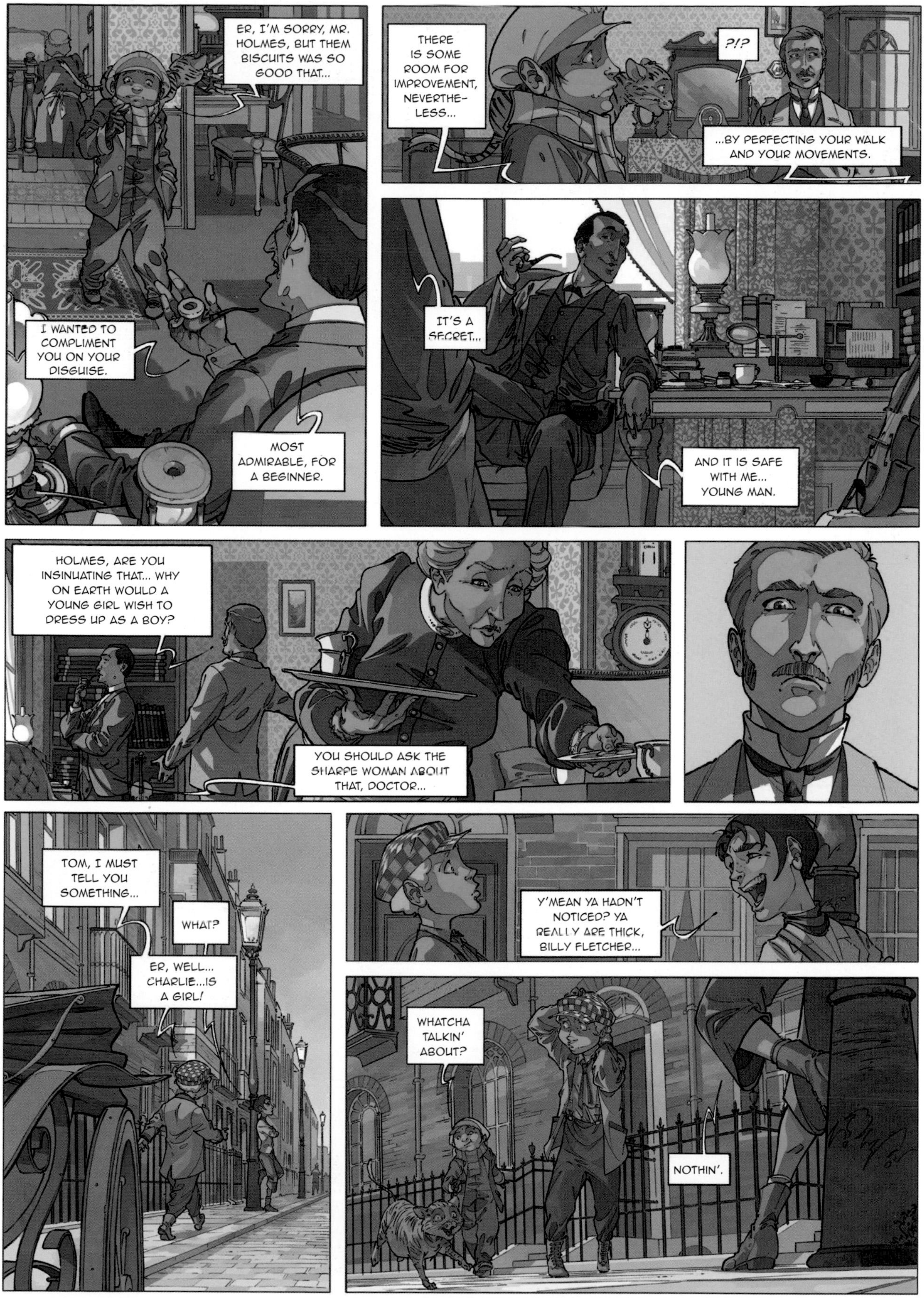
ER, I'M SORRY, MR. HOLMES, BUT THEM BISCUITS WAS SO GOOD THAT...
I WANTED TO COMPLIMENT YOU ON YOUR DISGUISE.
MOST ADMIRABLE, FOR A BEGINNER.
THERE IS SOME ROOM FOR IMPROVEMENT, NEVERTHE-LESS...
?!?
...BY PERFECTING YOUR WALK AND YOUR MOVEMENTS.
IT'S A SECRET...
AND IT IS SAFE WITH ME... YOUNG MAN.
HOLMES, ARE YOU INSINUATING THAT... WHY ON EARTH WOULD A YOUNG GIRL WISH TO DRESS UP AS A BOY?
YOU SHOULD ASK THE SHARPE WOMAN ABOUT THAT, DOCTOR...
TOM, I MUST TELL YOU SOMETHING...
WHAT?
ER, WELL... CHARLIE...IS A GIRL!
Y'MEAN YA HADN'T NOTICED? YA REALLY ARE THICK, BILLY FLETCHER...
WHATCHA TALKIN' ABOUT?
NOTHIN'.

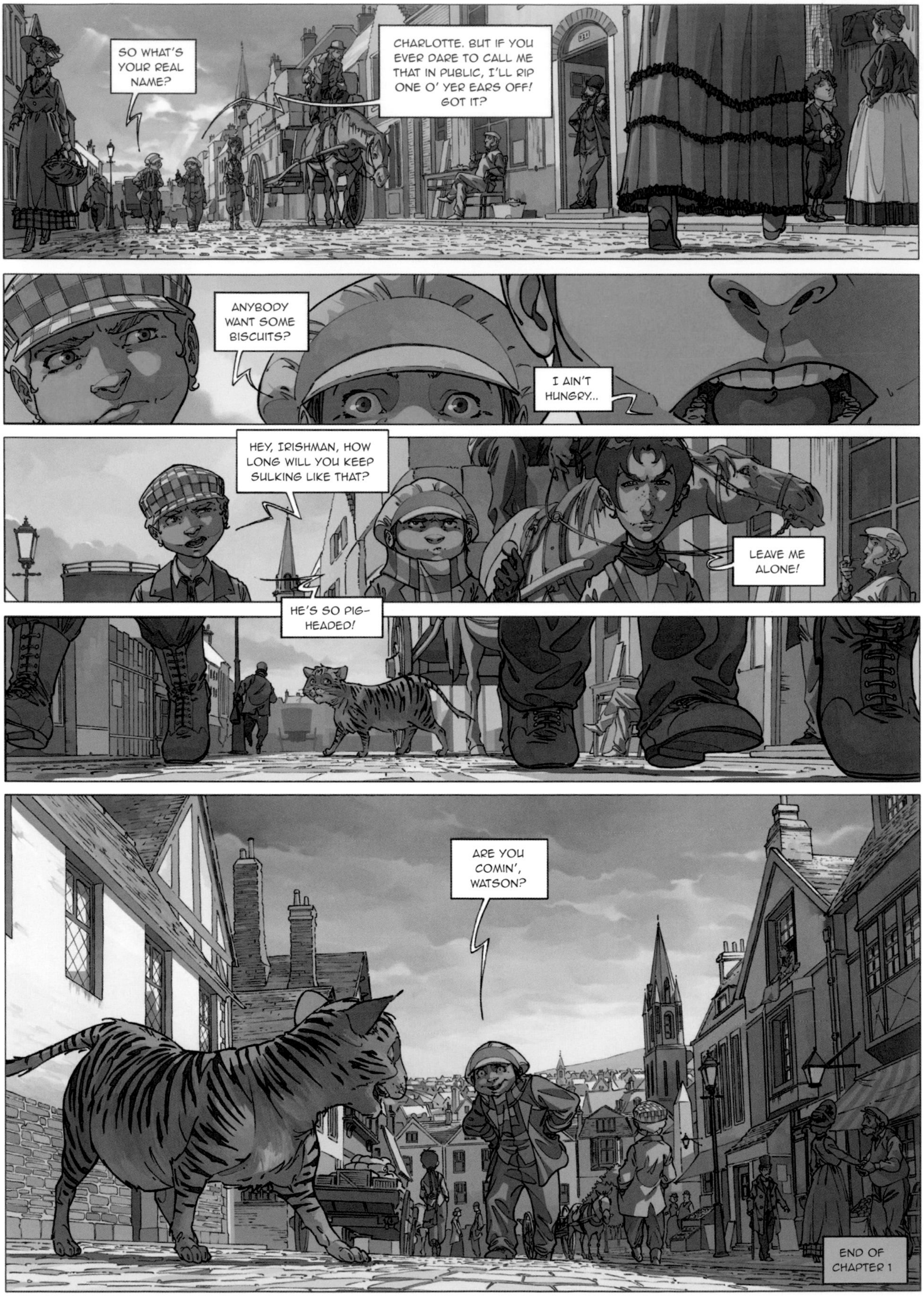
SO WHAT'S YOUR REAL NAME?
CHARLOTTE. BUT IF YOU EVER DARE TO CALL ME THAT IN PUBLIC, I'LL RIP ONE O' YER EARS OFF! GOT IT?
ANYBODY WANT SOME BISCUITS?
I AIN'T HUNGRY...
HEY, IRISHMAN, HOW LONG WILL YOU KEEP SULKING LIKE THAT?
LEAVE ME ALONE!
HE'S SO PIG-HEADED!
ARE YOU COMIN', WATSON?
END OF CHAPTER 1

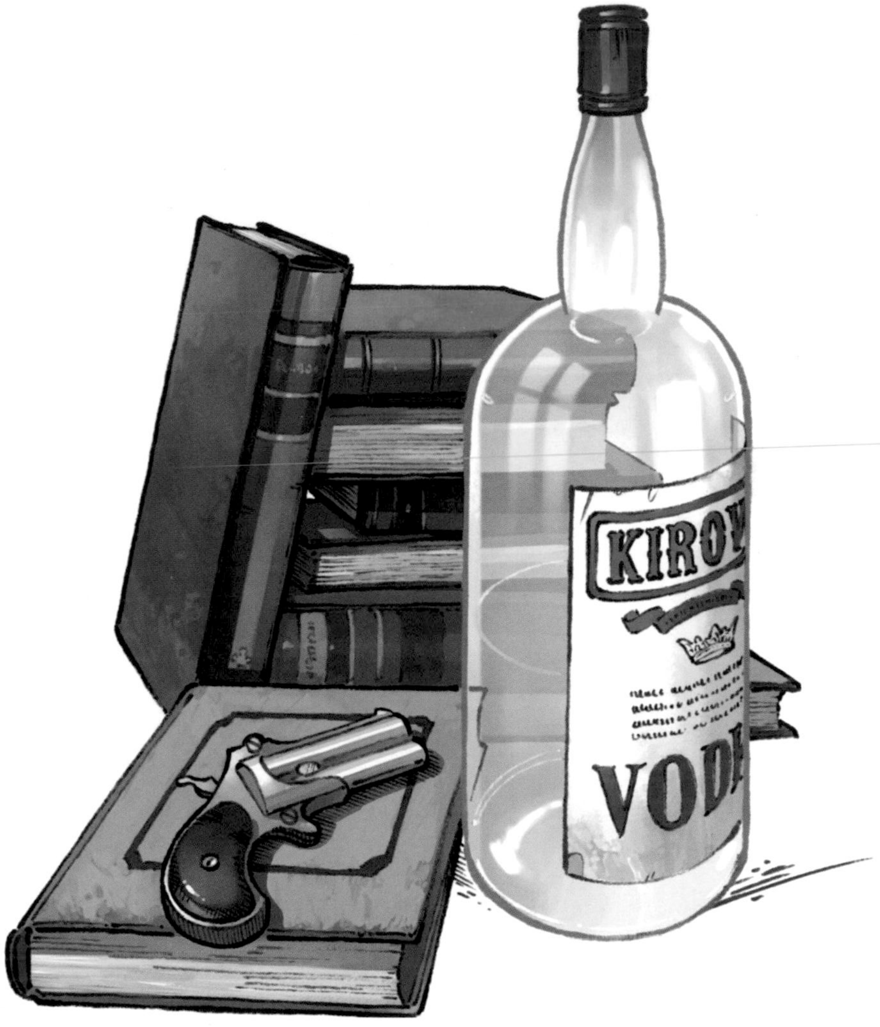
KIROV
VODK

The Rabúkin Case

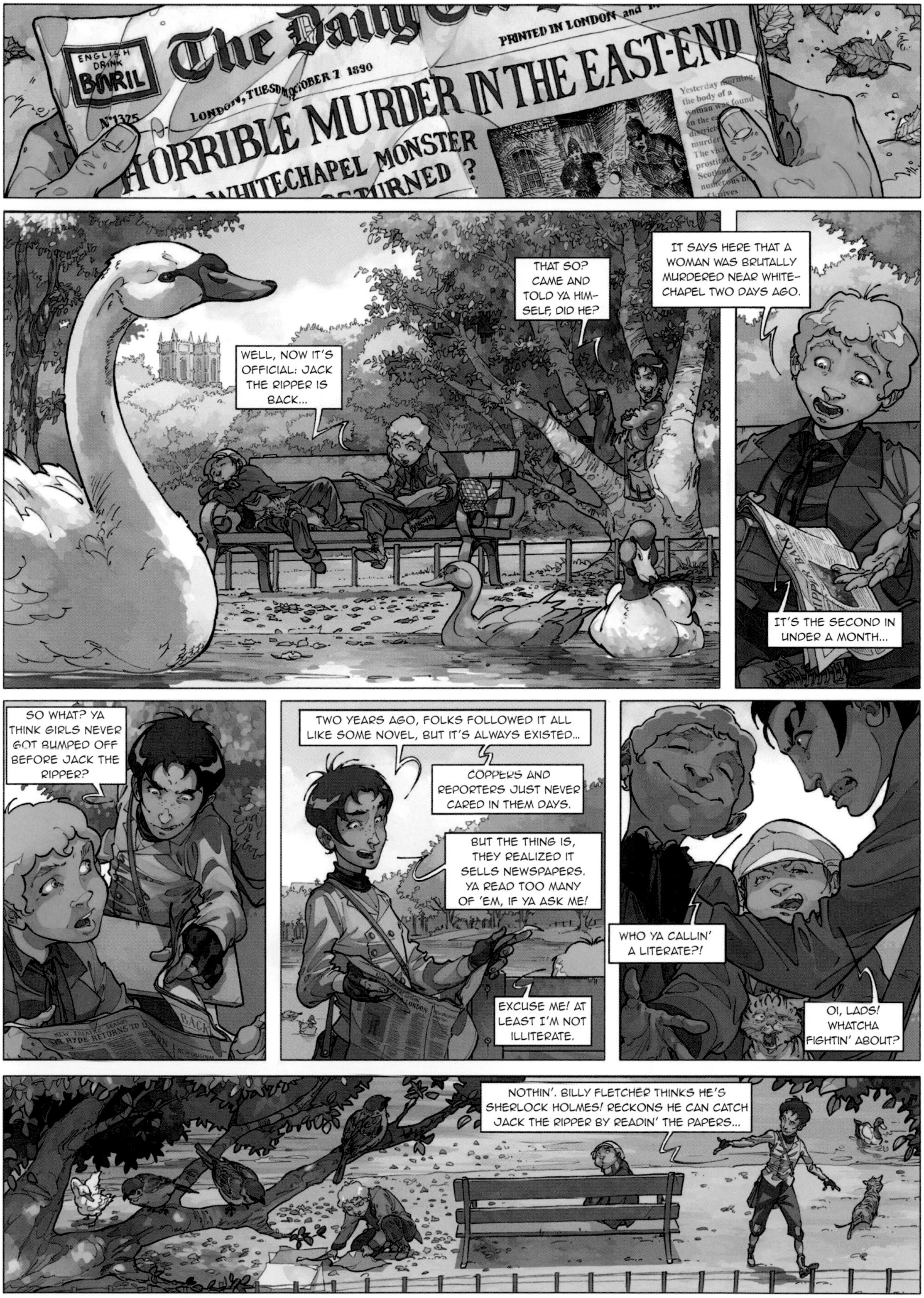
ENGLISH DRINK BOVRIL
The Daily
PRINTED IN LONDON and
LONDON, TUESDAY OCTOBER 7 1890
Nº1325
HORRIBLE MURDER IN THE EAST-END
WHITECHAPEL MONSTER RETURNED ?
WELL, NOW IT'S OFFICIAL: JACK THE RIPPER IS BACK...
THAT SO? CAME AND TOLD YA HIMSELF, DID HE?
IT SAYS HERE THAT A WOMAN WAS BRUTALLY MURDERED NEAR WHITECHAPEL TWO DAYS AGO.
IT'S THE SECOND IN UNDER A MONTH...
SO WHAT? YA THINK GIRLS NEVER GOT BUMPED OFF BEFORE JACK THE RIPPER?
TWO YEARS AGO, FOLKS FOLLOWED IT ALL LIKE SOME NOVEL, BUT IT'S ALWAYS EXISTED...
COPPERS AND REPORTERS JUST NEVER CARED IN THEM DAYS.
BUT THE THING IS, THEY REALIZED IT SELLS NEWSPAPERS. YA READ TOO MANY OF 'EM, IF YA ASK ME!
EXCUSE ME! AT LEAST I'M NOT ILLITERATE.
WHO YA CALLIN' A LITERATE?!
OI, LADS! WHATCHA FIGHTIN' ABOUT?
NOTHIN'. BILLY FLETCHER THINKS HE'S SHERLOCK HOLMES! RECKONS HE CAN CATCH JACK THE RIPPER BY READIN' THE PAPERS...

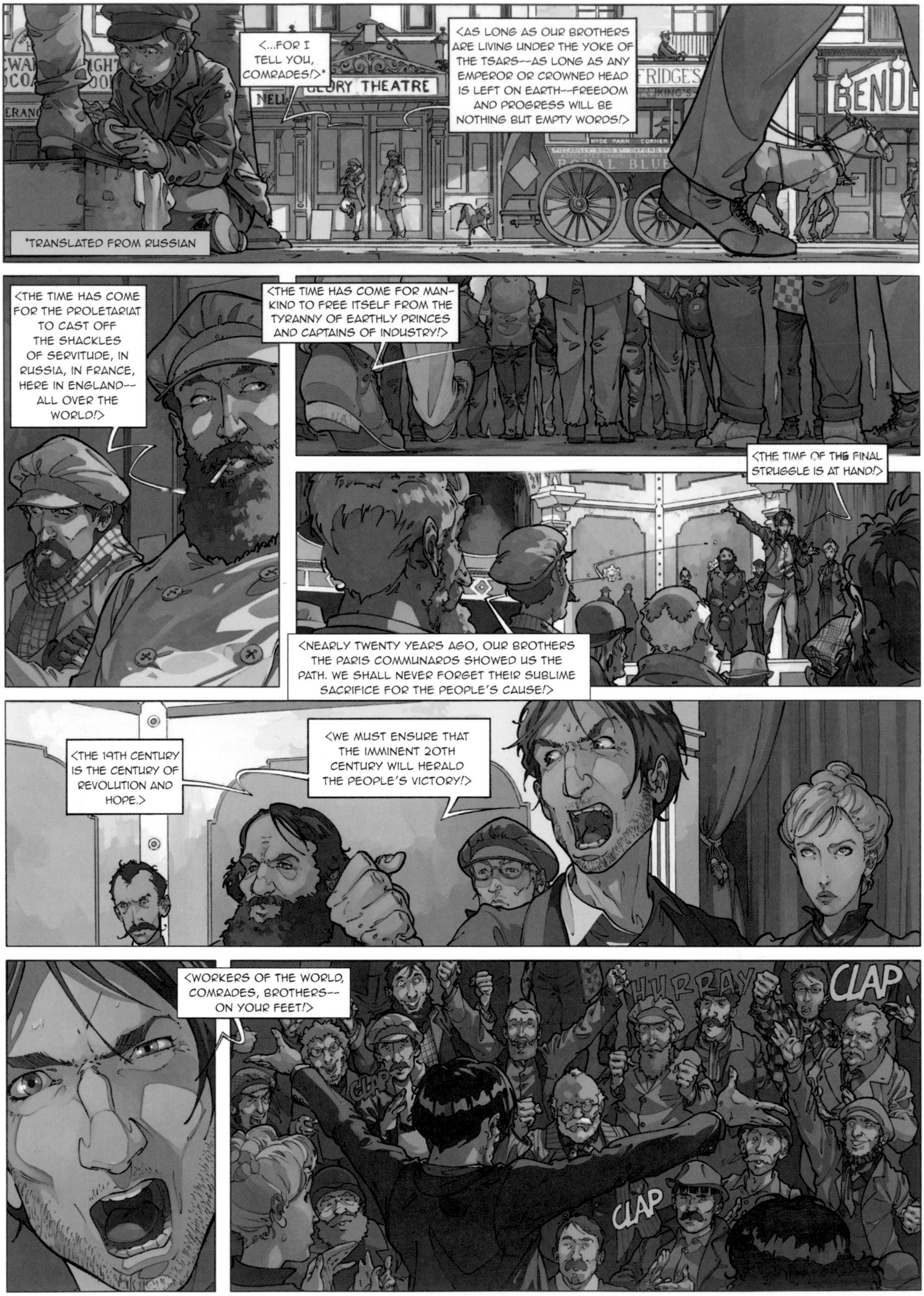
<...FOR I TELL YOU, COMRADES!>*
GLORY THEATRE
<AS LONG AS OUR BROTHERS ARE LIVING UNDER THE YOKE OF THE TSARS--AS LONG AS ANY EMPEROR OR CROWNED HEAD IS LEFT ON EARTH--FREEDOM AND PROGRESS WILL BE NOTHING BUT EMPTY WORDS!>
HYDE PARK CORNER
ROYAL BLUE
*TRANSLATED FROM RUSSIAN
<THE TIME HAS COME FOR THE PROLETARIAT TO CAST OFF THE SHACKLES OF SERVITUDE, IN RUSSIA, IN FRANCE, HERE IN ENGLAND-- ALL OVER THE WORLD!>
<THE TIME HAS COME FOR MAN-KIND TO FREE ITSELF FROM THE TYRANNY OF EARTHLY PRINCES AND CAPTAINS OF INDUSTRY!>
<THE TIME OF THE FINAL STRUGGLE IS AT HAND!>
<NEARLY TWENTY YEARS AGO, OUR BROTHERS THE PARIS COMMUNARDS SHOWED US THE PATH. WE SHALL NEVER FORGET THEIR SUBLIME SACRIFICE FOR THE PEOPLE'S CAUSE!>
<THE 19TH CENTURY IS THE CENTURY OF REVOLUTION AND HOPE.>
<WE MUST ENSURE THAT THE IMMINENT 20TH CENTURY WILL HERALD THE PEOPLE'S VICTORY!>
<WORKERS OF THE WORLD, COMRADES, BROTHERS-- ON YOUR FEET!>
HURRAY
CLAP
CLAP

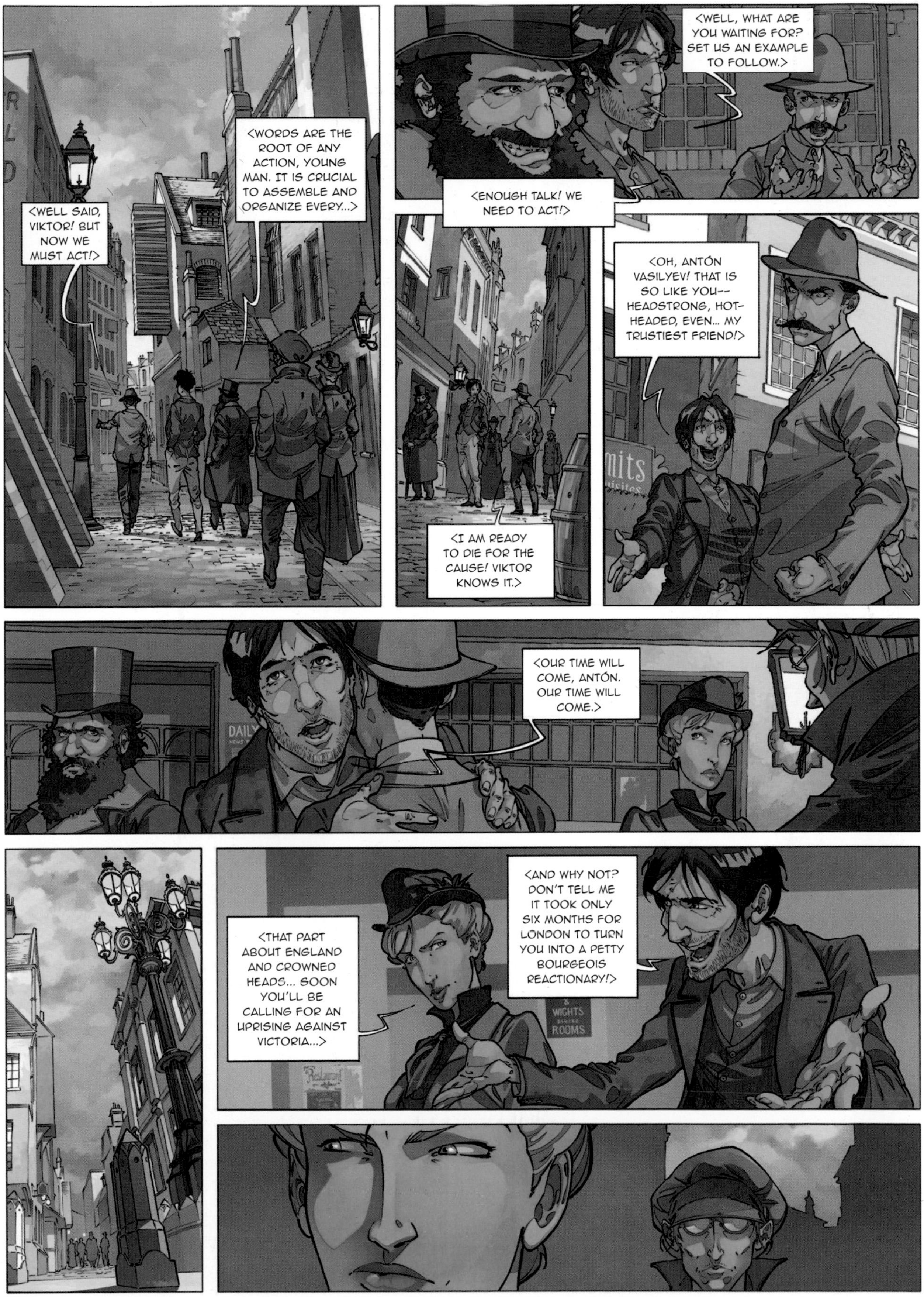
<WORDS ARE THE ROOT OF ANY ACTION, YOUNG MAN. IT IS CRUCIAL TO ASSEMBLE AND ORGANIZE EVERY...>
<WELL SAID, VIKTOR! BUT NOW WE MUST ACT!>
<WELL, WHAT ARE YOU WAITING FOR? SET US AN EXAMPLE TO FOLLOW.>
<ENOUGH TALK! WE NEED TO ACT!>
<I AM READY TO DIE FOR THE CAUSE! VIKTOR KNOWS IT.>
<OH, ANTÓN VASILYEV! THAT IS SO LIKE YOU-- HEADSTRONG, HOT-HEADED, EVEN... MY TRUSTIEST FRIEND!>
<OUR TIME WILL COME, ANTÓN. OUR TIME WILL COME.>
<THAT PART ABOUT ENGLAND AND CROWNED HEADS... SOON YOU'LL BE CALLING FOR AN UPRISING AGAINST VICTORIA...>
<AND WHY NOT? DON'T TELL ME IT TOOK ONLY SIX MONTHS FOR LONDON TO TURN YOU INTO A PETTY BOURGEOIS REACTIONARY!>

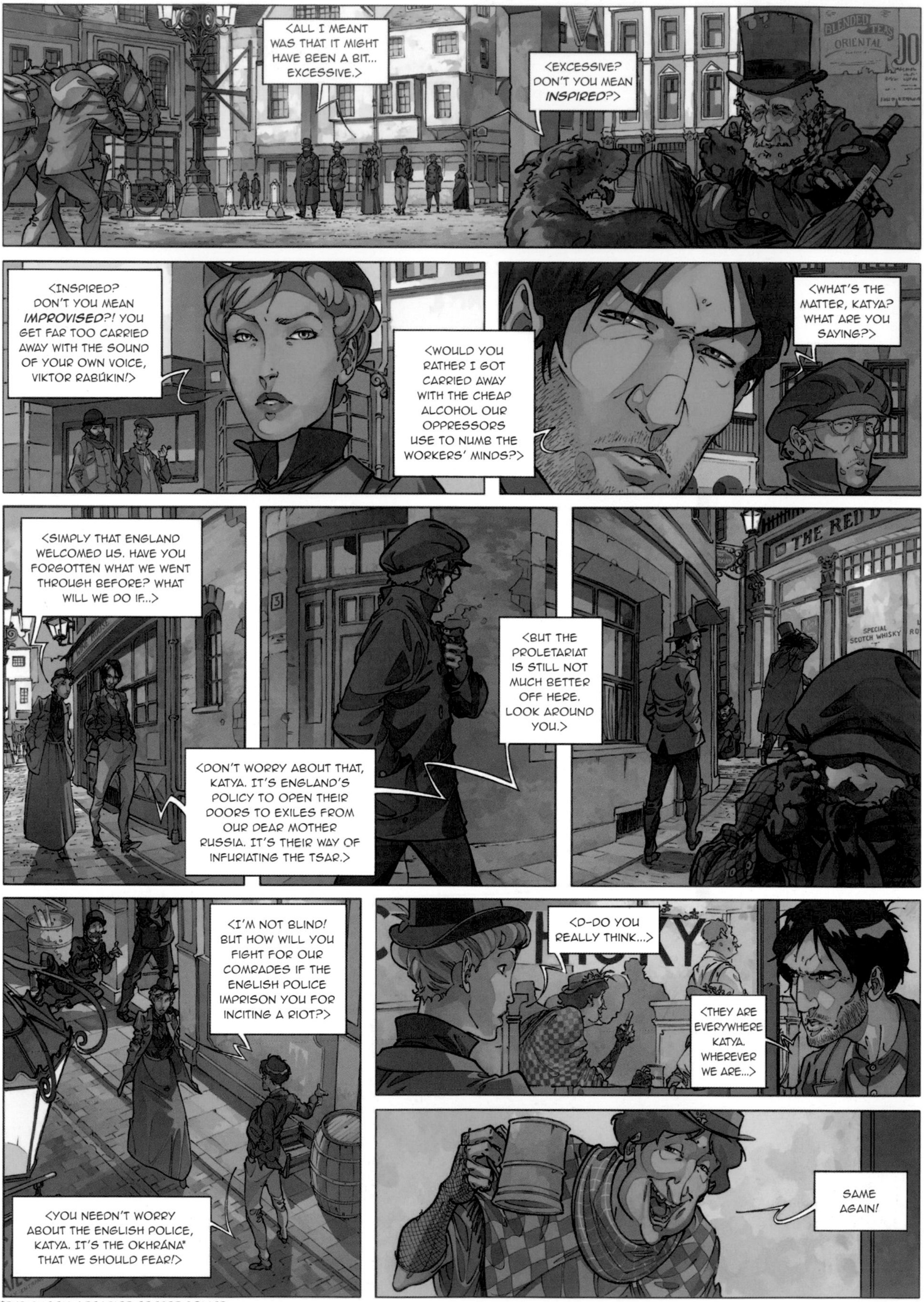
<ALL I MEANT WAS THAT IT MIGHT HAVE BEEN A BIT... EXCESSIVE.>
<EXCESSIVE? DON'T YOU MEAN INSPIRED?>
<INSPIRED? DON'T YOU MEAN IMPROVISED?! YOU GET FAR TOO CARRIED AWAY WITH THE SOUND OF YOUR OWN VOICE, VIKTOR RABÚKIN!>
<WOULD YOU RATHER I GOT CARRIED AWAY WITH THE CHEAP ALCOHOL OUR OPPRESSORS USE TO NUMB THE WORKERS' MINDS?>
<WHAT'S THE MATTER, KATYA? WHAT ARE YOU SAYING?>
<SIMPLY THAT ENGLAND WELCOMED US. HAVE YOU FORGOTTEN WHAT WE WENT THROUGH BEFORE? WHAT WILL WE DO IF...>
<DON'T WORRY ABOUT THAT, KATYA. IT'S ENGLAND'S POLICY TO OPEN THEIR DOORS TO EXILES FROM OUR DEAR MOTHER RUSSIA. IT'S THEIR WAY OF INFURIATING THE TSAR.>
<BUT THE PROLETARIAT IS STILL NOT MUCH BETTER OFF HERE. LOOK AROUND YOU.>
THE RED
SPECIAL SCOTCH WHISKY
<I'M NOT BLIND! BUT HOW WILL YOU FIGHT FOR OUR COMRADES IF THE ENGLISH POLICE IMPRISON YOU FOR INCITING A RIOT?>
<YOU NEEDN'T WORRY ABOUT THE ENGLISH POLICE, KATYA. IT'S THE OKHRÁNA* THAT WE SHOULD FEAR!>
<D-DO YOU REALLY THINK...>
<THEY ARE EVERYWHERE KATYA. WHEREVER WE ARE...>
SAME AGAIN!

*THE RUSSIAN TSARIST SECRET POLICE.

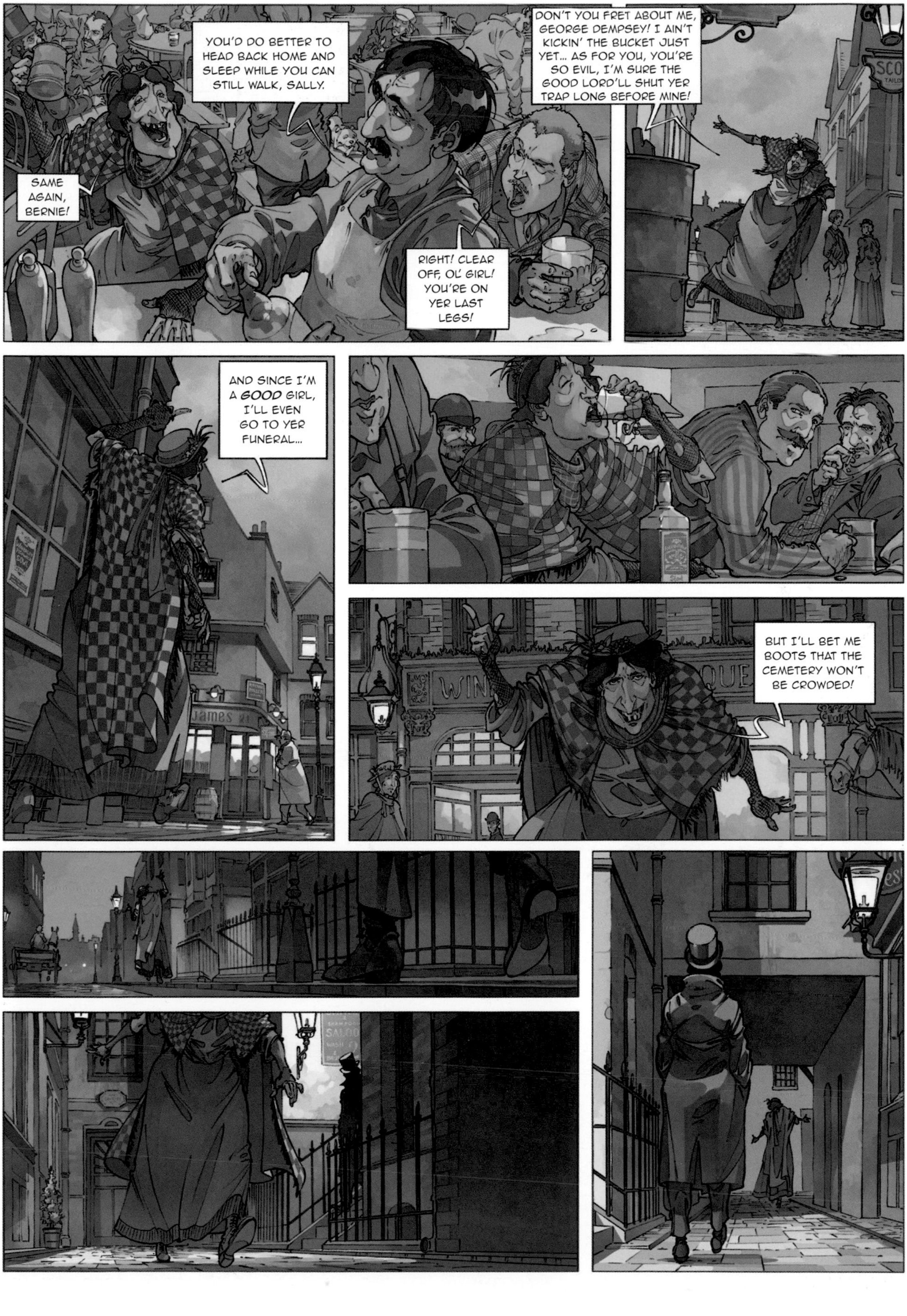
SAME AGAIN, BERNIE!
YOU'D DO BETTER TO HEAD BACK HOME AND SLEEP WHILE YOU CAN STILL WALK, SALLY.
RIGHT! CLEAR OFF, OL' GIRL! YOU'RE ON YER LAST LEGS!
DON'T YOU FRET ABOUT ME, GEORGE DEMPSEY! I AIN'T KICKIN' THE BUCKET JUST YET... AS FOR YOU, YOU'RE SO EVIL, I'M SURE THE GOOD LORD'LL SHUT YER TRAP LONG BEFORE MINE!
AND SINCE I'M A GOOD GIRL, I'LL EVEN GO TO YER FUNERAL...
BUT I'LL BET ME BOOTS THAT THE CEMETERY WON'T BE CROWDED!

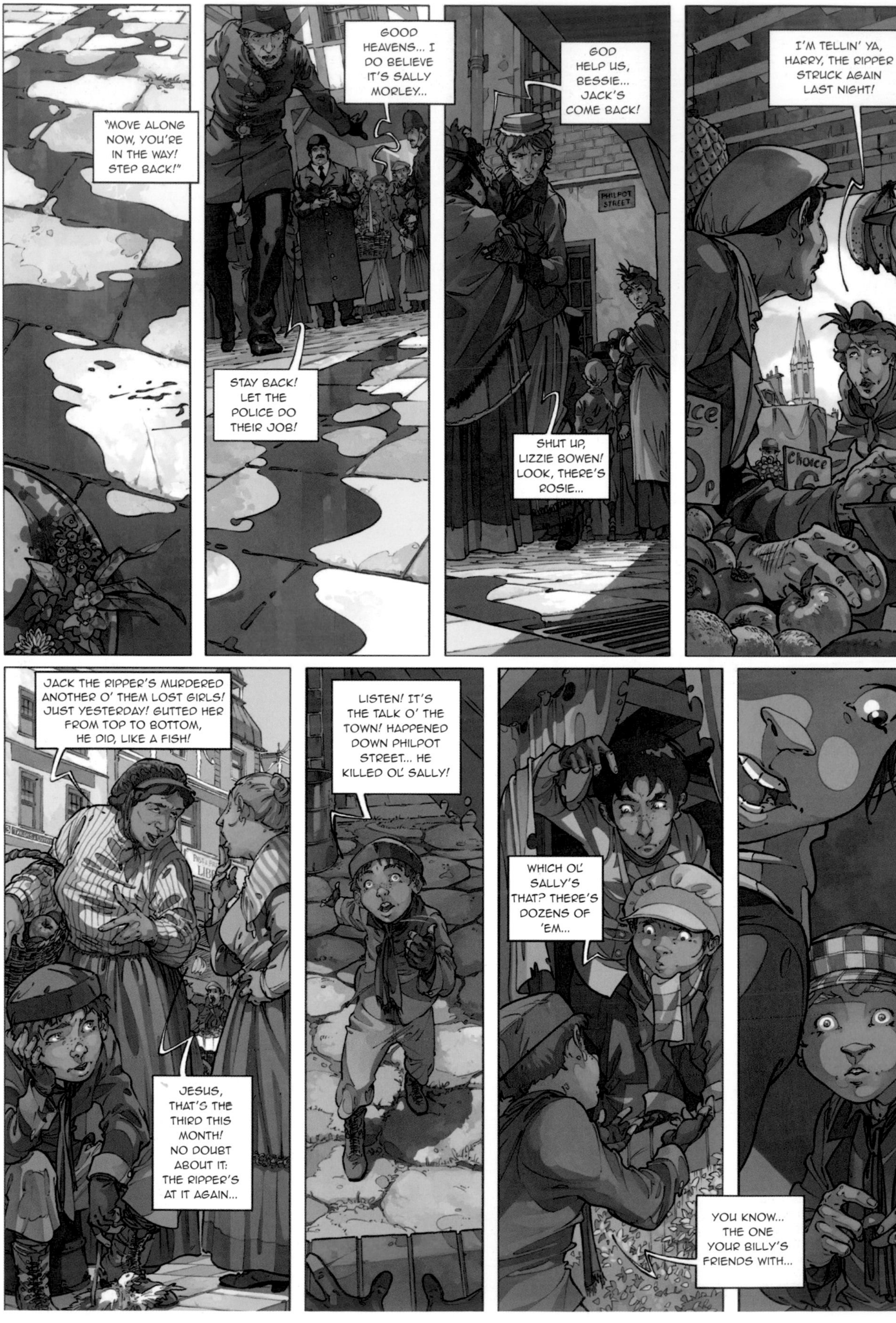
"MOVE ALONG NOW, YOU'RE IN THE WAY! STEP BACK!"
GOOD HEAVENS... I DO BELIEVE IT'S SALLY MORLEY...
STAY BACK! LET THE POLICE DO THEIR JOB!
GOD HELP US, BESSIE... JACK'S COME BACK!
PHILPOT STREET
SHUT UP, LIZZIE BOWEN! LOOK, THERE'S ROSIE...
I'M TELLIN' YA, HARRY, THE RIPPER STRUCK AGAIN LAST NIGHT!
JACK THE RIPPER'S MURDERED ANOTHER O' THEM LOST GIRLS! JUST YESTERDAY! GUTTED HER FROM TOP TO BOTTOM, HE DID, LIKE A FISH!
JESUS, THAT'S THE THIRD THIS MONTH! NO DOUBT ABOUT IT: THE RIPPER'S AT IT AGAIN...
LISTEN! IT'S THE TALK O' THE TOWN! HAPPENED DOWN PHILPOT STREET... HE KILLED OL' SALLY!
WHICH OL' SALLY'S THAT? THERE'S DOZENS OF 'EM...
YOU KNOW... THE ONE YOUR BILLY'S FRIENDS WITH...

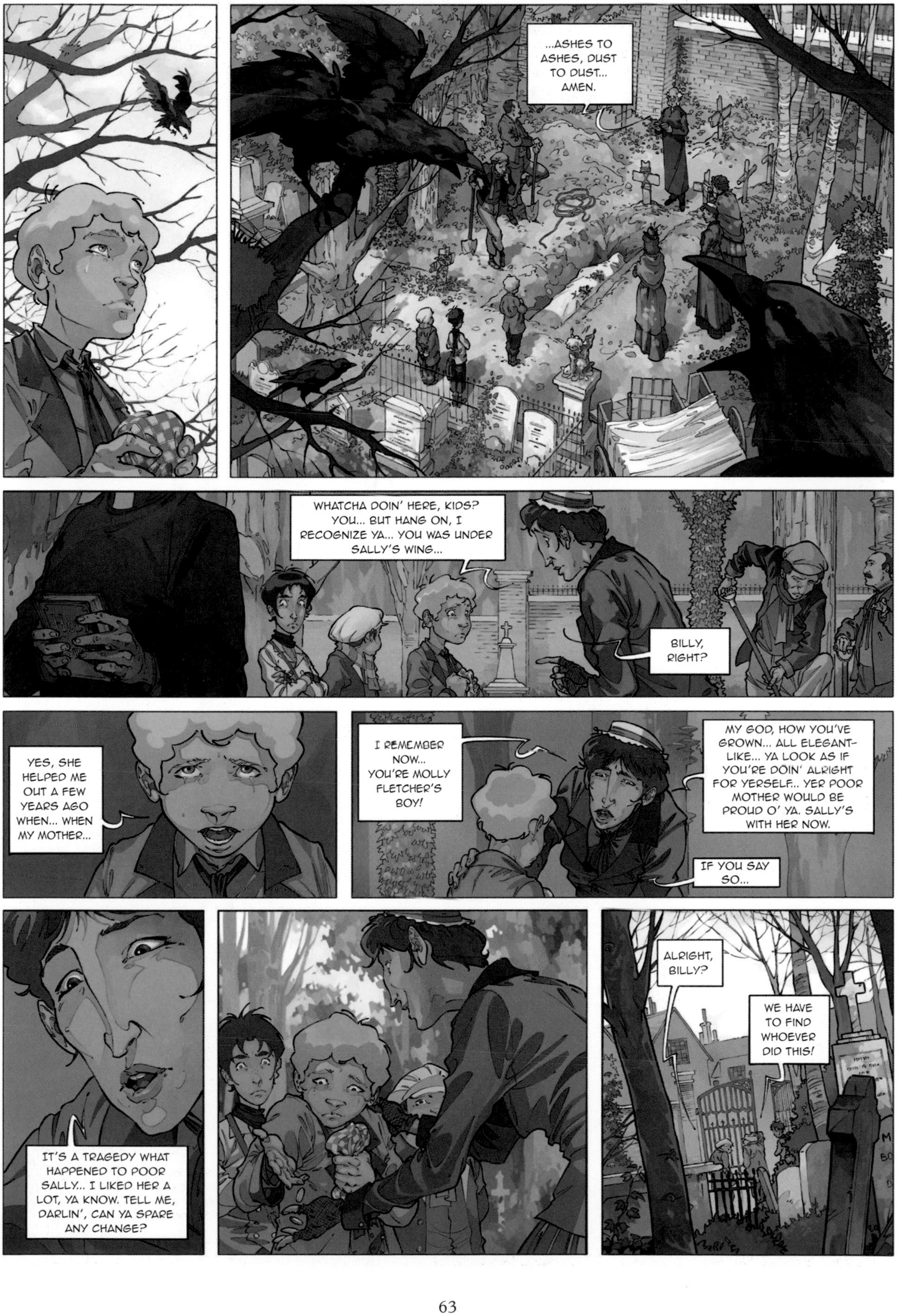
...ASHES TO ASHES, DUST TO DUST... AMEN.
WHATCHA DOIN' HERE, KIDS? YOU... BUT HANG ON, I RECOGNIZE YA... YOU WAS UNDER SALLY'S WING...
BILLY, RIGHT?
YES, SHE HELPED ME OUT A FEW YEARS AGO WHEN... WHEN MY MOTHER...
I REMEMBER NOW... YOU'RE MOLLY FLETCHER'S BOY!
MY GOD, HOW YOU'VE GROWN... ALL ELEGANT-LIKE... YA LOOK AS IF YOU'RE DOIN' ALRIGHT FOR YERSELF... YER POOR MOTHER WOULD BE PROUD O' YA. SALLY'S WITH HER NOW.
IF YOU SAY SO...
IT'S A TRAGEDY WHAT HAPPENED TO POOR SALLY... I LIKED HER A LOT, YA KNOW. TELL ME, DARLIN', CAN YA SPARE ANY CHANGE?
ALRIGHT, BILLY?
WE HAVE TO FIND WHOEVER DID THIS!

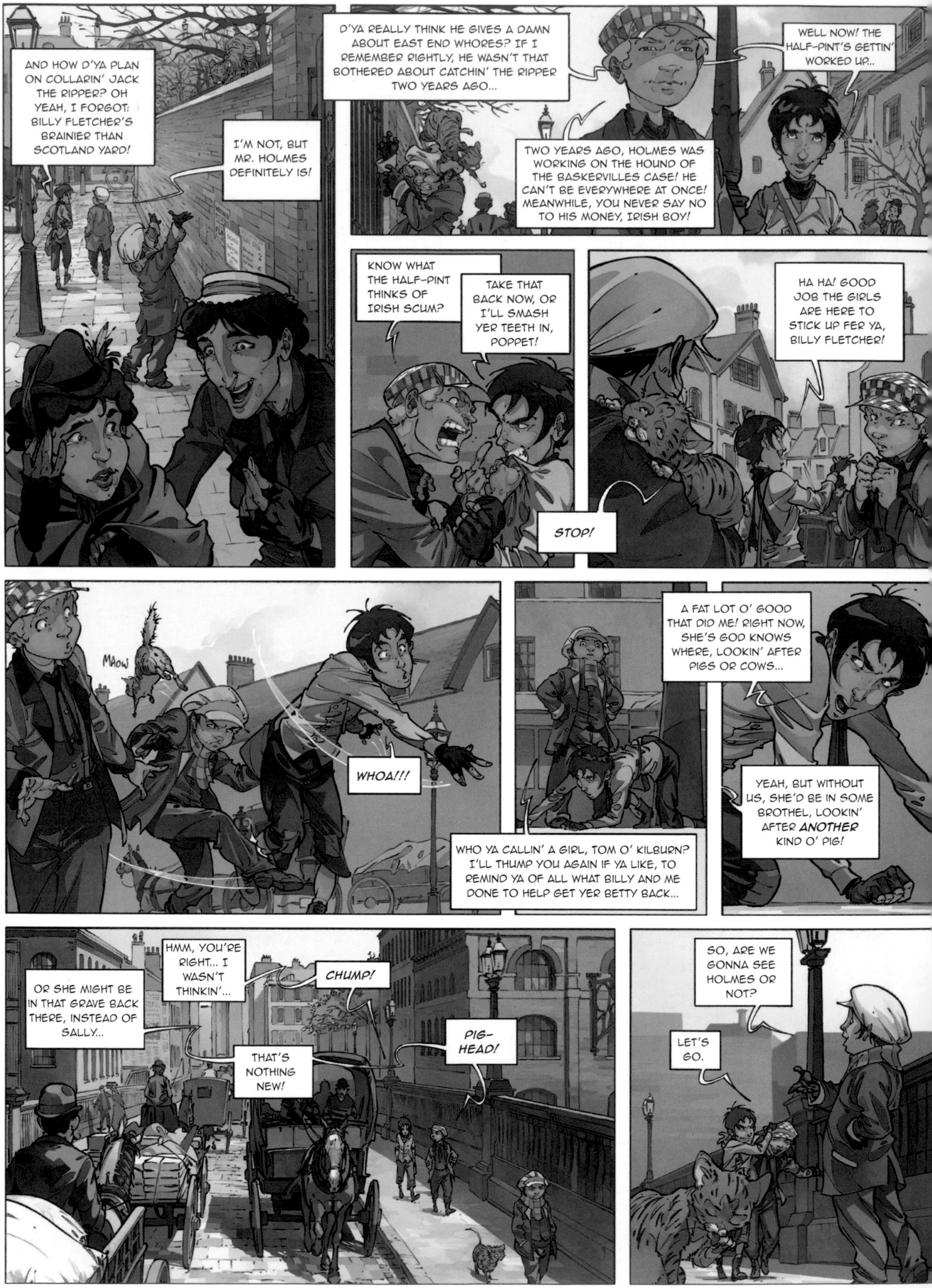
AND HOW D'YA PLAN ON COLLARIN' JACK THE RIPPER? OH YEAH, I FORGOT: BILLY FLETCHER'S BRAINIER THAN SCOTLAND YARD!
I'M NOT, BUT MR. HOLMES DEFINITELY IS!
D'YA REALLY THINK HE GIVES A DAMN ABOUT EAST END WHORES? IF I REMEMBER RIGHTLY, HE WASN'T THAT BOTHERED ABOUT CATCHIN' THE RIPPER TWO YEARS AGO...
TWO YEARS AGO, HOLMES WAS WORKING ON THE HOUND OF THE BASKERVILLES CASE! HE CAN'T BE EVERYWHERE AT ONCE! MEANWHILE, YOU NEVER SAY NO TO HIS MONEY, IRISH BOY!
WELL NOW! THE HALF-PINT'S GETTIN' WORKED UP...
KNOW WHAT THE HALF-PINT THINKS OF IRISH SCUM?
TAKE THAT BACK NOW, OR I'LL SMASH YER TEETH IN, POPPET!
STOP!
HA HA! GOOD JOB THE GIRLS ARE HERE TO STICK UP FER YA, BILLY FLETCHER!
MAOW
WHOA!!!
WHO YA CALLIN' A GIRL, TOM O' KILBURN? I'LL THUMP YOU AGAIN IF YA LIKE, TO REMIND YA OF ALL WHAT BILLY AND ME DONE TO HELP GET YER BETTY BACK...
A FAT LOT O' GOOD THAT DID ME! RIGHT NOW, SHE'S GOD KNOWS WHERE, LOOKIN' AFTER PIGS OR COWS...
YEAH, BUT WITHOUT US, SHE'D BE IN SOME BROTHEL, LOOKIN' AFTER ANOTHER KIND O' PIG!
OR SHE MIGHT BE IN THAT GRAVE BACK THERE, INSTEAD OF SALLY...
HMM, YOU'RE RIGHT... I WASN'T THINKIN'...
CHUMP!
THAT'S NOTHING NEW!
PIG-HEAD!
SO, ARE WE GONNA SEE HOLMES OR NOT?
LET'S GO.

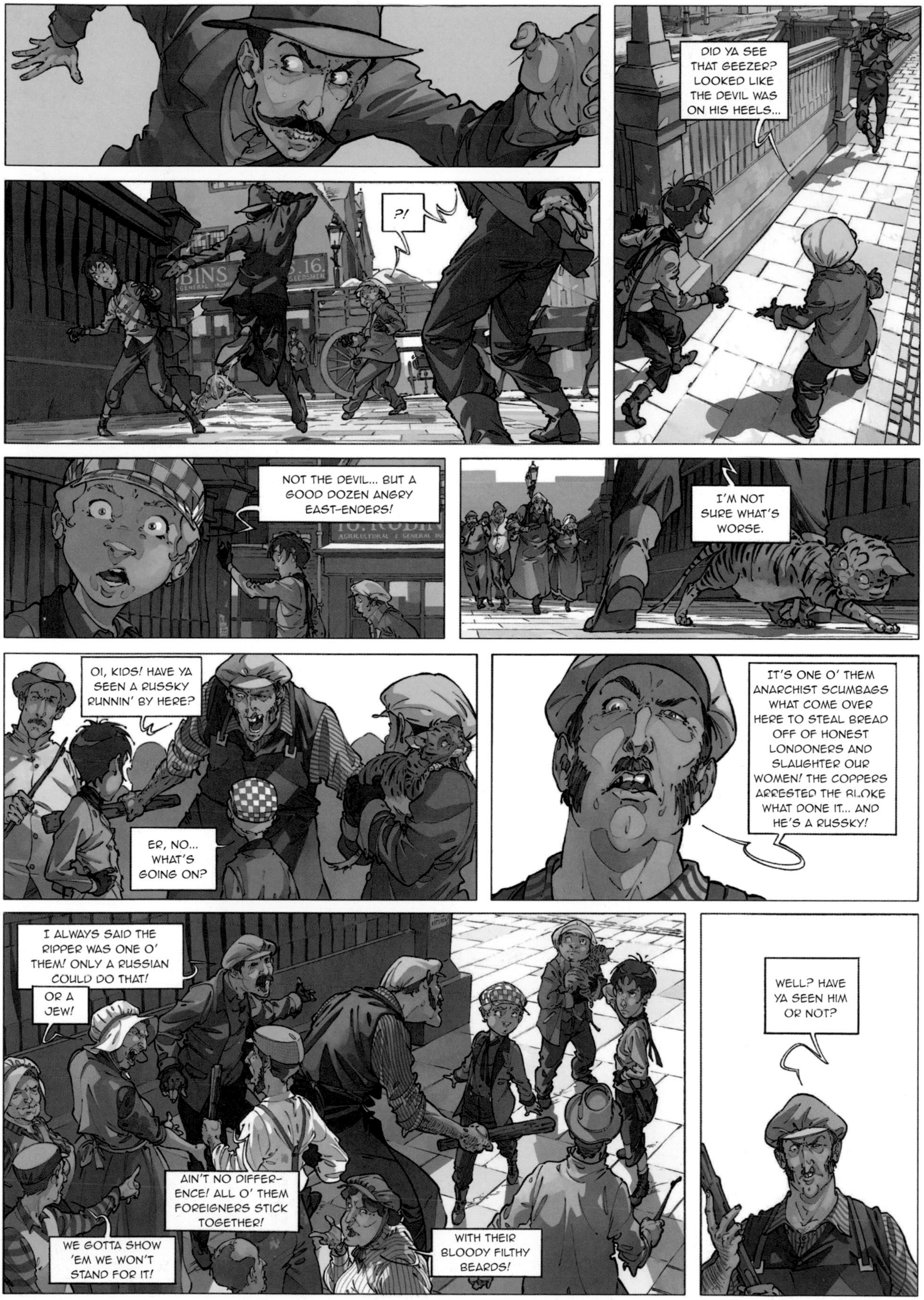
DID YA SEE THAT GEEZER? LOOKED LIKE THE DEVIL WAS ON HIS HEELS...
?!
NOT THE DEVIL... BUT A GOOD DOZEN ANGRY EAST-ENDERS!
I'M NOT SURE WHAT'S WORSE.
OI, KIDS! HAVE YA SEEN A RUSSKY RUNNIN' BY HERE?
ER, NO... WHAT'S GOING ON?
IT'S ONE O' THEM ANARCHIST SCUMBAGS WHAT COME OVER HERE TO STEAL BREAD OFF OF HONEST LONDONERS AND SLAUGHTER OUR WOMEN! THE COPPERS ARRESTED THE BLOKE WHAT DONE IT... AND HE'S A RUSSKY!
I ALWAYS SAID THE RIPPER WAS ONE O' THEM! ONLY A RUSSIAN COULD DO THAT!
OR A JEW!
AIN'T NO DIFFERENCE! ALL O' THEM FOREIGNERS STICK TOGETHER!
WE GOTTA SHOW 'EM WE WON'T STAND FOR IT!
WITH THEIR BLOODY FILTHY BEARDS!
WELL? HAVE YA SEEN HIM OR NOT?

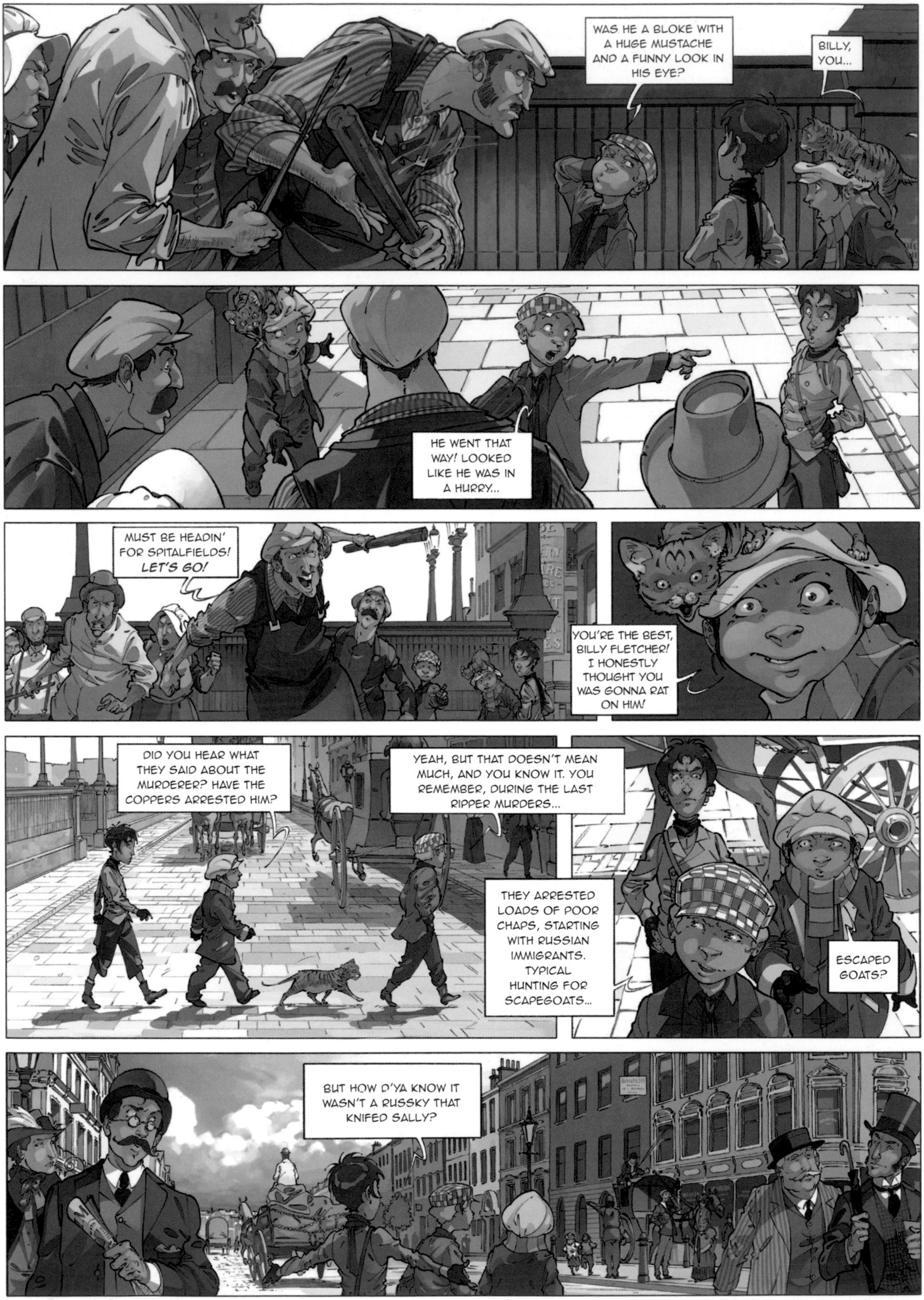
WAS HE A BLOKE WITH A HUGE MUSTACHE AND A FUNNY LOOK IN HIS EYE?
BILLY, YOU...
HE WENT THAT WAY! LOOKED LIKE HE WAS IN A HURRY...
MUST BE HEADIN' FOR SPITALFIELDS! LET'S GO!
YOU'RE THE BEST, BILLY FLETCHER! I HONESTLY THOUGHT YOU WAS GONNA RAT ON HIM!
DID YOU HEAR WHAT THEY SAID ABOUT THE MURDERER? HAVE THE COPPERS ARRESTED HIM?
YEAH, BUT THAT DOESN'T MEAN MUCH, AND YOU KNOW IT. YOU REMEMBER, DURING THE LAST RIPPER MURDERS...
THEY ARRESTED LOADS OF POOR CHAPS, STARTING WITH RUSSIAN IMMIGRANTS. TYPICAL HUNTING FOR SCAPEGOATS...
ESCAPED GOATS?
BUT HOW D'YA KNOW IT WASN'T A RUSSKY THAT KNIFED SALLY?

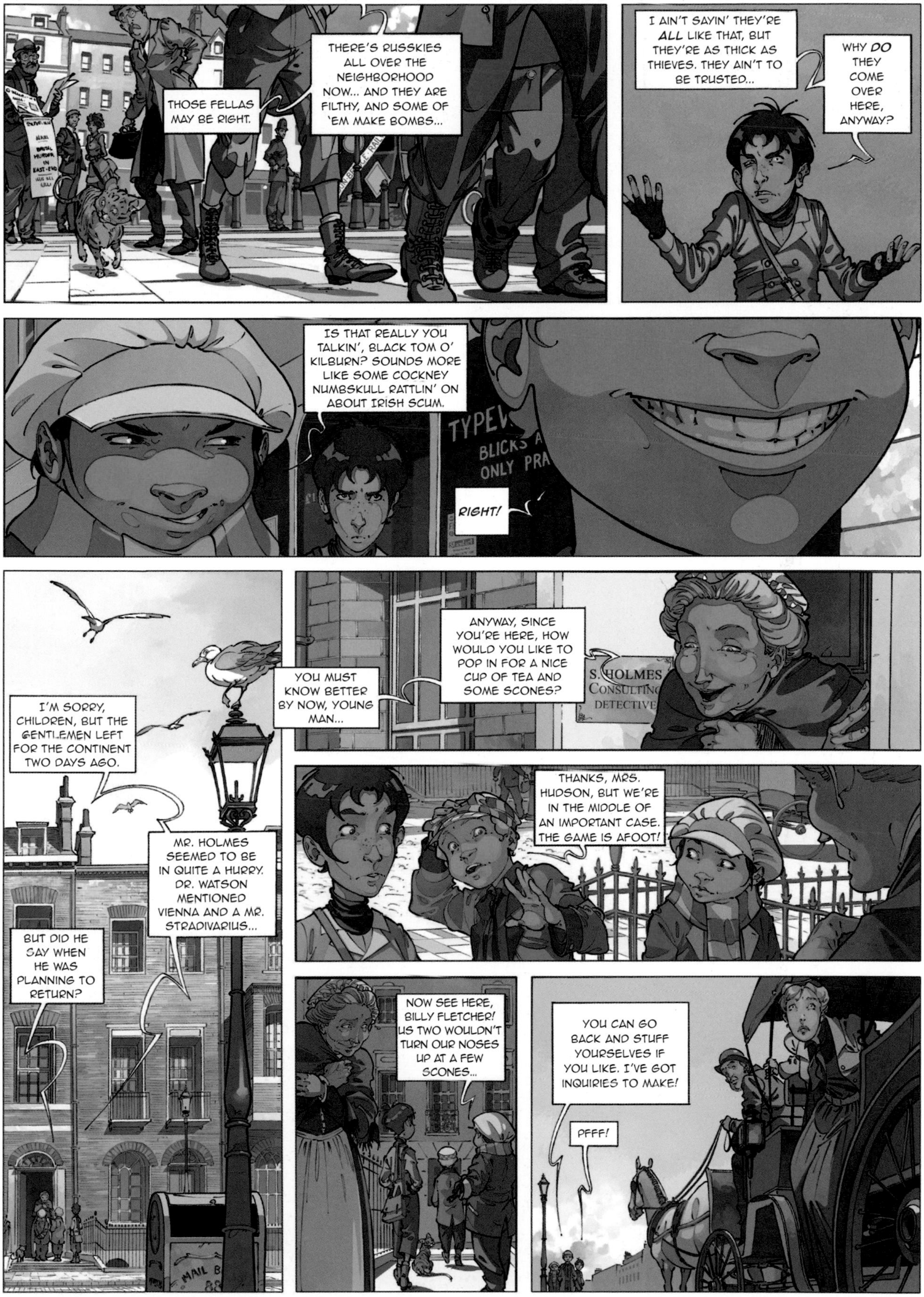
THOSE FELLAS MAY BE RIGHT.
THERE'S RUSSKIES ALL OVER THE NEIGHBORHOOD NOW... AND THEY ARE FILTHY, AND SOME OF 'EM MAKE BOMBS...
I AIN'T SAYIN' THEY'RE ALL LIKE THAT, BUT THEY'RE AS THICK AS THIEVES. THEY AIN'T TO BE TRUSTED...
WHY DO THEY COME OVER HERE, ANYWAY?
IS THAT REALLY YOU TALKIN', BLACK TOM O' KILBURN? SOUNDS MORE LIKE SOME COCKNEY NUMBSKULL RATTLIN' ON ABOUT IRISH SCUM.
RIGHT!
I'M SORRY, CHILDREN, BUT THE GENTLEMEN LEFT FOR THE CONTINENT TWO DAYS AGO.
MR. HOLMES SEEMED TO BE IN QUITE A HURRY. DR. WATSON MENTIONED VIENNA AND A MR. STRADIVARIUS...
BUT DID HE SAY WHEN HE WAS PLANNING TO RETURN?
YOU MUST KNOW BETTER BY NOW, YOUNG MAN...
ANYWAY, SINCE YOU'RE HERE, HOW WOULD YOU LIKE TO POP IN FOR A NICE CUP OF TEA AND SOME SCONES?
S. HOLMES
CONSULTING
DETECTIVE
THANKS, MRS. HUDSON, BUT WE'RE IN THE MIDDLE OF AN IMPORTANT CASE. THE GAME IS AFOOT!
NOW SEE HERE, BILLY FLETCHER! US TWO WOULDN'T TURN OUR NOSES UP AT A FEW SCONES...
YOU CAN GO BACK AND STUFF YOURSELVES IF YOU LIKE. I'VE GOT INQUIRIES TO MAKE!
PFFF!

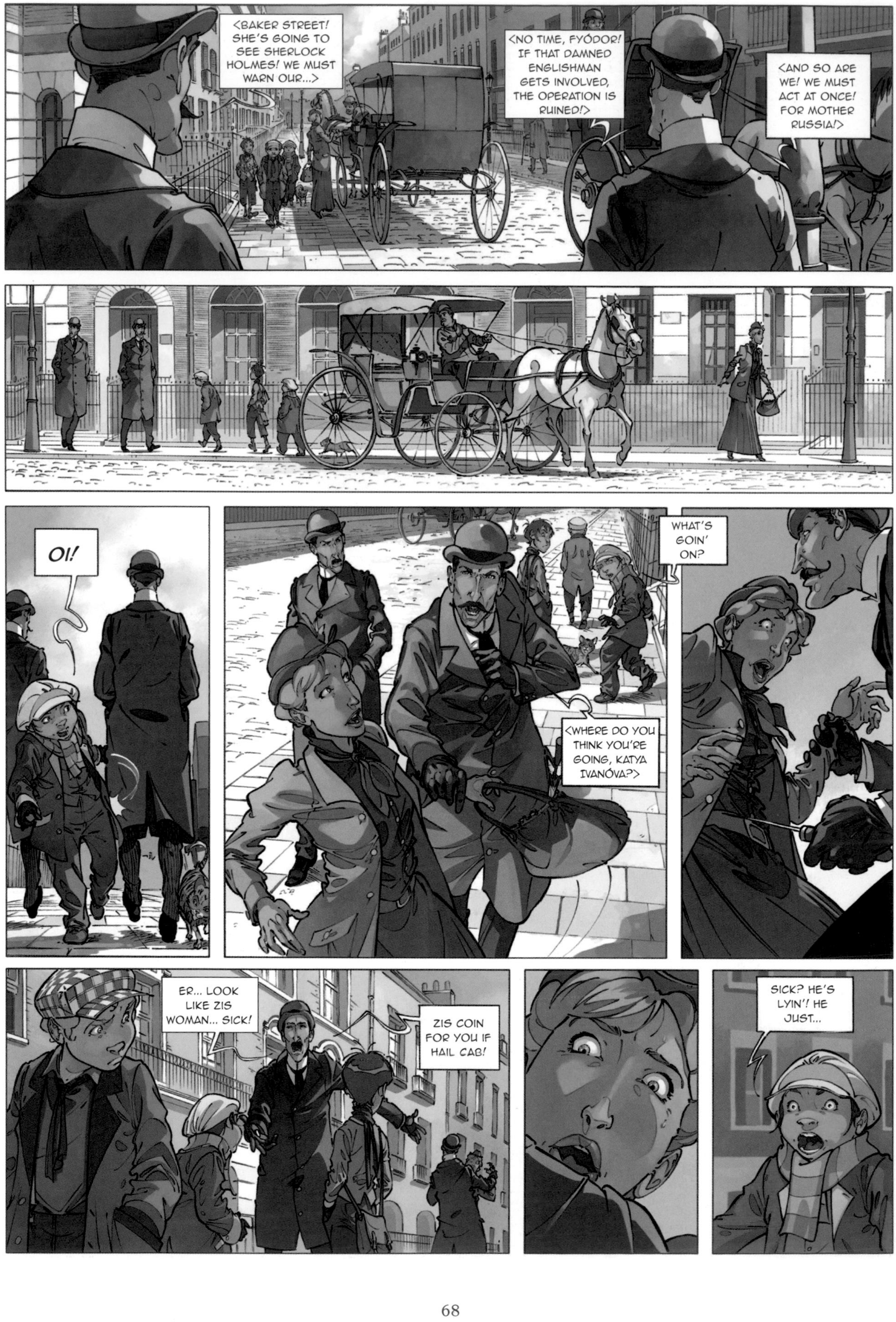
<BAKER STREET! SHE'S GOING TO SEE SHERLOCK HOLMES! WE MUST WARN OUR...>
<NO TIME, FYÓDOR! IF THAT DAMNED ENGLISHMAN GETS INVOLVED, THE OPERATION IS RUINED!>
<AND SO ARE WE! WE MUST ACT AT ONCE! FOR MOTHER RUSSIA!>
OI!
<WHERE DO YOU THINK YOU'RE GOING, KATYA IVANÓVA?>
WHAT'S GOIN' ON?
ER... LOOK LIKE ZIS WOMAN... SICK!
ZIS COIN FOR YOU IF HAIL CAB!
SICK? HE'S LYIN'! HE JUST...

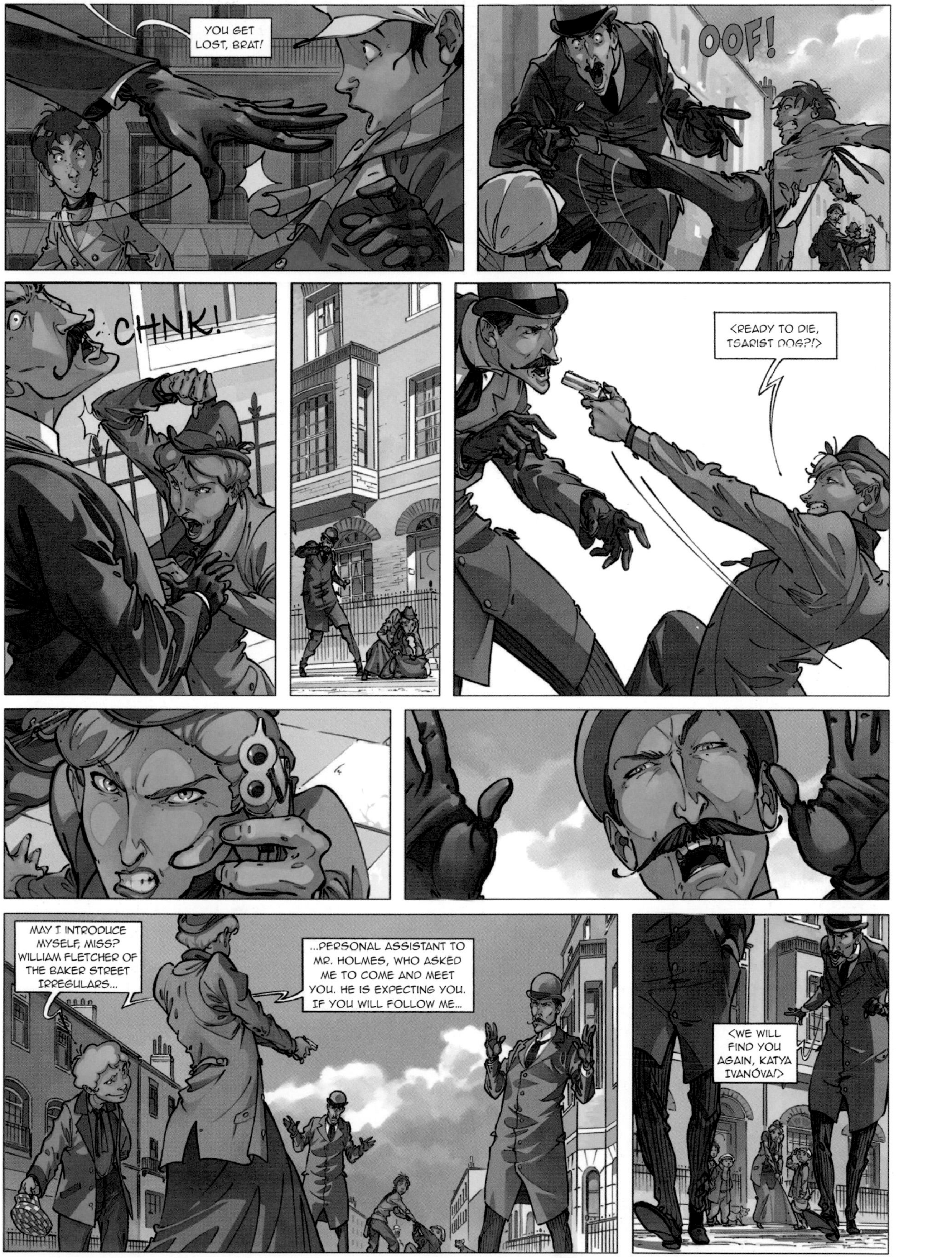
YOU GET LOST, BRAT!
OOF!
CHNK!
<READY TO DIE, TSARIST DOG?!>
MAY I INTRODUCE MYSELF, MISS? WILLIAM FLETCHER OF THE BAKER STREET IRREGULARS...
...PERSONAL ASSISTANT TO MR. HOLMES, WHO ASKED ME TO COME AND MEET YOU. HE IS EXPECTING YOU. IF YOU WILL FOLLOW ME...
<WE WILL FIND YOU AGAIN, KATYA IVANÓVA!>

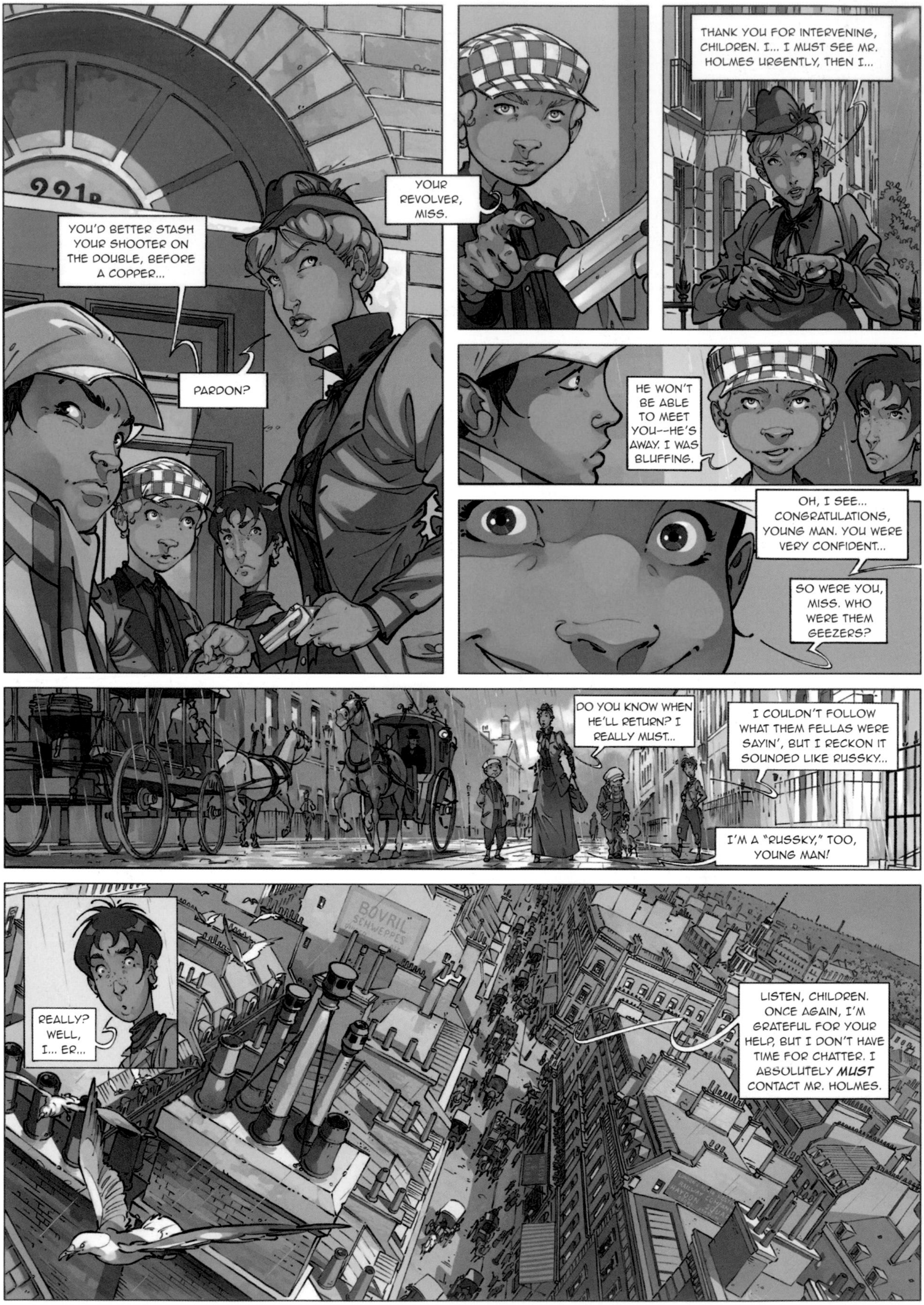
YOU'D BETTER STASH YOUR SHOOTER ON THE DOUBLE, BEFORE A COPPER...
PARDON?
221B
YOUR REVOLVER, MISS.
THANK YOU FOR INTERVENING, CHILDREN. I... I MUST SEE MR. HOLMES URGENTLY, THEN I...
HE WON'T BE ABLE TO MEET YOU--HE'S AWAY. I WAS BLUFFING.
OH, I SEE... CONGRATULATIONS, YOUNG MAN. YOU WERE VERY CONFIDENT...
SO WERE YOU, MISS. WHO WERE THEM GEEZERS?
DO YOU KNOW WHEN HE'LL RETURN? I REALLY MUST...
I COULDN'T FOLLOW WHAT THEM FELLAS WERE SAYIN', BUT I RECKON IT SOUNDED LIKE RUSSKY...
I'M A "RUSSKY," TOO, YOUNG MAN!
BOVRIL
SCHWEPPES
REALLY? WELL, I... ER...
LISTEN, CHILDREN. ONCE AGAIN, I'M GRATEFUL FOR YOUR HELP, BUT I DON'T HAVE TIME FOR CHATTER. I ABSOLUTELY ***MUST*** CONTACT MR. HOLMES.

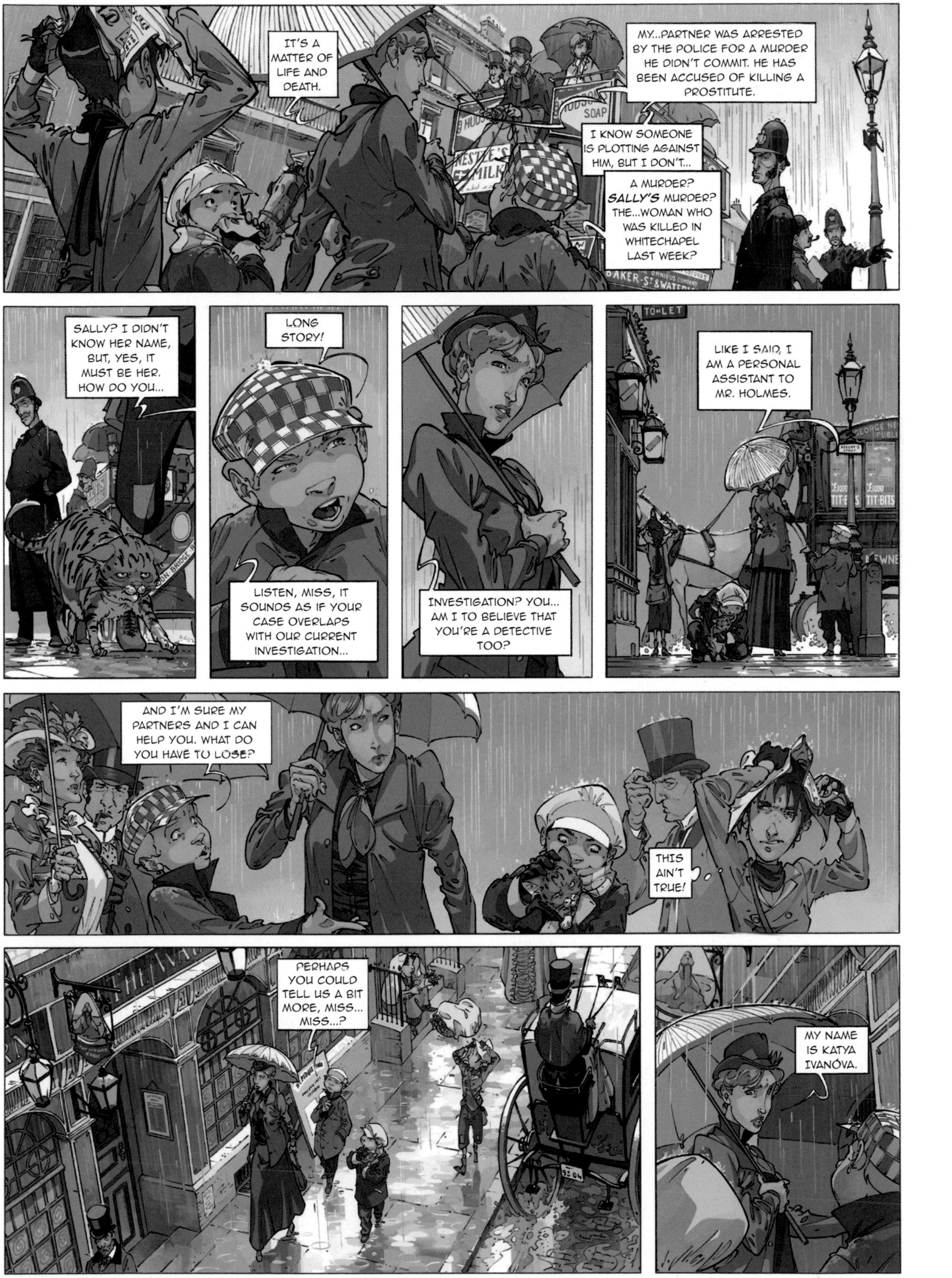
IT'S A MATTER OF LIFE AND DEATH.
MY...PARTNER WAS ARRESTED BY THE POLICE FOR A MURDER HE DIDN'T COMMIT. HE HAS BEEN ACCUSED OF KILLING A PROSTITUTE.
I KNOW SOMEONE IS PLOTTING AGAINST HIM, BUT I DON'T...
A MURDER? **SALLY'S** MURDER? THE...WOMAN WHO WAS KILLED IN WHITECHAPEL LAST WEEK?
SALLY? I DIDN'T KNOW HER NAME, BUT, YES, IT MUST BE HER. HOW DO YOU...
LONG STORY!
LISTEN, MISS, IT SOUNDS AS IF YOUR CASE OVERLAPS WITH OUR CURRENT INVESTIGATION...
INVESTIGATION? YOU... AM I TO BELIEVE THAT YOU'RE A DETECTIVE TOO?
TO LET
LIKE I SAID, I AM A PERSONAL ASSISTANT TO MR. HOLMES.
TIT-BITS
AND I'M SURE MY PARTNERS AND I CAN HELP YOU. WHAT DO YOU HAVE TO LOSE?
THIS AIN'T TRUE!
PERHAPS YOU COULD TELL US A BIT MORE, MISS... MISS...?
MY NAME IS KATYA IVANÓVA.

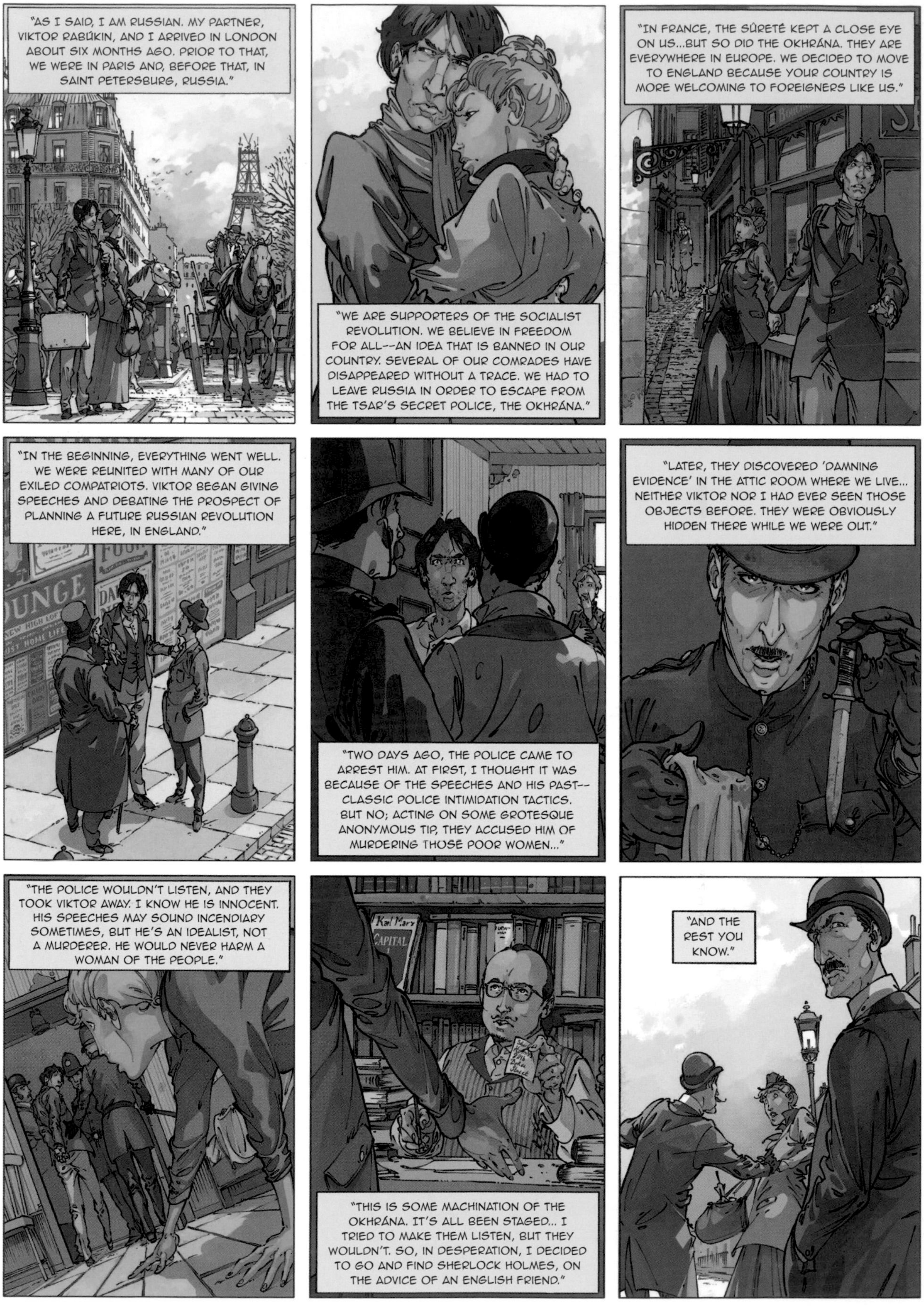
"AS I SAID, I AM RUSSIAN. MY PARTNER, VIKTOR RABÚKIN, AND I ARRIVED IN LONDON ABOUT SIX MONTHS AGO. PRIOR TO THAT, WE WERE IN PARIS AND, BEFORE THAT, IN SAINT PETERSBURG, RUSSIA."
"WE ARE SUPPORTERS OF THE SOCIALIST REVOLUTION. WE BELIEVE IN FREEDOM FOR ALL--AN IDEA THAT IS BANNED IN OUR COUNTRY. SEVERAL OF OUR COMRADES HAVE DISAPPEARED WITHOUT A TRACE. WE HAD TO LEAVE RUSSIA IN ORDER TO ESCAPE FROM THE TSAR'S SECRET POLICE, THE OKHRÁNA."
"IN FRANCE, THE SÛRETÉ KEPT A CLOSE EYE ON US...BUT SO DID THE OKHRÁNA. THEY ARE EVERYWHERE IN EUROPE. WE DECIDED TO MOVE TO ENGLAND BECAUSE YOUR COUNTRY IS MORE WELCOMING TO FOREIGNERS LIKE US."
"IN THE BEGINNING, EVERYTHING WENT WELL. WE WERE REUNITED WITH MANY OF OUR EXILED COMPATRIOTS. VIKTOR BEGAN GIVING SPEECHES AND DEBATING THE PROSPECT OF PLANNING A FUTURE RUSSIAN REVOLUTION HERE, IN ENGLAND."
LOUNGE
"TWO DAYS AGO, THE POLICE CAME TO ARREST HIM. AT FIRST, I THOUGHT IT WAS BECAUSE OF THE SPEECHES AND HIS PAST--CLASSIC POLICE INTIMIDATION TACTICS. BUT NO; ACTING ON SOME GROTESQUE ANONYMOUS TIP, THEY ACCUSED HIM OF MURDERING THOSE POOR WOMEN..."
"LATER, THEY DISCOVERED 'DAMNING EVIDENCE' IN THE ATTIC ROOM WHERE WE LIVE... NEITHER VIKTOR NOR I HAD EVER SEEN THOSE OBJECTS BEFORE. THEY WERE OBVIOUSLY HIDDEN THERE WHILE WE WERE OUT."
"THE POLICE WOULDN'T LISTEN, AND THEY TOOK VIKTOR AWAY. I KNOW HE IS INNOCENT. HIS SPEECHES MAY SOUND INCENDIARY SOMETIMES, BUT HE'S AN IDEALIST, NOT A MURDERER. HE WOULD NEVER HARM A WOMAN OF THE PEOPLE."
CAPITAL
"THIS IS SOME MACHINATION OF THE OKHRÁNA. IT'S ALL BEEN STAGED... I TRIED TO MAKE THEM LISTEN, BUT THEY WOULDN'T. SO, IN DESPERATION, I DECIDED TO GO AND FIND SHERLOCK HOLMES, ON THE ADVICE OF AN ENGLISH FRIEND."
"AND THE REST YOU KNOW."

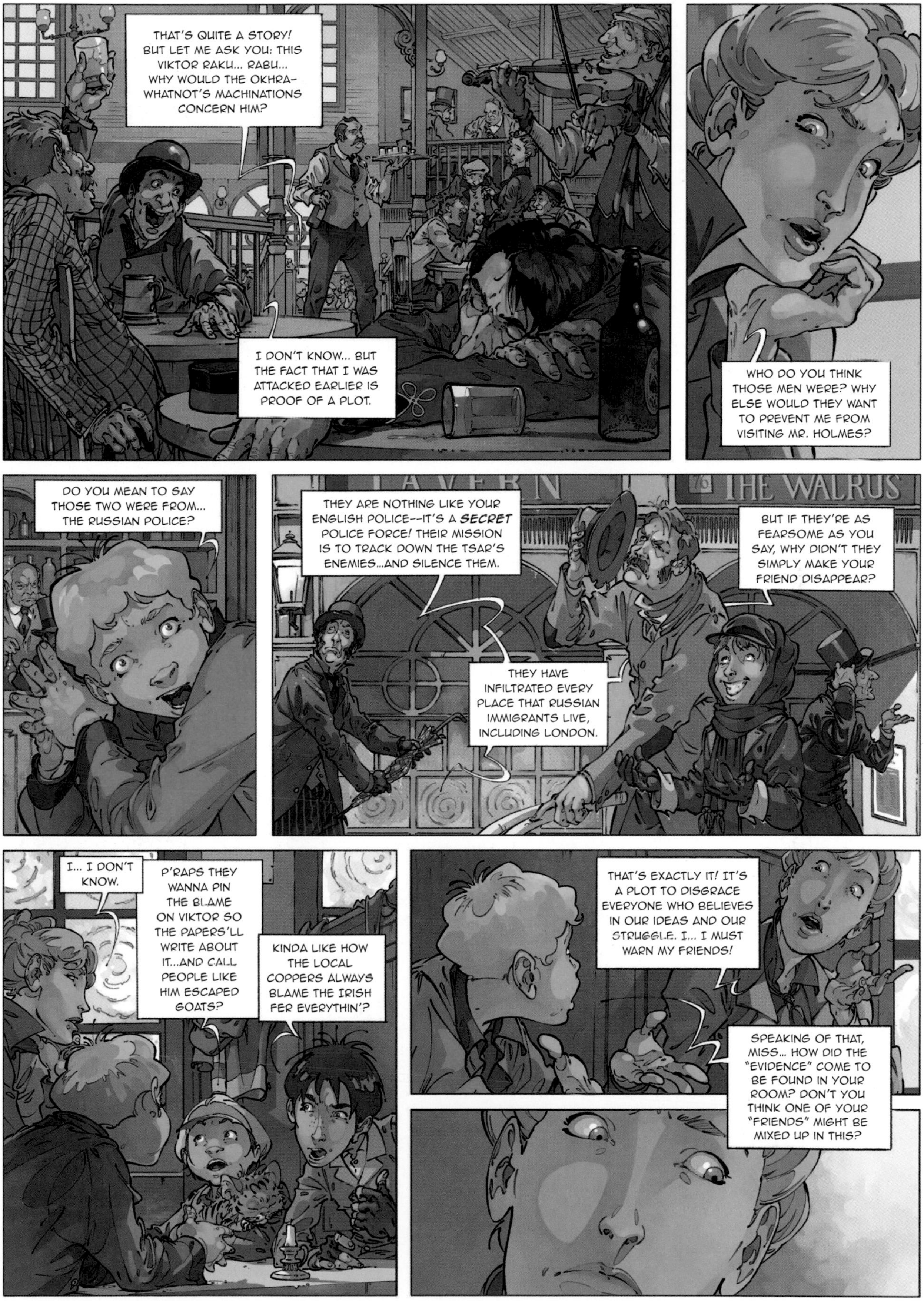
THAT'S QUITE A STORY! BUT LET ME ASK YOU: THIS VIKTOR RAKU... RABU... WHY WOULD THE OKHRA-WHATNOT'S MACHINATIONS CONCERN HIM?
I DON'T KNOW... BUT THE FACT THAT I WAS ATTACKED EARLIER IS PROOF OF A PLOT.
WHO DO YOU THINK THOSE MEN WERE? WHY ELSE WOULD THEY WANT TO PREVENT ME FROM VISITING MR. HOLMES?
DO YOU MEAN TO SAY THOSE TWO WERE FROM... THE RUSSIAN POLICE?
TAVERN
THE WALRUS
THEY ARE NOTHING LIKE YOUR ENGLISH POLICE--IT'S A SECRET POLICE FORCE! THEIR MISSION IS TO TRACK DOWN THE TSAR'S ENEMIES...AND SILENCE THEM.
THEY HAVE INFILTRATED EVERY PLACE THAT RUSSIAN IMMIGRANTS LIVE, INCLUDING LONDON.
BUT IF THEY'RE AS FEARSOME AS YOU SAY, WHY DIDN'T THEY SIMPLY MAKE YOUR FRIEND DISAPPEAR?
I... I DON'T KNOW.
P'RAPS THEY WANNA PIN THE BLAME ON VIKTOR SO THE PAPERS'LL WRITE ABOUT IT...AND CALL PEOPLE LIKE HIM ESCAPED GOATS?
KINDA LIKE HOW THE LOCAL COPPERS ALWAYS BLAME THE IRISH FER EVERYTHIN'?
THAT'S EXACTLY IT! IT'S A PLOT TO DISGRACE EVERYONE WHO BELIEVES IN OUR IDEAS AND OUR STRUGGLE. I... I MUST WARN MY FRIENDS!
SPEAKING OF THAT, MISS... HOW DID THE "EVIDENCE" COME TO BE FOUND IN YOUR ROOM? DON'T YOU THINK ONE OF YOUR "FRIENDS" MIGHT BE MIXED UP IN THIS?

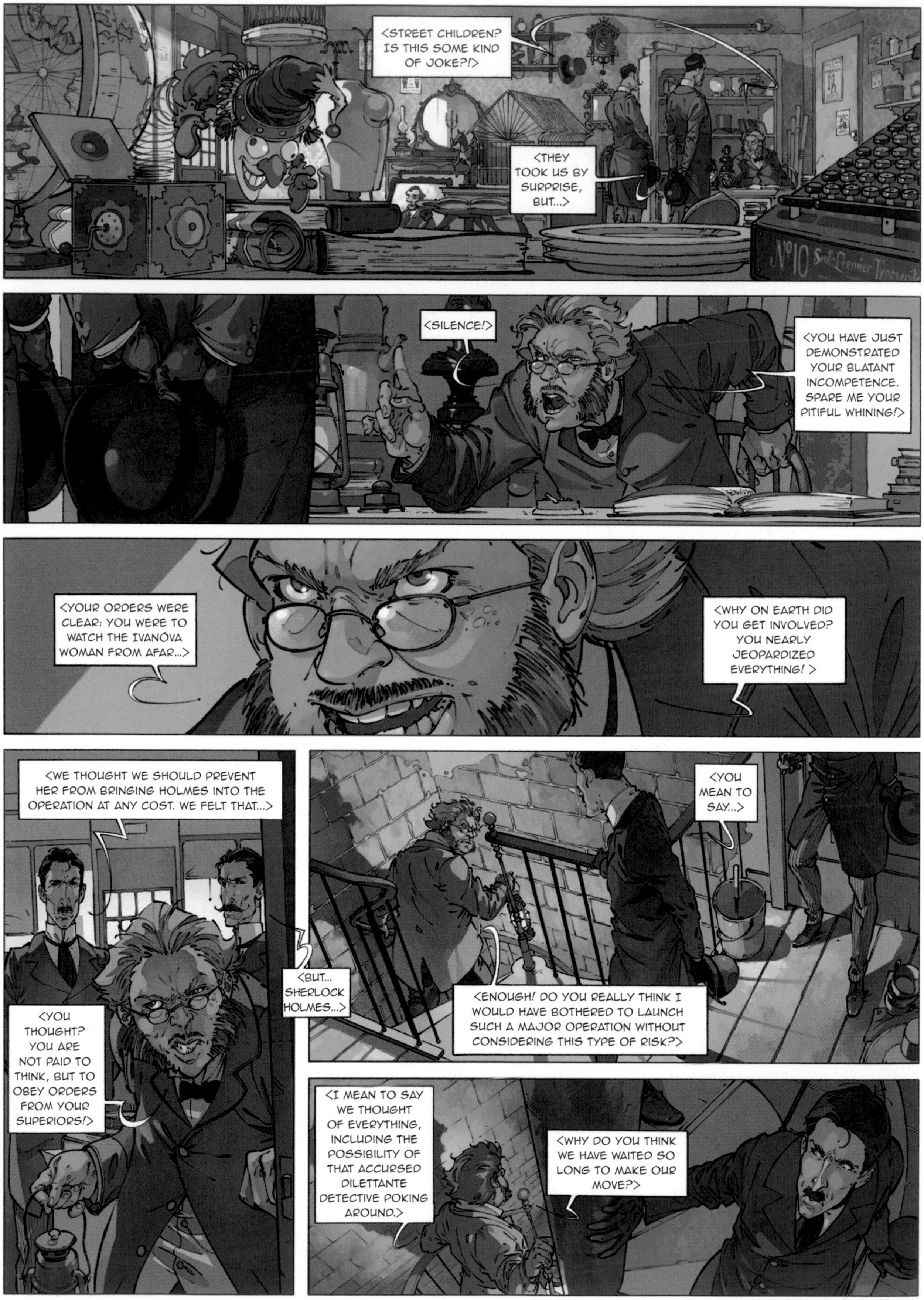
<STREET CHILDREN? IS THIS SOME KIND OF JOKE?!>
<THEY TOOK US BY SURPRISE, BUT...>
<SILENCE!>
<YOU HAVE JUST DEMONSTRATED YOUR BLATANT INCOMPETENCE. SPARE ME YOUR PITIFUL WHINING!>
<YOUR ORDERS WERE CLEAR: YOU WERE TO WATCH THE IVANÓVA WOMAN FROM AFAR...>
<WHY ON EARTH DID YOU GET INVOLVED? YOU NEARLY JEOPARDIZED EVERYTHING! >
<WE THOUGHT WE SHOULD PREVENT HER FROM BRINGING HOLMES INTO THE OPERATION AT ANY COST. WE FELT THAT...>
<YOU THOUGHT? YOU ARE NOT PAID TO THINK, BUT TO OBEY ORDERS FROM YOUR SUPERIORS!>
<BUT... SHERLOCK HOLMES...>
<ENOUGH! DO YOU REALLY THINK I WOULD HAVE BOTHERED TO LAUNCH SUCH A MAJOR OPERATION WITHOUT CONSIDERING THIS TYPE OF RISK?>
<YOU MEAN TO SAY...>
<I MEAN TO SAY WE THOUGHT OF EVERYTHING, INCLUDING THE POSSIBILITY OF THAT ACCURSED DILETTANTE DETECTIVE POKING AROUND.>
<WHY DO YOU THINK WE HAVE WAITED SO LONG TO MAKE OUR MOVE?>

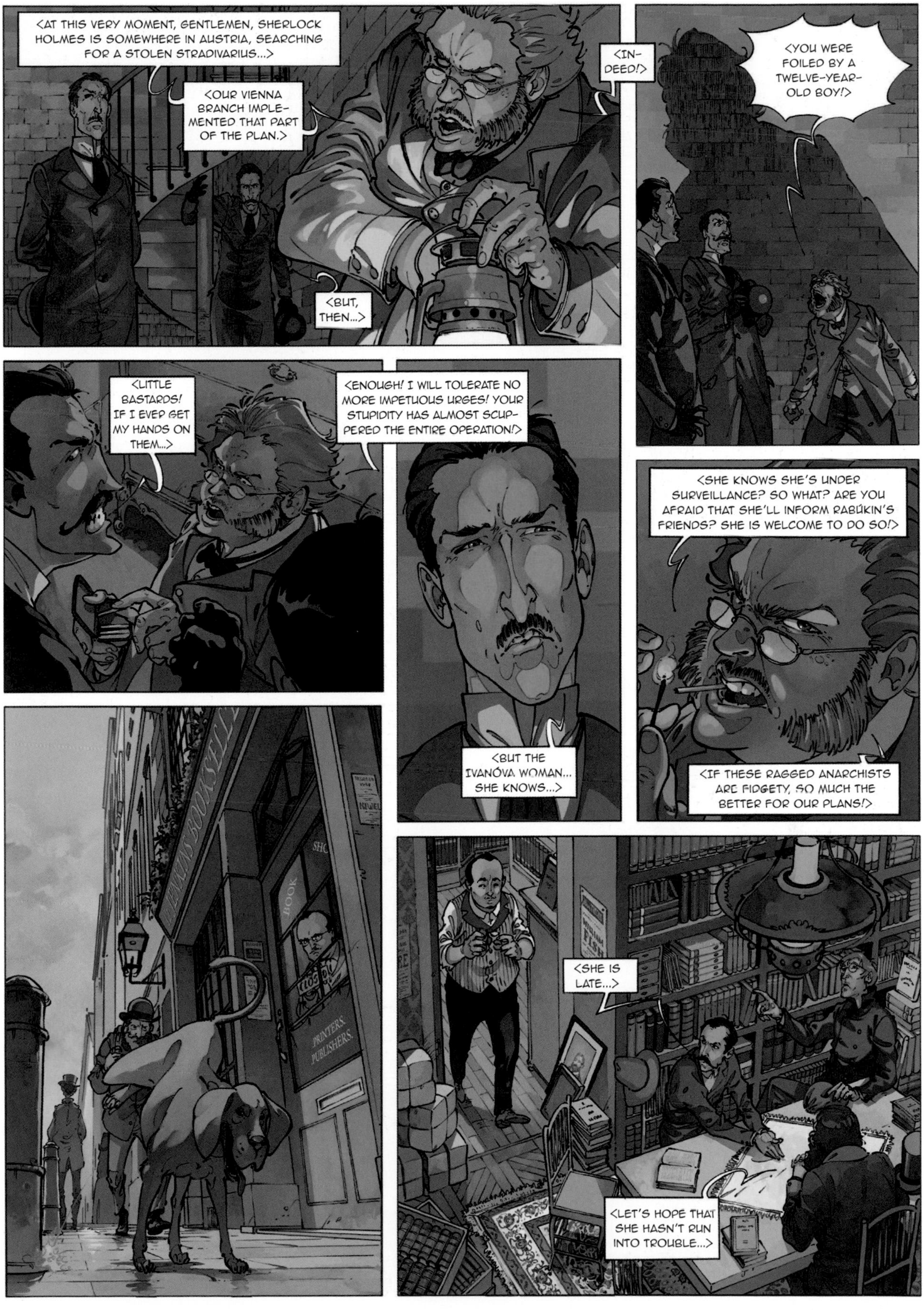

<AT THIS VERY MOMENT, GENTLEMEN, SHERLOCK HOLMES IS SOMEWHERE IN AUSTRIA, SEARCHING FOR A STOLEN STRADIVARIUS...>
<OUR VIENNA BRANCH IMPLEMENTED THAT PART OF THE PLAN.>
<INDEED!>
<BUT, THEN...>
<YOU WERE FOILED BY A TWELVE-YEAR-OLD BOY!>
<LITTLE BASTARDS! IF I EVER GET MY HANDS ON THEM...>
<ENOUGH! I WILL TOLERATE NO MORE IMPETUOUS URGES! YOUR STUPIDITY HAS ALMOST SCUPPERED THE ENTIRE OPERATION!>
<BUT THE IVANÓVA WOMAN... SHE KNOWS...>
<SHE KNOWS SHE'S UNDER SURVEILLANCE? SO WHAT? ARE YOU AFRAID THAT SHE'LL INFORM RABÚKIN'S FRIENDS? SHE IS WELCOME TO DO SO!>
<IF THESE RAGGED ANARCHISTS ARE FIDGETY, SO MUCH THE BETTER FOR OUR PLANS!>
BOOKSELLERS
BOOK
SHO
CLOSED
PRINTERS. PUBLISHERS.
<SHE IS LATE...>
<LET'S HOPE THAT SHE HASN'T RUN INTO TROUBLE...>

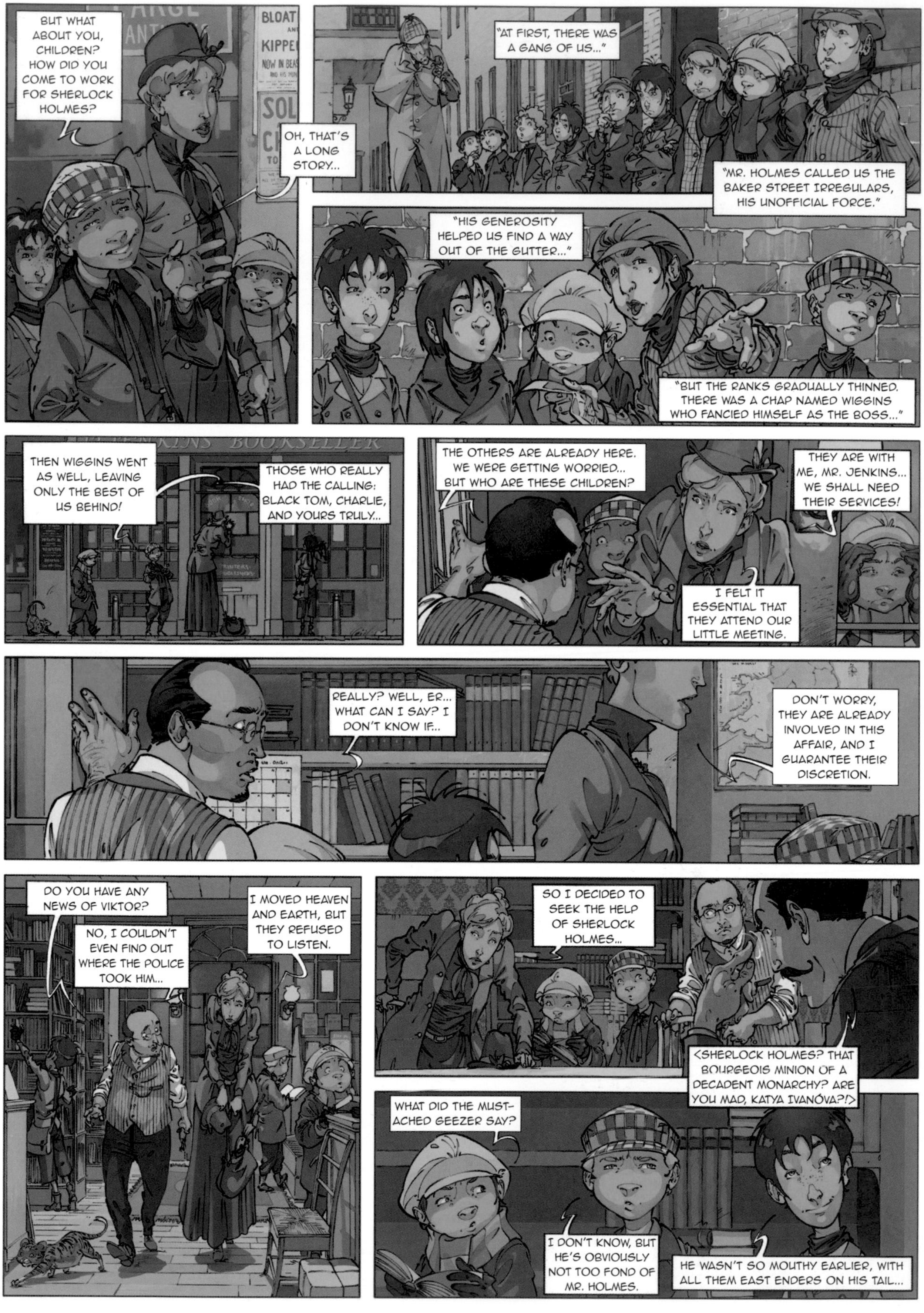
BUT WHAT ABOUT YOU, CHILDREN? HOW DID YOU COME TO WORK FOR SHERLOCK HOLMES?
OH, THAT'S A LONG STORY...
"AT FIRST, THERE WAS A GANG OF US..."
"MR. HOLMES CALLED US THE BAKER STREET IRREGULARS, HIS UNOFFICIAL FORCE."
"HIS GENEROSITY HELPED US FIND A WAY OUT OF THE GUTTER..."
"BUT THE RANKS GRADUALLY THINNED. THERE WAS A CHAP NAMED WIGGINS WHO FANCIED HIMSELF AS THE BOSS..."
THEN WIGGINS WENT AS WELL, LEAVING ONLY THE BEST OF US BEHIND!
THOSE WHO REALLY HAD THE CALLING: BLACK TOM, CHARLIE, AND YOURS TRULY...
THE OTHERS ARE ALREADY HERE. WE WERE GETTING WORRIED... BUT WHO ARE THESE CHILDREN?
THEY ARE WITH ME, MR. JENKINS... WE SHALL NEED THEIR SERVICES!
I FELT IT ESSENTIAL THAT THEY ATTEND OUR LITTLE MEETING.
REALLY? WELL, ER... WHAT CAN I SAY? I DON'T KNOW IF...
DON'T WORRY, THEY ARE ALREADY INVOLVED IN THIS AFFAIR, AND I GUARANTEE THEIR DISCRETION.
DO YOU HAVE ANY NEWS OF VIKTOR?
NO, I COULDN'T EVEN FIND OUT WHERE THE POLICE TOOK HIM...
I MOVED HEAVEN AND EARTH, BUT THEY REFUSED TO LISTEN.
SO I DECIDED TO SEEK THE HELP OF SHERLOCK HOLMES...
<SHERLOCK HOLMES? THAT BOURGEOIS MINION OF A DECADENT MONARCHY? ARE YOU MAD, KATYA IVANÓVA?!>
WHAT DID THE MUST-ACHED GEEZER SAY?
I DON'T KNOW, BUT HE'S OBVIOUSLY NOT TOO FOND OF MR. HOLMES.
HE WASN'T SO MOUTHY EARLIER, WITH ALL THEM EAST ENDERS ON HIS TAIL...

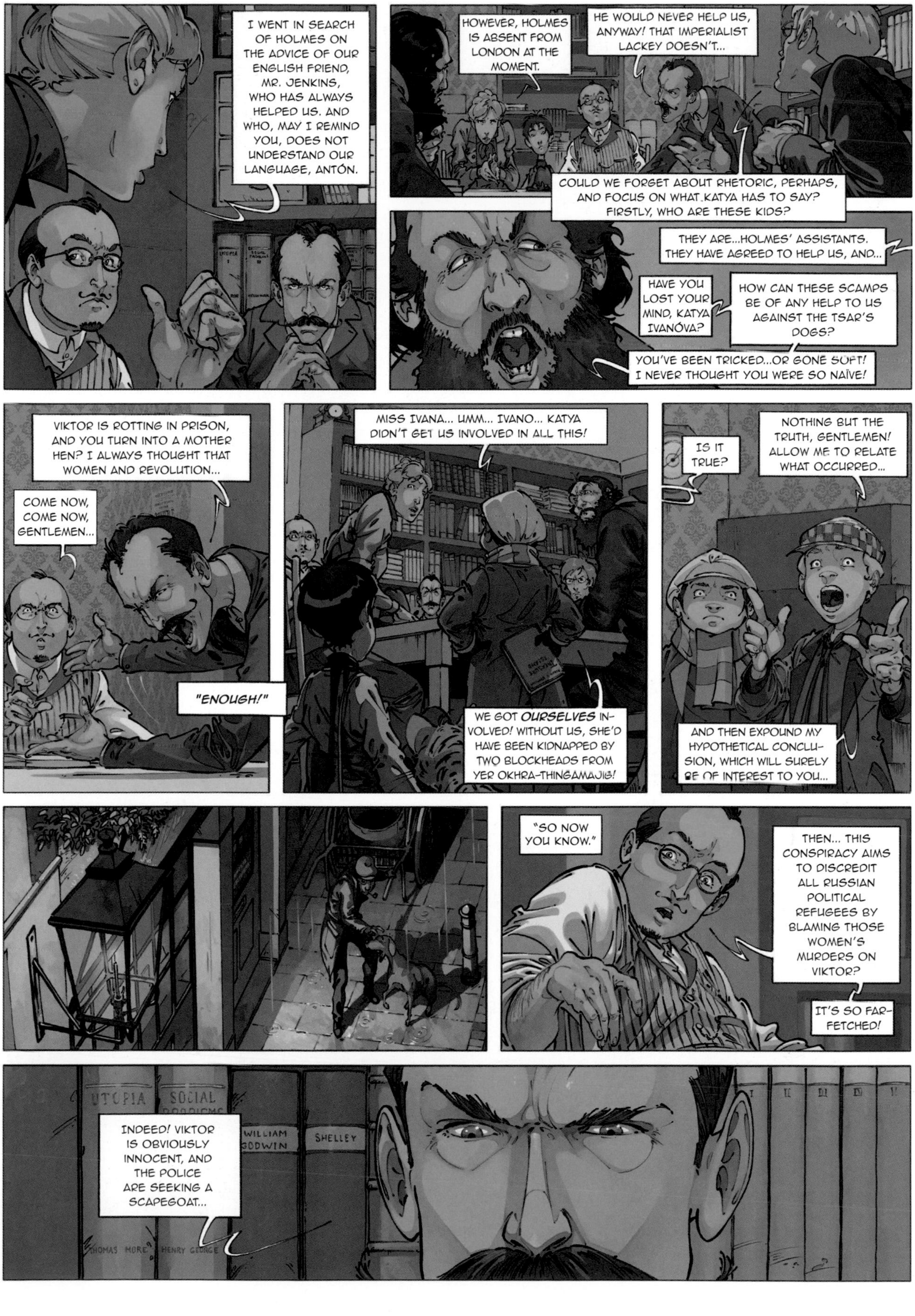
I WENT IN SEARCH OF HOLMES ON THE ADVICE OF OUR ENGLISH FRIEND, MR. JENKINS, WHO HAS ALWAYS HELPED US. AND WHO, MAY I REMIND YOU, DOES NOT UNDERSTAND OUR LANGUAGE, ANTÓN.
HOWEVER, HOLMES IS ABSENT FROM LONDON AT THE MOMENT.
HE WOULD NEVER HELP US, ANYWAY! THAT IMPERIALIST LACKEY DOESN'T...
COULD WE FORGET ABOUT RHETORIC, PERHAPS, AND FOCUS ON WHAT KATYA HAS TO SAY? FIRSTLY, WHO ARE THESE KIDS?
THEY ARE...HOLMES' ASSISTANTS. THEY HAVE AGREED TO HELP US, AND...
HAVE YOU LOST YOUR MIND, KATYA IVANÓVA?
HOW CAN THESE SCAMPS BE OF ANY HELP TO US AGAINST THE TSAR'S DOGS?
YOU'VE BEEN TRICKED...OR GONE SOFT! I NEVER THOUGHT YOU WERE SO NAÏVE!
VIKTOR IS ROTTING IN PRISON, AND YOU TURN INTO A MOTHER HEN? I ALWAYS THOUGHT THAT WOMEN AND REVOLUTION...
COME NOW, COME NOW, GENTLEMEN...
"ENOUGH!"
MISS IVANA... UMM... IVANO... KATYA DIDN'T GET US INVOLVED IN ALL THIS!
WE GOT *OURSELVES* INVOLVED! WITHOUT US, SHE'D HAVE BEEN KIDNAPPED BY TWO BLOCKHEADS FROM YER OKHRA-THINGAMAJIG!
IS IT TRUE?
NOTHING BUT THE TRUTH, GENTLEMEN! ALLOW ME TO RELATE WHAT OCCURRED...
AND THEN EXPOUND MY HYPOTHETICAL CONCLUSION, WHICH WILL SURELY BE OF INTEREST TO YOU...
"SO NOW YOU KNOW."
THEN... THIS CONSPIRACY AIMS TO DISCREDIT ALL RUSSIAN POLITICAL REFUGEES BY BLAMING THOSE WOMEN'S MURDERS ON VIKTOR?
IT'S SO FARFETCHED!
UTOPIA
SOCIAL
WILLIAM GODWIN
SHELLEY
INDEED! VIKTOR IS OBVIOUSLY INNOCENT, AND THE POLICE ARE SEEKING A SCAPEGOAT...
THOMAS MORE
HENRY GEORGE

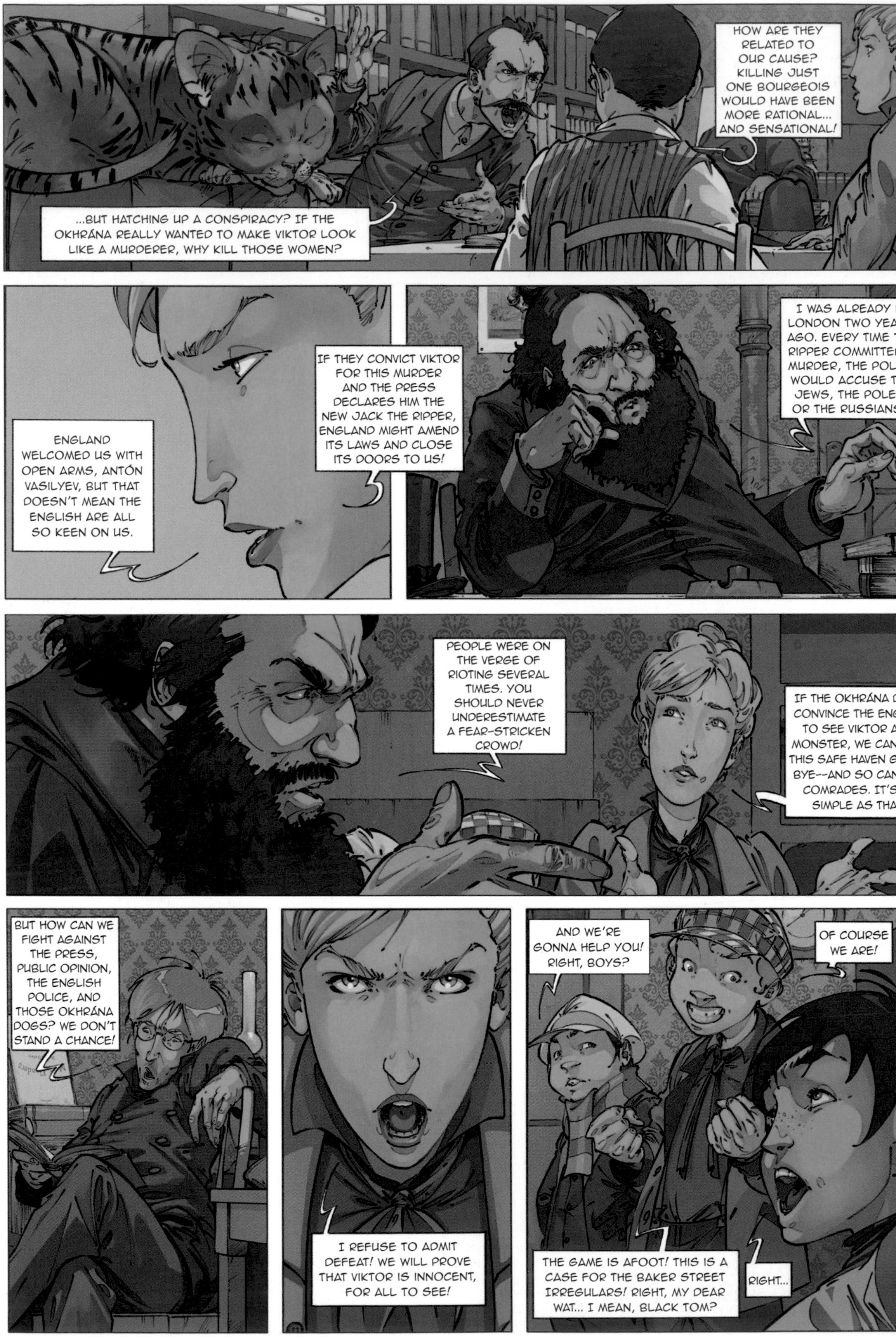
...BUT HATCHING UP A CONSPIRACY? IF THE OKHRÁNA REALLY WANTED TO MAKE VIKTOR LOOK LIKE A MURDERER, WHY KILL THOSE WOMEN?
HOW ARE THEY RELATED TO OUR CAUSE? KILLING JUST ONE BOURGEOIS WOULD HAVE BEEN MORE RATIONAL... AND SENSATIONAL!
ENGLAND WELCOMED US WITH OPEN ARMS, ANTÓN VASILYEV, BUT THAT DOESN'T MEAN THE ENGLISH ARE ALL SO KEEN ON US.
IF THEY CONVICT VIKTOR FOR THIS MURDER AND THE PRESS DECLARES HIM THE NEW JACK THE RIPPER, ENGLAND MIGHT AMEND ITS LAWS AND CLOSE ITS DOORS TO US!
I WAS ALREADY IN LONDON TWO YEARS AGO. EVERY TIME THE RIPPER COMMITTED A MURDER, THE POLICE WOULD ACCUSE THE JEWS, THE POLES, OR THE RUSSIANS...
PEOPLE WERE ON THE VERGE OF RIOTING SEVERAL TIMES. YOU SHOULD NEVER UNDERESTIMATE A FEAR-STRICKEN CROWD!
IF THE OKHRÁNA DOES CONVINCE THE ENGLISH TO SEE VIKTOR AS A MONSTER, WE CAN KISS THIS SAFE HAVEN GOOD-BYE--AND SO CAN OUR COMRADES. IT'S AS SIMPLE AS THAT...
BUT HOW CAN WE FIGHT AGAINST THE PRESS, PUBLIC OPINION, THE ENGLISH POLICE, AND THOSE OKHRÁNA DOGS? WE DON'T STAND A CHANCE!
I REFUSE TO ADMIT DEFEAT! WE WILL PROVE THAT VIKTOR IS INNOCENT, FOR ALL TO SEE!
AND WE'RE GONNA HELP YOU! RIGHT, BOYS?
OF COURSE WE ARE!
THE GAME IS AFOOT! THIS IS A CASE FOR THE BAKER STREET IRREGULARS! RIGHT, MY DEAR WAT... I MEAN, BLACK TOM?
RIGHT...

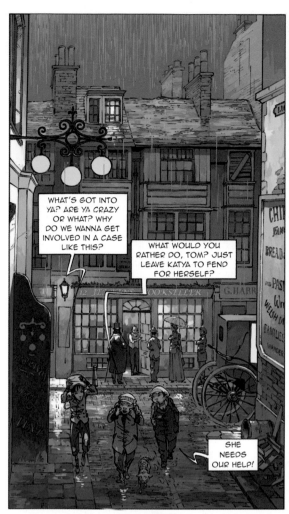

WHAT'S GOT INTO YA? ARE YA CRAZY OR WHAT? WHY DO WE WANNA GET INVOLVED IN A CASE LIKE THIS?

WHAT WOULD YOU RATHER DO, TOM? JUST LEAVE KATYA TO FEND FOR HERSELF?

SHE NEEDS OUR HELP!

SHE WON'T GET MINE!

THEM RUSSKIES AIN'T NONE OF OUR BUSINESS! THEY'RE NOTHIN' TO DO WITH US, CHARLIE!

I SEE! ALL YA CARE ABOUT'S YER HIDE, BLACK TOM O' KILBURN!

MY HIDE, YOUR HIDE, AND EVEN BILLY'S, TOO!

I DON'T MIND PLAYIN' THE ACROBAT OR WATCHMAN FER HOLMES, SO LONG AS HE'S COUGHIN' UP THE CASH... BUT THIS HAS NOTHIN' TO DO WITH US!

ALWAYS A FIRST TIME!

WE CAN AT LEAST TAKE CARE OF THINGS UNTIL MR. HOLMES GETS BACK.

AH, THE APPRENTICE DETECTIVE'S OFF AGAIN! IT'S BEEN A WHILE...

D'YA CARE TO SHARE YER LATEST DEDUCTIONS WITH US, MR. EXPERT?

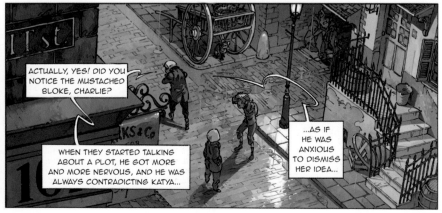

ACTUALLY, YES! DID YOU NOTICE THE MUSTACHED BLOKE, CHARLIE?

WHEN THEY STARTED TALKING ABOUT A PLOT, HE GOT MORE AND MORE NERVOUS, AND HE WAS ALWAYS CONTRADICTING KATYA...

...AS IF HE WAS ANXIOUS TO DISMISS HER IDEA...

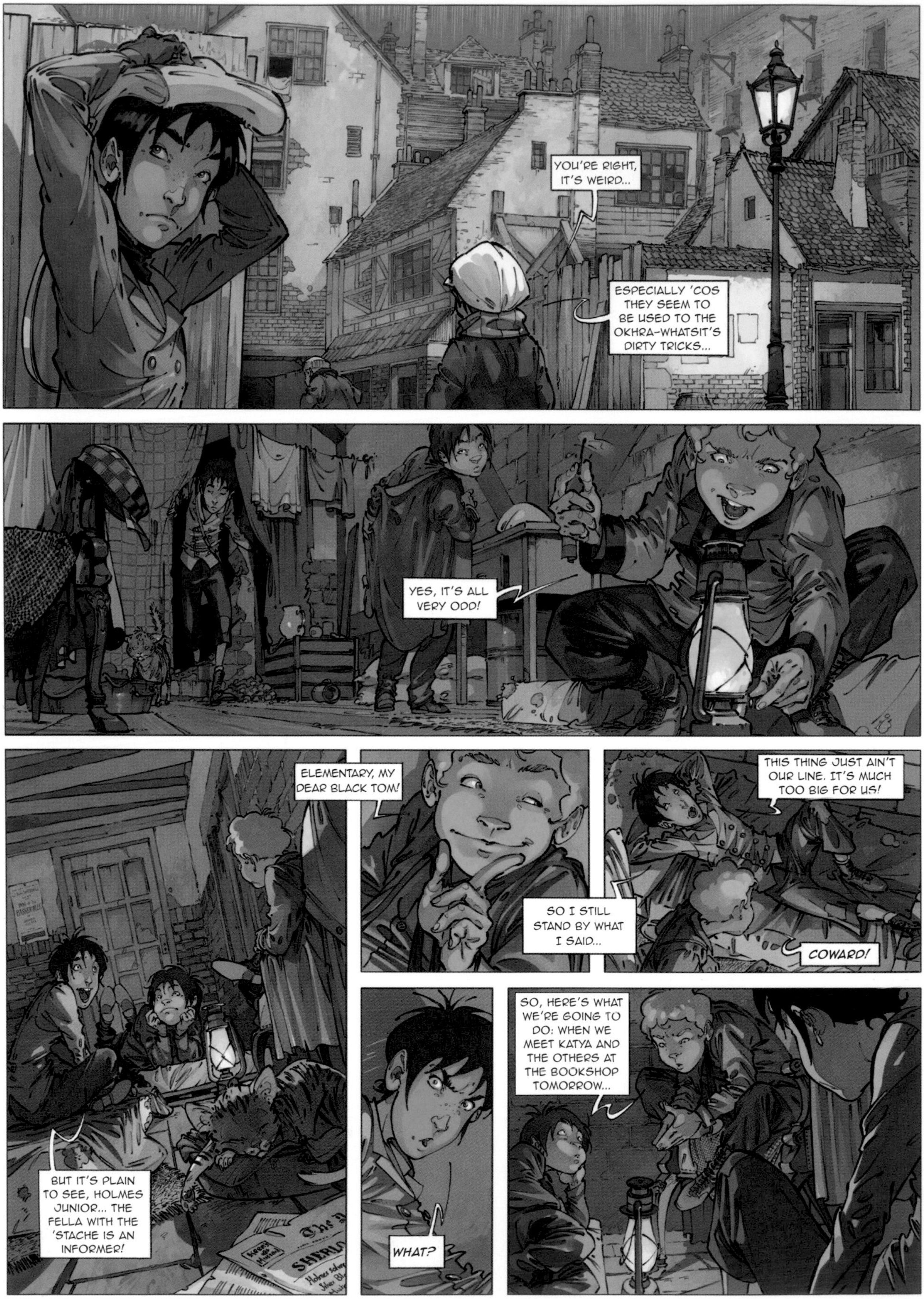
YOU'RE RIGHT, IT'S WEIRD...
ESPECIALLY 'COS THEY SEEM TO BE USED TO THE OKHRA-WHATSIT'S DIRTY TRICKS...
YES, IT'S ALL VERY ODD!
BUT IT'S PLAIN TO SEE, HOLMES JUNIOR... THE FELLA WITH THE 'STACHE IS AN INFORMER!
ELEMENTARY, MY DEAR BLACK TOM!
SO I STILL STAND BY WHAT I SAID...
THIS THING JUST AIN'T OUR LINE. IT'S MUCH TOO BIG FOR US!
COWARD!
WHAT?
SO, HERE'S WHAT WE'RE GOING TO DO: WHEN WE MEET KATYA AND THE OTHERS AT THE BOOKSHOP TOMORROW...

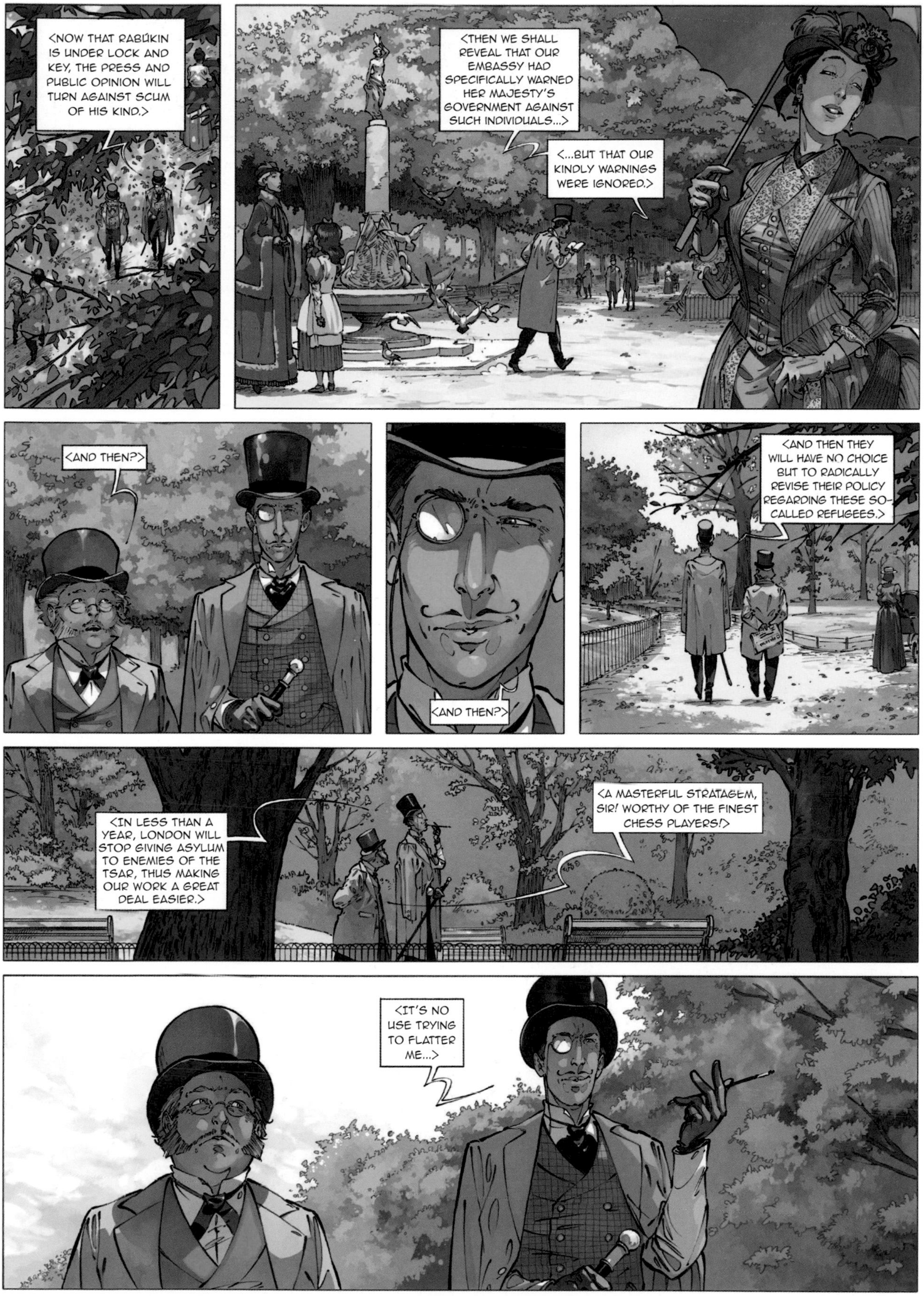
<NOW THAT RABÚKIN IS UNDER LOCK AND KEY, THE PRESS AND PUBLIC OPINION WILL TURN AGAINST SCUM OF HIS KIND.>
<THEN WE SHALL REVEAL THAT OUR EMBASSY HAD SPECIFICALLY WARNED HER MAJESTY'S GOVERNMENT AGAINST SUCH INDIVIDUALS...>
<...BUT THAT OUR KINDLY WARNINGS WERE IGNORED.>
<AND THEN?>
<AND THEN?>
<AND THEN THEY WILL HAVE NO CHOICE BUT TO RADICALLY REVISE THEIR POLICY REGARDING THESE SO-CALLED REFUGEES.>
<IN LESS THAN A YEAR, LONDON WILL STOP GIVING ASYLUM TO ENEMIES OF THE TSAR, THUS MAKING OUR WORK A GREAT DEAL EASIER.>
<A MASTERFUL STRATAGEM, SIR! WORTHY OF THE FINEST CHESS PLAYERS!>
<IT'S NO USE TRYING TO FLATTER ME...>

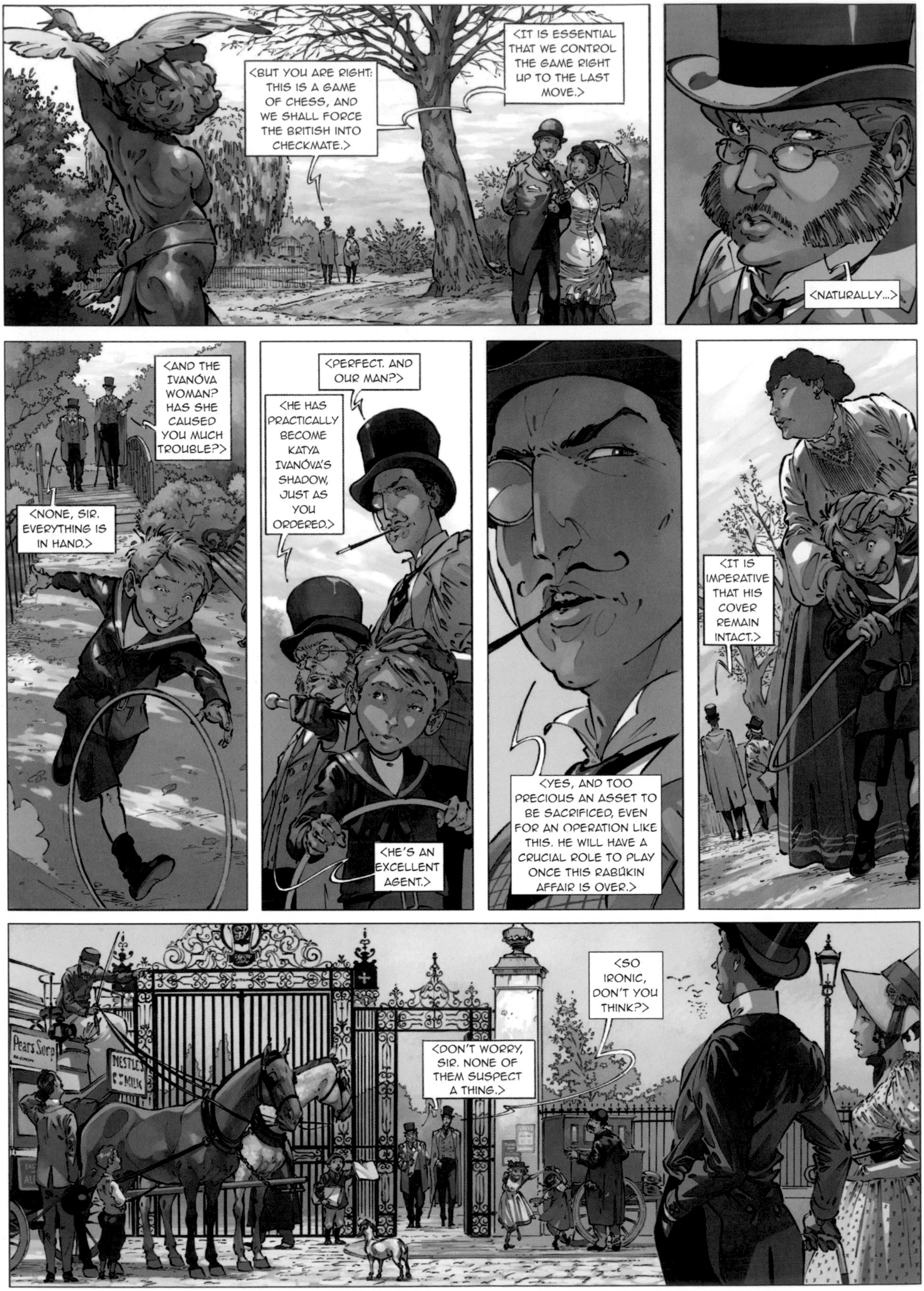
<BUT YOU ARE RIGHT: THIS IS A GAME OF CHESS, AND WE SHALL FORCE THE BRITISH INTO CHECKMATE.>
<IT IS ESSENTIAL THAT WE CONTROL THE GAME RIGHT UP TO THE LAST MOVE.>
<NATURALLY...>
<AND THE IVANÓVA WOMAN? HAS SHE CAUSED YOU MUCH TROUBLE?>
<NONE, SIR. EVERYTHING IS IN HAND.>
<PERFECT. AND OUR MAN?>
<HE HAS PRACTICALLY BECOME KATYA IVANÓVA'S SHADOW, JUST AS YOU ORDERED.>
<HE'S AN EXCELLENT AGENT.>
<YES, AND TOO PRECIOUS AN ASSET TO BE SACRIFICED, EVEN FOR AN OPERATION LIKE THIS. HE WILL HAVE A CRUCIAL ROLE TO PLAY ONCE THIS RABÚKIN AFFAIR IS OVER.>
<IT IS IMPERATIVE THAT HIS COVER REMAIN INTACT.>
Pears Soap
NESTLE'S MILK
<DON'T WORRY, SIR. NONE OF THEM SUSPECT A THING.>
<SO IRONIC, DON'T YOU THINK?>

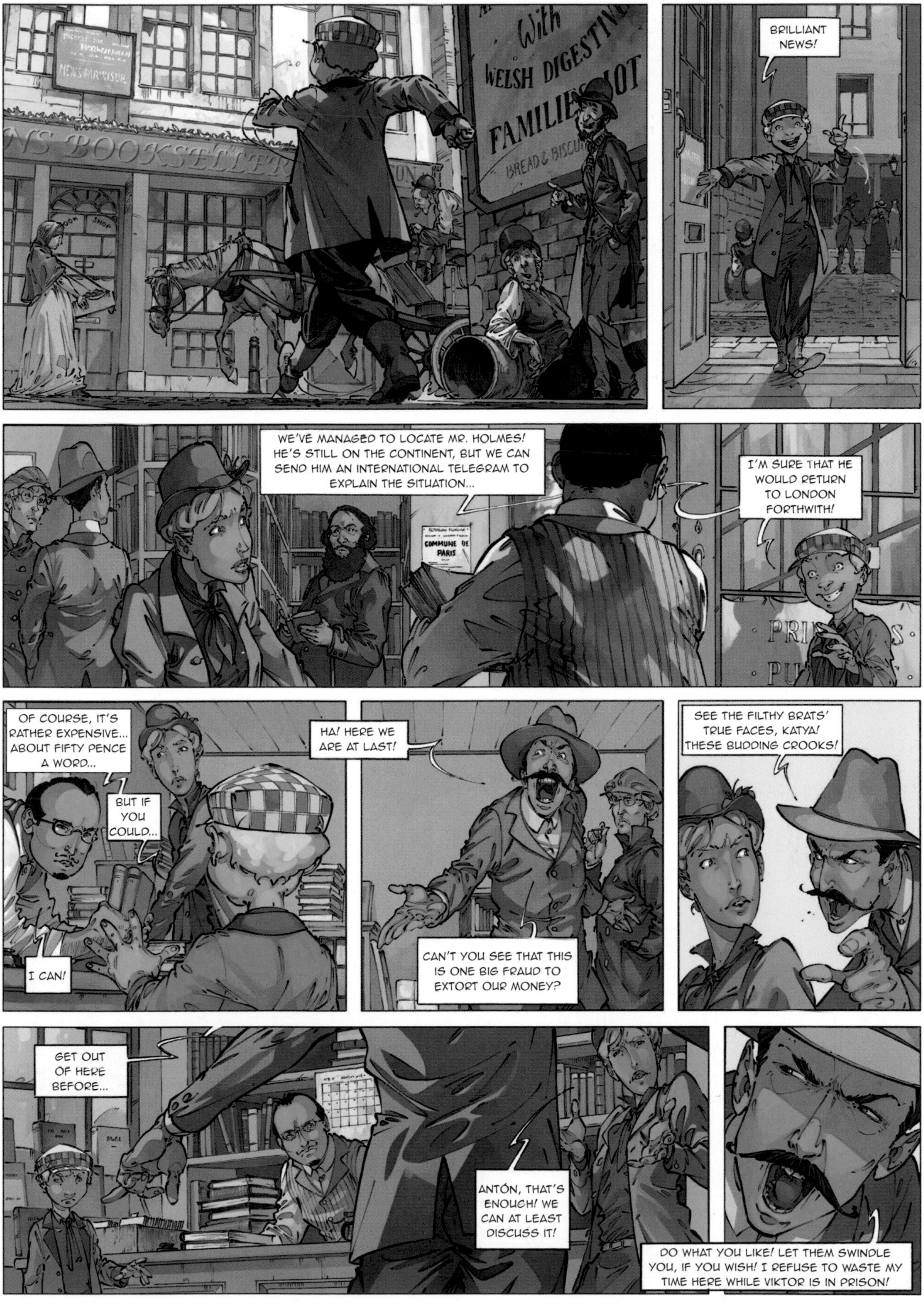
BRILLIANT NEWS!
WE'VE MANAGED TO LOCATE MR. HOLMES! HE'S STILL ON THE CONTINENT, BUT WE CAN SEND HIM AN INTERNATIONAL TELEGRAM TO EXPLAIN THE SITUATION...
I'M SURE THAT HE WOULD RETURN TO LONDON FORTHWITH!
OF COURSE, IT'S RATHER EXPENSIVE... ABOUT FIFTY PENCE A WORD...
BUT IF YOU COULD...
I CAN!
HA! HERE WE ARE AT LAST!
CAN'T YOU SEE THAT THIS IS ONE BIG FRAUD TO EXTORT OUR MONEY?
SEE THE FILTHY BRATS' TRUE FACES, KATYA! THESE BUDDING CROOKS!
GET OUT OF HERE BEFORE...
ANTÓN, THAT'S ENOUGH! WE CAN AT LEAST DISCUSS IT!
DO WHAT YOU LIKE! LET THEM SWINDLE YOU, IF YOU WISH! I REFUSE TO WASTE MY TIME HERE WHILE VIKTOR IS IN PRISON!

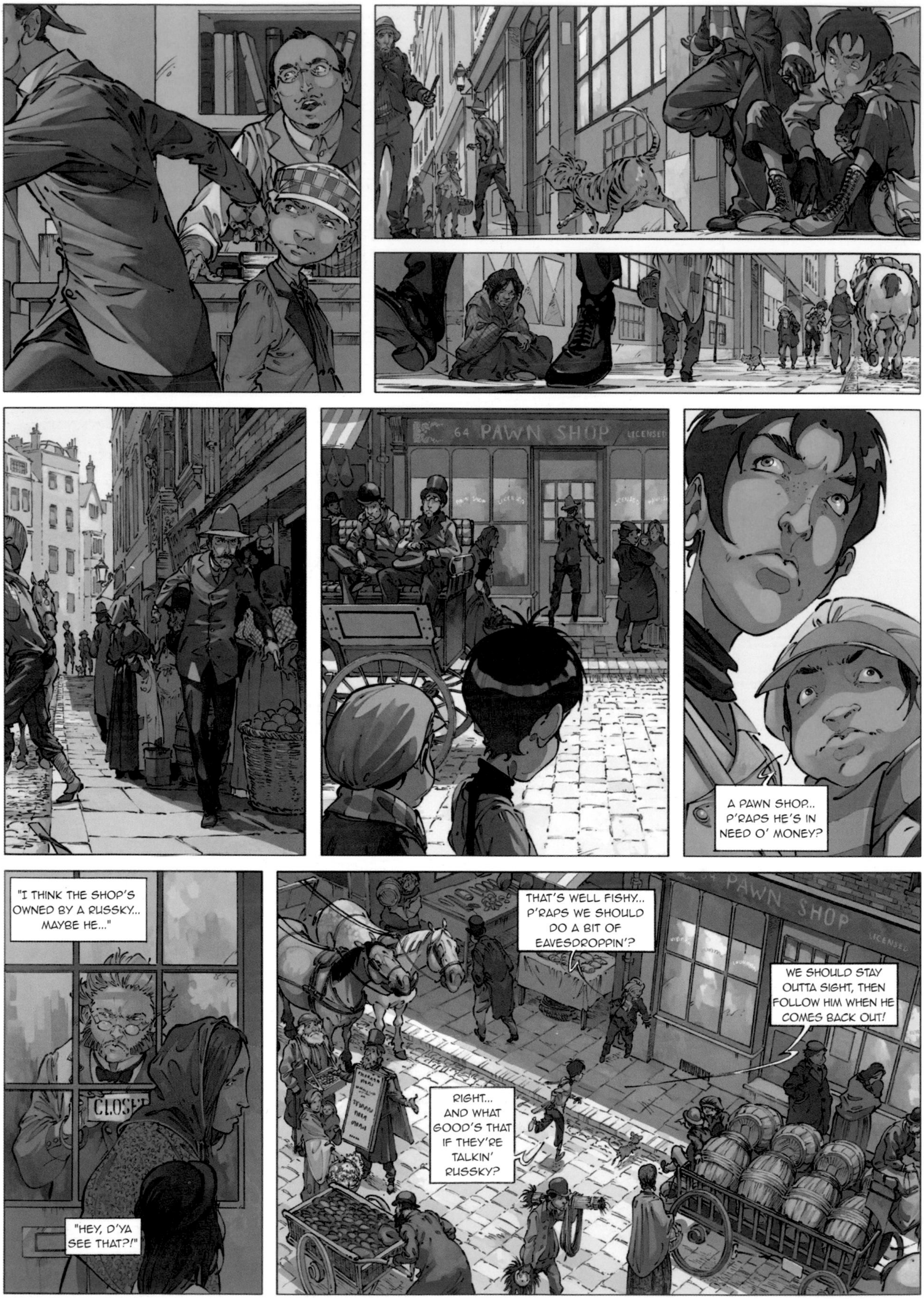
64 PAWN SHOP LICENSED
A PAWN SHOP... P'RAPS HE'S IN NEED O' MONEY?
"I THINK THE SHOP'S OWNED BY A RUSSKY... MAYBE HE..."
"HEY, D'YA SEE THAT?!"
THAT'S WELL FISHY... P'RAPS WE SHOULD DO A BIT OF EAVESDROPPIN'?
RIGHT... AND WHAT GOOD'S THAT IF THEY'RE TALKIN' RUSSKY?
WE SHOULD STAY OUTTA SIGHT, THEN FOLLOW HIM WHEN HE COMES BACK OUT!

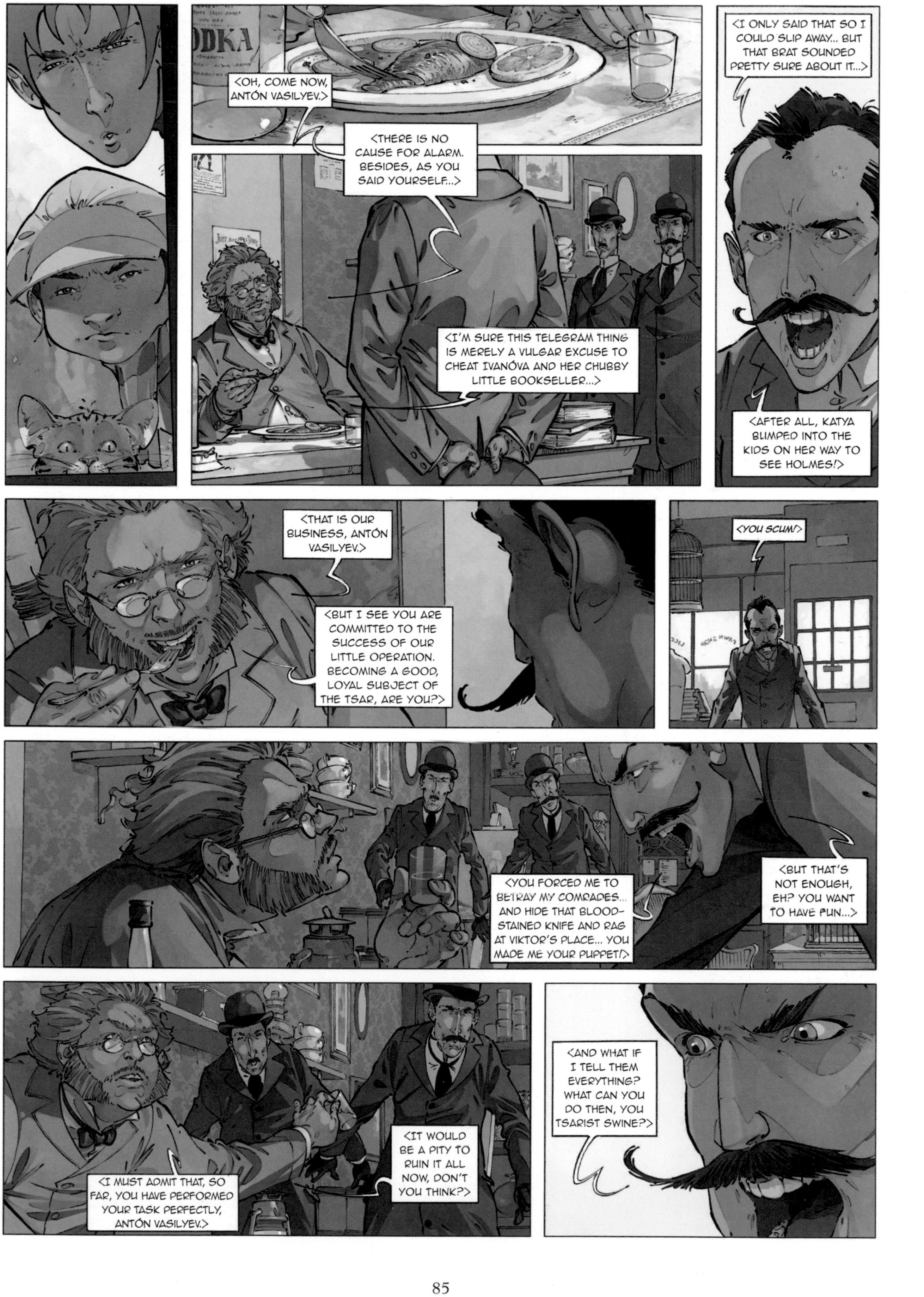
<OH, COME NOW, ANTÓN VASILYEV.>
<THERE IS NO CAUSE FOR ALARM. BESIDES, AS YOU SAID YOURSELF...>
<I'M SURE THIS TELEGRAM THING IS MERELY A VULGAR EXCUSE TO CHEAT IVANÓVA AND HER CHUBBY LITTLE BOOKSELLER...>
<I ONLY SAID THAT SO I COULD SLIP AWAY... BUT THAT BRAT SOUNDED PRETTY SURE ABOUT IT...>
<AFTER ALL, KATYA BUMPED INTO THE KIDS ON HER WAY TO SEE HOLMES!>
<THAT IS OUR BUSINESS, ANTÓN VASILYEV.>
<BUT I SEE YOU ARE COMMITTED TO THE SUCCESS OF OUR LITTLE OPERATION. BECOMING A GOOD, LOYAL SUBJECT OF THE TSAR, ARE YOU?>
<YOU SCUM!>
<YOU FORCED ME TO BETRAY MY COMRADES... AND HIDE THAT BLOOD-STAINED KNIFE AND RAG AT VIKTOR'S PLACE... YOU MADE ME YOUR PUPPET!>
<BUT THAT'S NOT ENOUGH, EH? YOU WANT TO HAVE FUN...>
<I MUST ADMIT THAT, SO FAR, YOU HAVE PERFORMED YOUR TASK PERFECTLY, ANTÓN VASILYEV.>
<IT WOULD BE A PITY TO RUIN IT ALL NOW, DON'T YOU THINK?>
<AND WHAT IF I TELL THEM EVERYTHING? WHAT CAN YOU DO THEN, YOU TSARIST SWINE?>

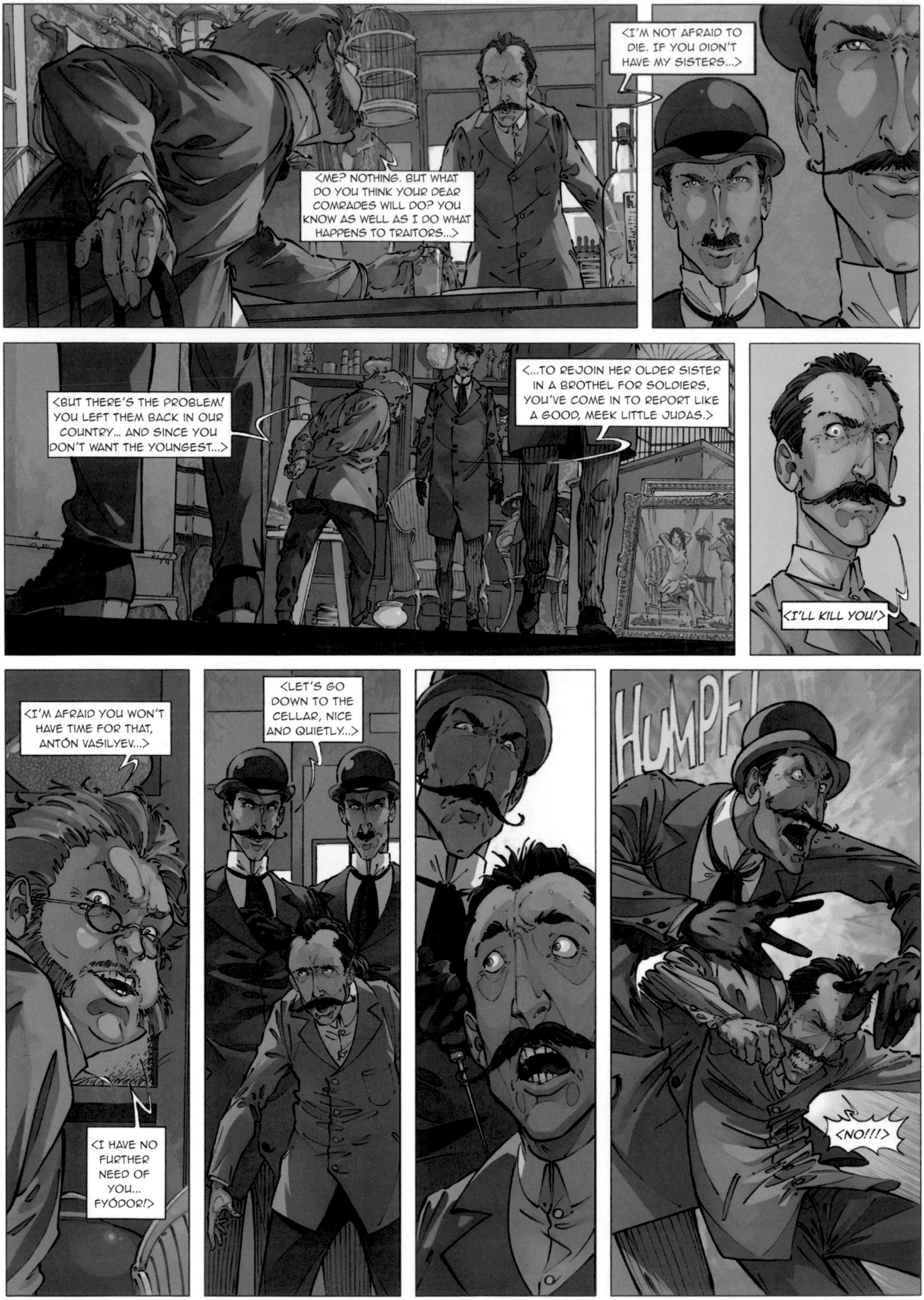
<ME? NOTHING. BUT WHAT DO YOU THINK YOUR DEAR COMRADES WILL DO? YOU KNOW AS WELL AS I DO WHAT HAPPENS TO TRAITORS...>
<I'M NOT AFRAID TO DIE. IF YOU DIDN'T HAVE MY SISTERS...>
<BUT THERE'S THE PROBLEM! YOU LEFT THEM BACK IN OUR COUNTRY... AND SINCE YOU DON'T WANT THE YOUNGEST...>
<...TO REJOIN HER OLDER SISTER IN A BROTHEL FOR SOLDIERS, YOU'VE COME IN TO REPORT LIKE A GOOD, MEEK LITTLE JUDAS.>
<I'LL KILL YOU!>
<I'M AFRAID YOU WON'T HAVE TIME FOR THAT, ANTÓN VASILYEV...>
<I HAVE NO FURTHER NEED OF YOU... FYÓDOR!>
<LET'S GO DOWN TO THE CELLAR, NICE AND QUIETLY...>
HUMPF!
<NO!!!>

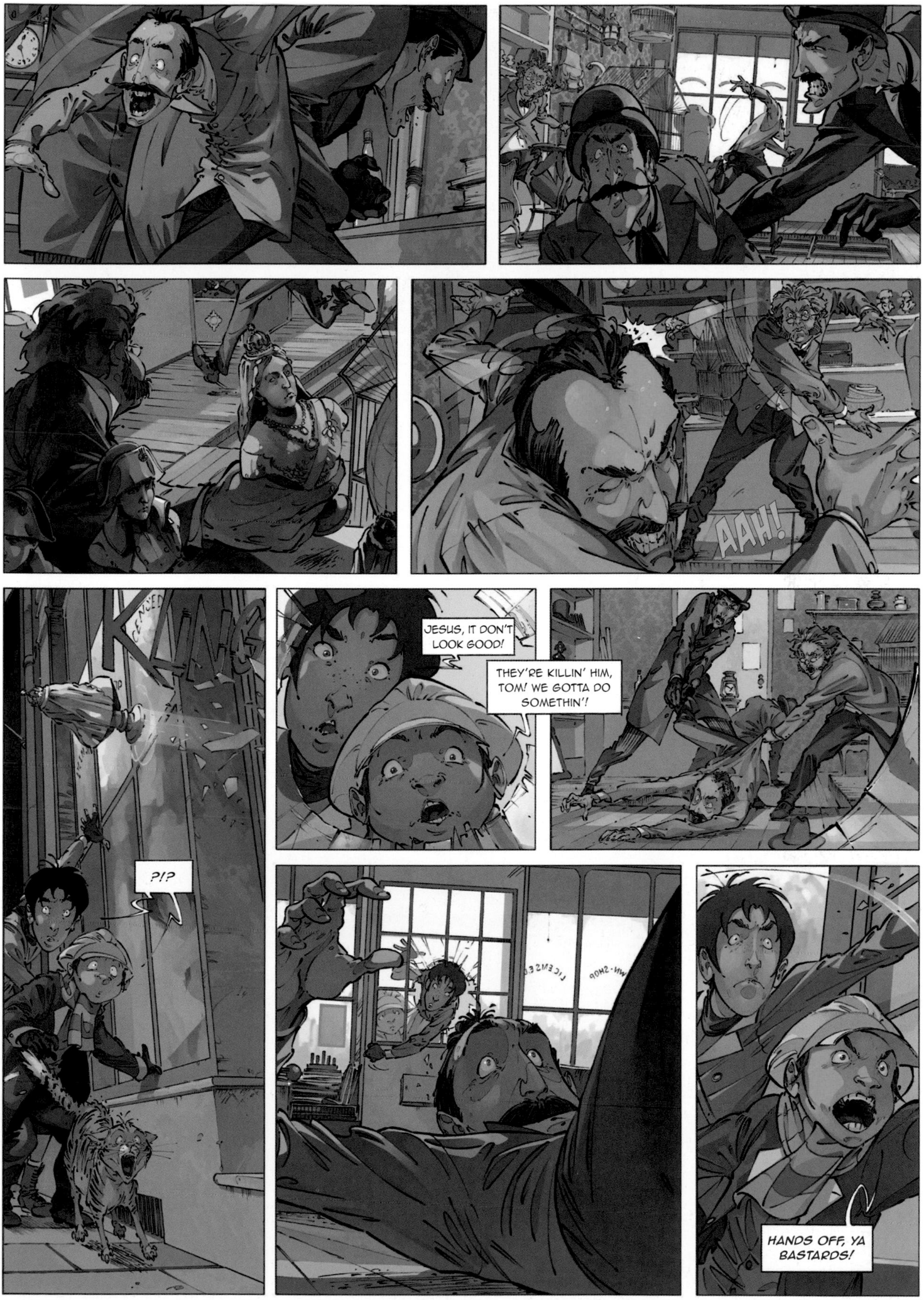
AAH!
JESUS, IT DON'T LOOK GOOD!
THEY'RE KILLIN' HIM, TOM! WE GOTTA DO SOMETHIN'!
?!?
HANDS OFF, YA BASTARDS!

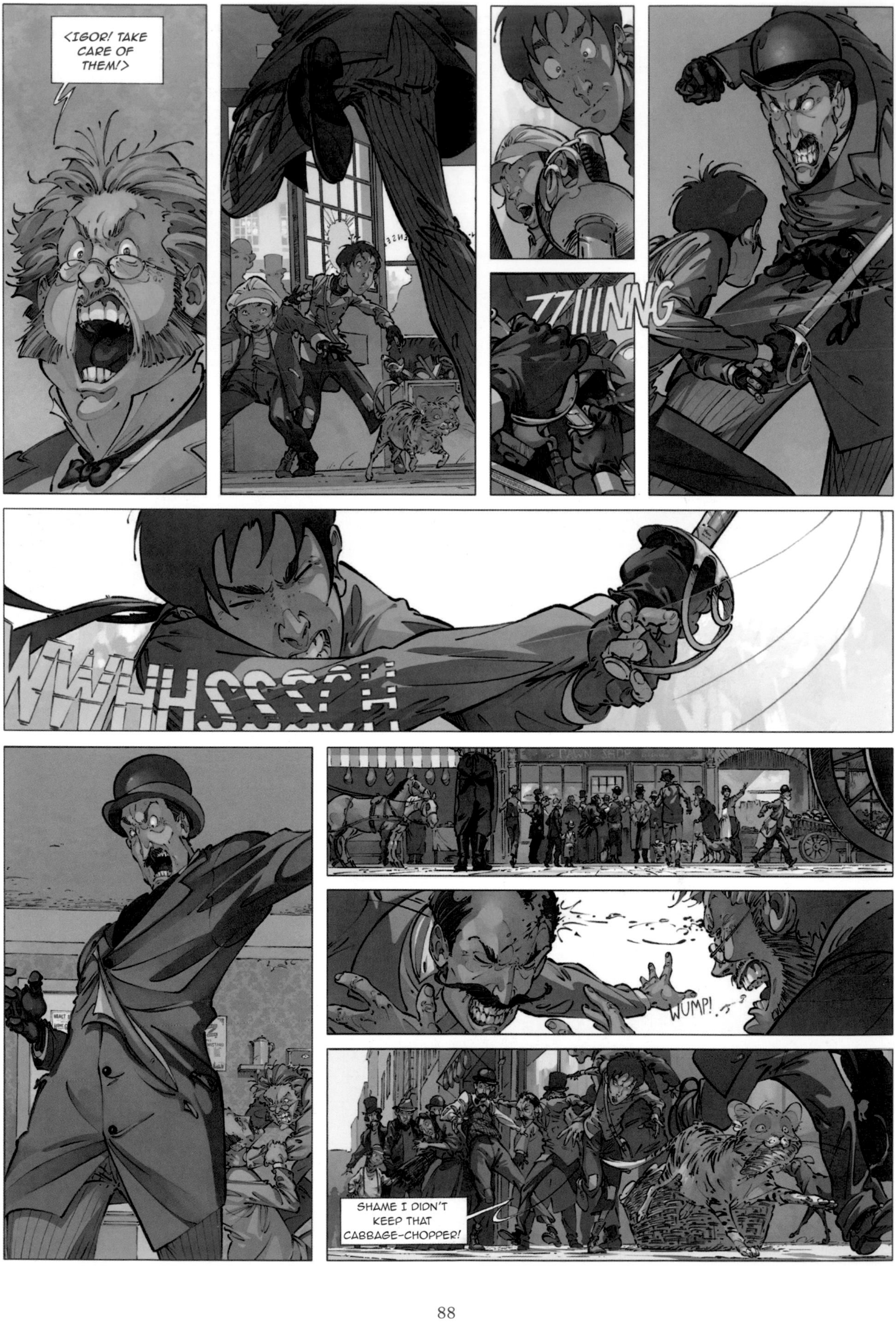
<IGOR! TAKE CARE OF THEM!>
ZZIIINNG
PAWN SHOP
WUMP!
SHAME I DIDN'T KEEP THAT CABBAGE-CHOPPER!

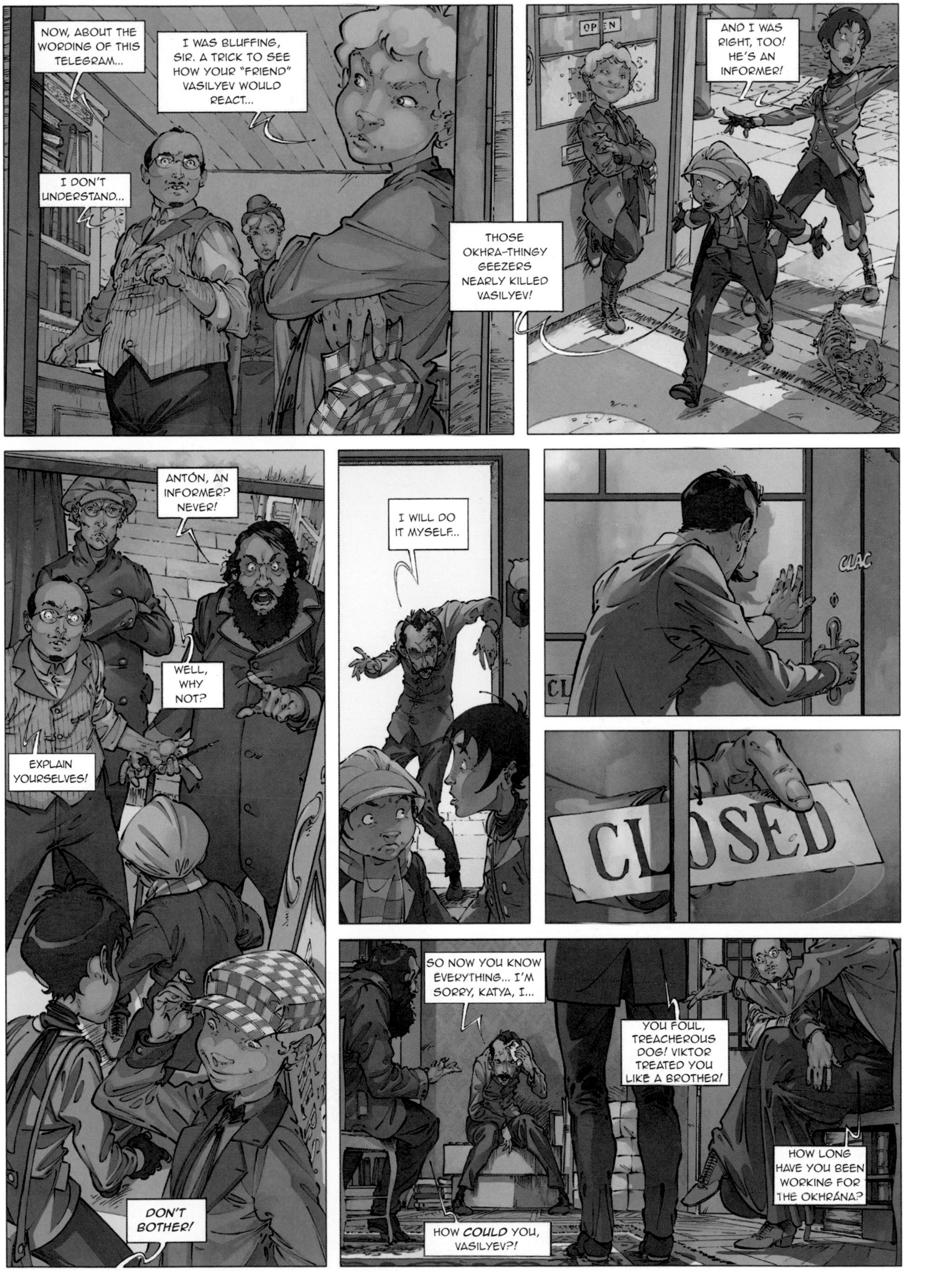
NOW, ABOUT THE WORDING OF THIS TELEGRAM...
I WAS BLUFFING, SIR. A TRICK TO SEE HOW YOUR "FRIEND" VASILYEV WOULD REACT...
I DON'T UNDERSTAND...
OPEN
AND I WAS RIGHT, TOO! HE'S AN INFORMER!
THOSE OKHRA-THINGY GEEZERS NEARLY KILLED VASILYEV!
ANTÓN, AN INFORMER? NEVER!
WELL, WHY NOT?
EXPLAIN YOURSELVES!
DON'T BOTHER!
I WILL DO IT MYSELF...
CLAC
CLOSED
SO NOW YOU KNOW EVERYTHING... I'M SORRY, KATYA, I...
YOU FOUL, TREACHEROUS DOG! VIKTOR TREATED YOU LIKE A BROTHER!
HOW LONG HAVE YOU BEEN WORKING FOR THE OKHRÁNA?
HOW COULD YOU, VASILYEV?!

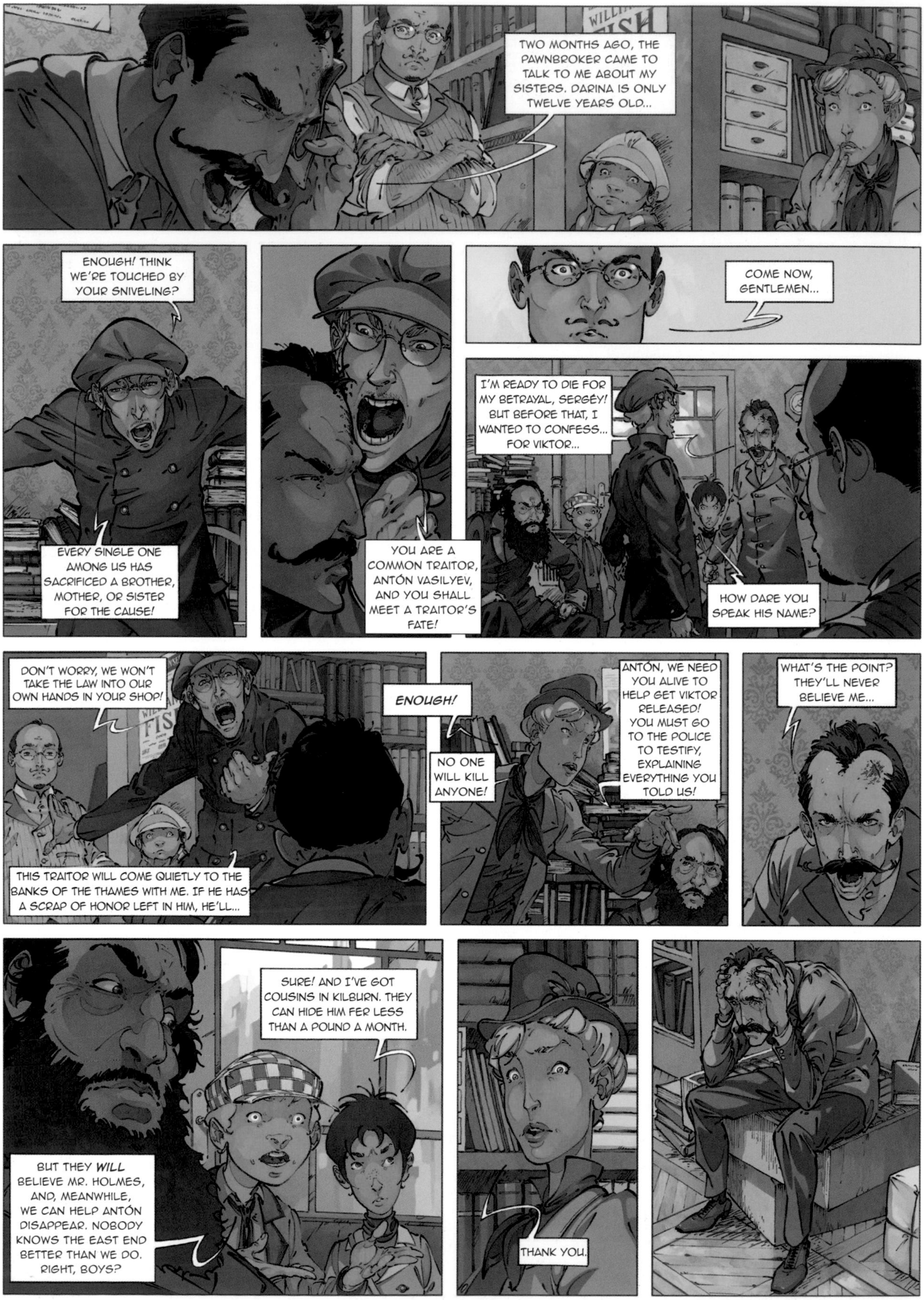
TWO MONTHS AGO, THE PAWNBROKER CAME TO TALK TO ME ABOUT MY SISTERS. DARINA IS ONLY TWELVE YEARS OLD...
ENOUGH! THINK WE'RE TOUCHED BY YOUR SNIVELING?
EVERY SINGLE ONE AMONG US HAS SACRIFICED A BROTHER, MOTHER, OR SISTER FOR THE CAUSE!
YOU ARE A COMMON TRAITOR, ANTÓN VASILYEV, AND YOU SHALL MEET A TRAITOR'S FATE!
COME NOW, GENTLEMEN...
I'M READY TO DIE FOR MY BETRAYAL, SERGÉY! BUT BEFORE THAT, I WANTED TO CONFESS... FOR VIKTOR...
HOW DARE YOU SPEAK HIS NAME?
DON'T WORRY, WE WON'T TAKE THE LAW INTO OUR OWN HANDS IN YOUR SHOP!
THIS TRAITOR WILL COME QUIETLY TO THE BANKS OF THE THAMES WITH ME. IF HE HAS A SCRAP OF HONOR LEFT IN HIM, HE'LL...
ENOUGH!
NO ONE WILL KILL ANYONE!
ANTÓN, WE NEED YOU ALIVE TO HELP GET VIKTOR RELEASED! YOU MUST GO TO THE POLICE TO TESTIFY, EXPLAINING EVERYTHING YOU TOLD US!
WHAT'S THE POINT? THEY'LL NEVER BELIEVE ME...
BUT THEY WILL BELIEVE MR. HOLMES, AND, MEANWHILE, WE CAN HELP ANTÓN DISAPPEAR. NOBODY KNOWS THE EAST END BETTER THAN WE DO. RIGHT, BOYS?
SURE! AND I'VE GOT COUSINS IN KILBURN. THEY CAN HIDE HIM FER LESS THAN A POUND A MONTH.
THANK YOU.

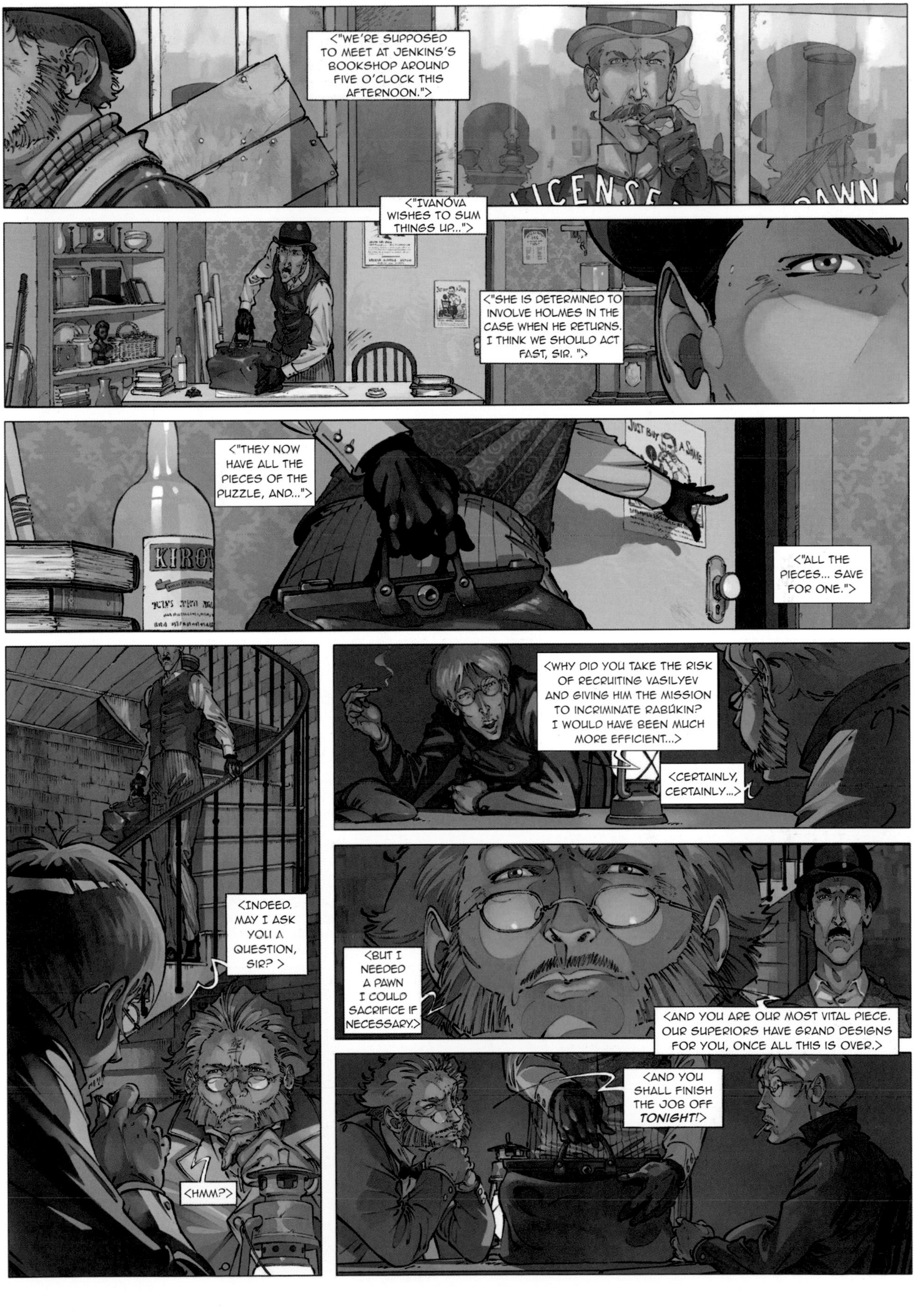
<"WE'RE SUPPOSED TO MEET AT JENKINS'S BOOKSHOP AROUND FIVE O'CLOCK THIS AFTERNOON.">
<"IVANÓVA WISHES TO SUM THINGS UP...">
<"SHE IS DETERMINED TO INVOLVE HOLMES IN THE CASE WHEN HE RETURNS. I THINK WE SHOULD ACT FAST, SIR. ">
<"THEY NOW HAVE ALL THE PIECES OF THE PUZZLE, AND...">
<"ALL THE PIECES... SAVE FOR ONE.">
<INDEED. MAY I ASK YOU A QUESTION, SIR? >
<HMM?>
<WHY DID YOU TAKE THE RISK OF RECRUITING VASILYEV AND GIVING HIM THE MISSION TO INCRIMINATE RABÚKIN? I WOULD HAVE BEEN MUCH MORE EFFICIENT...>
<CERTAINLY, CERTAINLY...>
<BUT I NEEDED A PAWN I COULD SACRIFICE IF NECESSARY.>
<AND YOU ARE OUR MOST VITAL PIECE. OUR SUPERIORS HAVE GRAND DESIGNS FOR YOU, ONCE ALL THIS IS OVER.>
<AND YOU SHALL FINISH THE JOB OFF *TONIGHT!*>

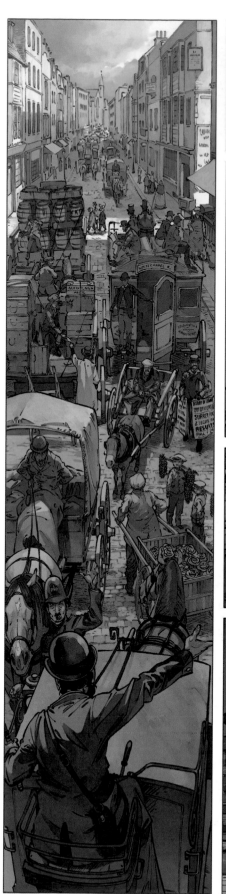

WELL? DID YOUR COUSINS AGREE TO HIDE ANTÓN?

IT'S NEVER A PROBLEM IF YA PAY 'EM IN ADVANCE...

HMM... BUT IS HE SAFE?

DON'T YA WORRY, GRANDDAD...

THERE ARE FELLAS IN KILBURN THAT THE ENGLISH COPPERS HAVE BEEN AFTER FER YEARS... SO *YOUR* COPPERS AIN'T LIKELY TO FLUSH HIM OUT!

I DON'T SEE WHY WE'RE TAKING SUCH CARE OF A TRAITOR...

MUST WE BRING THAT UP AGAIN, SERGÉY? ANTÓN SWORE TO TESTIFY AS SOON AS HOLMES TAKES UP OUR CASE.

SO, A TRAITOR'S WORD SUFFICES FOR YOU?

A *FRIEND'S* WORD.

WHAT'S THE SITUATION WITH THIS SHERLOCK HOLMES?

DO WE HAVE ANY IDEA WHERE HE IS AT THE MOMENT? HOW LONG MUST WE WAIT FOR HIM TO RETURN?

"AND HOW CAN WE BE SURE THAT HE'LL AGREE TO HELP US?"

EXACTLY. I WOULD LIKE TO SUM THINGS UP WITH YOU...

MIAOW!

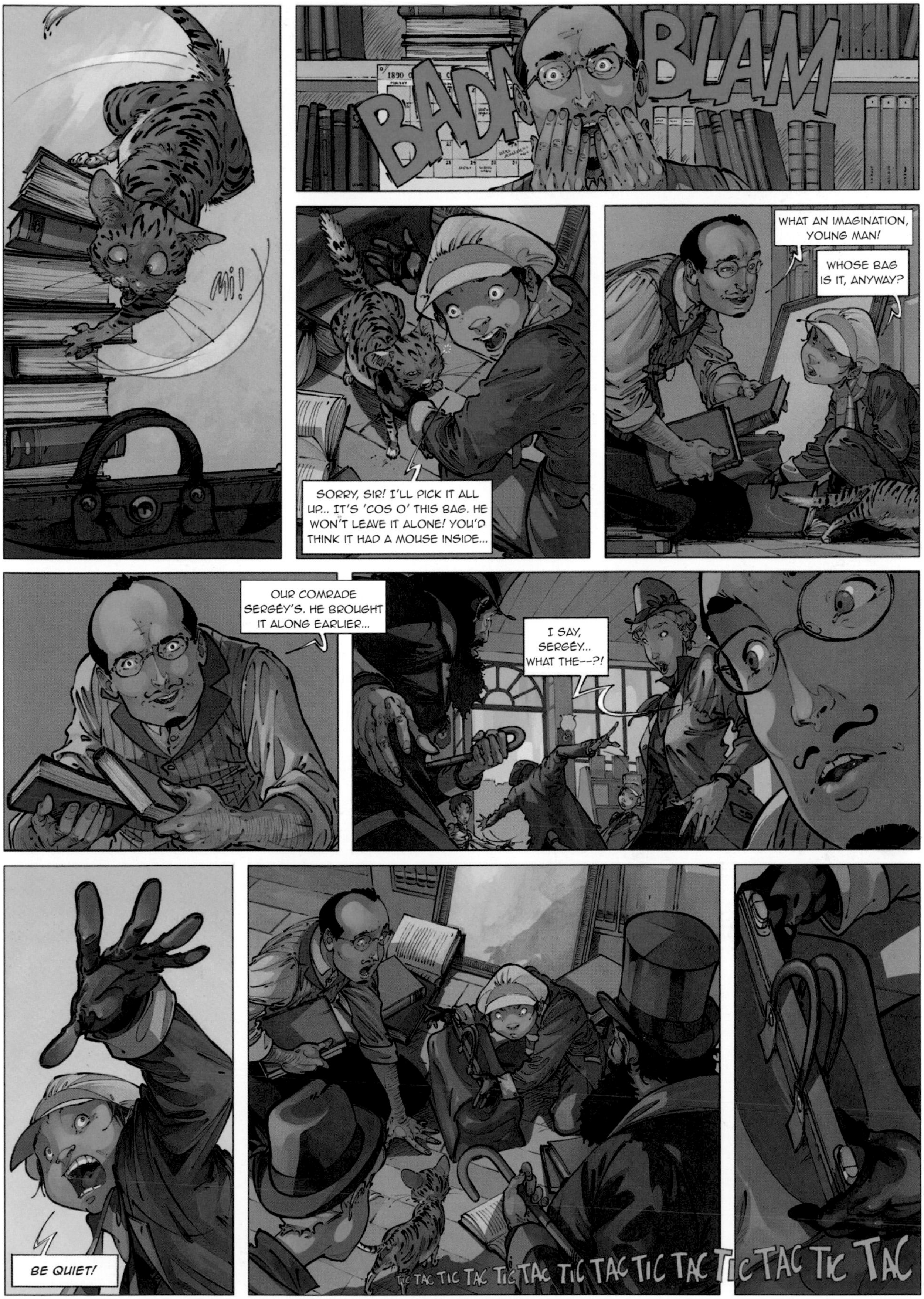
Mi!
BADA
BLAM
SORRY, SIR! I'LL PICK IT ALL UP... IT'S 'COS O' THIS BAG. HE WON'T LEAVE IT ALONE! YOU'D THINK IT HAD A MOUSE INSIDE...
WHAT AN IMAGINATION, YOUNG MAN!
WHOSE BAG IS IT, ANYWAY?
OUR COMRADE SERGEY'S. HE BROUGHT IT ALONG EARLIER...
I SAY, SERGEY... WHAT THE--?!
BE QUIET!
TIC TAC TIC TAC TIC TAC TIC TAC TIC TAC TIC TAC TIC TAC

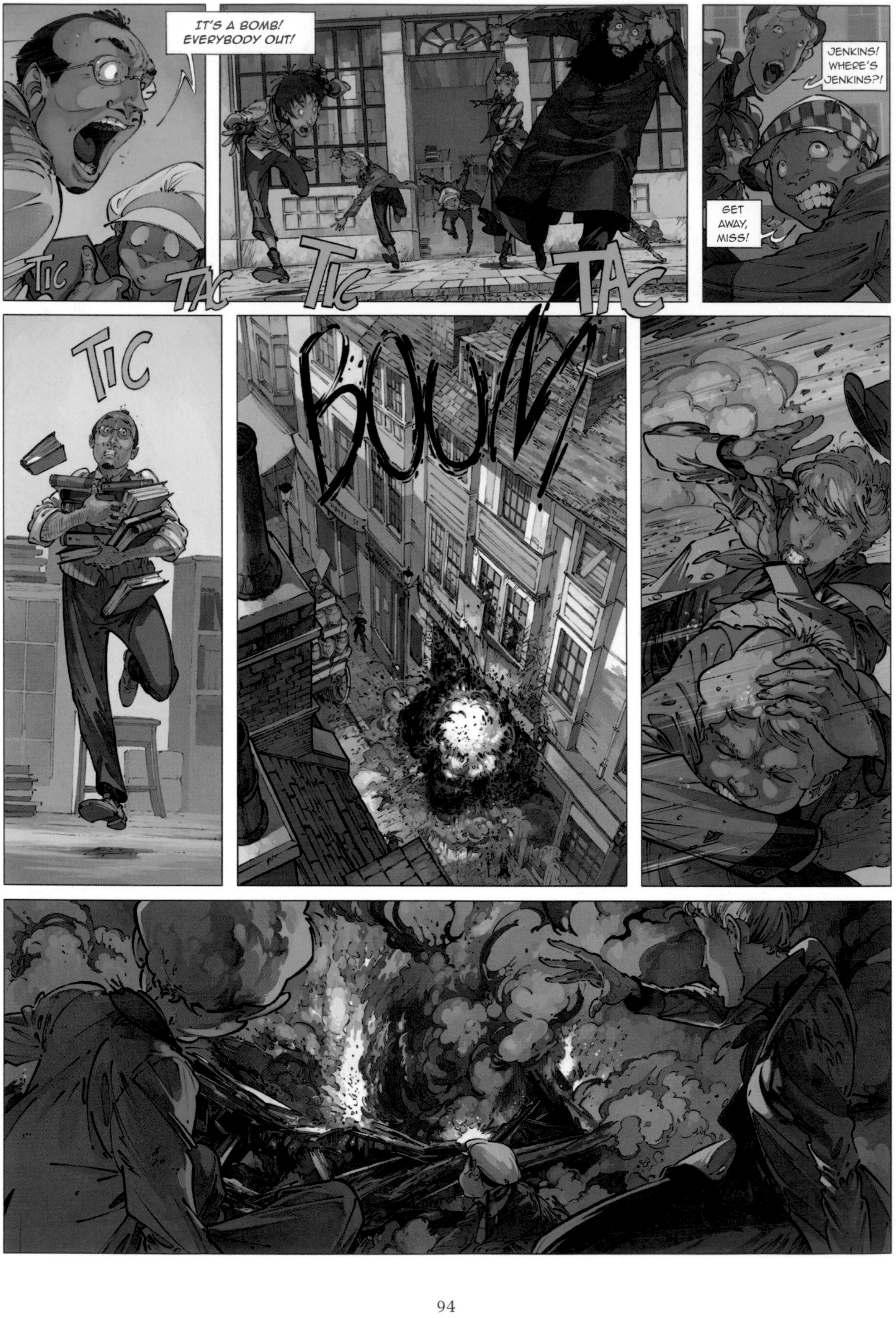
IT'S A BOMB! EVERYBODY OUT!
TIC
TAC
TIC
TAC
JENKINS! WHERE'S JENKINS?!
GET AWAY, MISS!
TIC
BOOM!

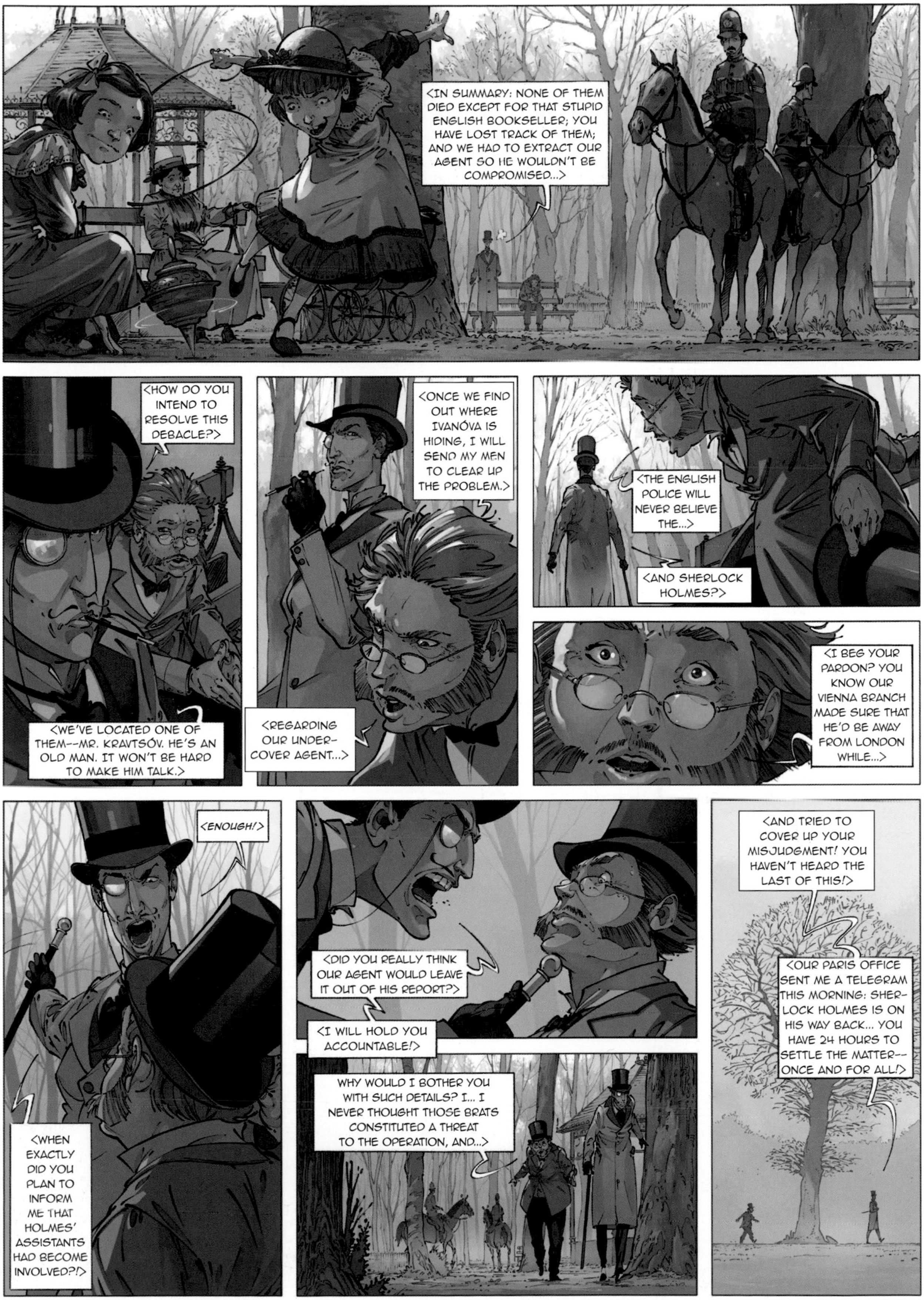
<IN SUMMARY: NONE OF THEM DIED EXCEPT FOR THAT STUPID ENGLISH BOOKSELLER; YOU HAVE LOST TRACK OF THEM; AND WE HAD TO EXTRACT OUR AGENT SO HE WOULDN'T BE COMPROMISED...>
<HOW DO YOU INTEND TO RESOLVE THIS DEBACLE?>
<WE'VE LOCATED ONE OF THEM--MR. KRAVTSÓV. HE'S AN OLD MAN. IT WON'T BE HARD TO MAKE HIM TALK.>
<ONCE WE FIND OUT WHERE IVANÓVA IS HIDING, I WILL SEND MY MEN TO CLEAR UP THE PROBLEM.>
<REGARDING OUR UNDER-COVER AGENT...>
<THE ENGLISH POLICE WILL NEVER BELIEVE THE...>
<AND SHERLOCK HOLMES?>
<I BEG YOUR PARDON? YOU KNOW OUR VIENNA BRANCH MADE SURE THAT HE'D BE AWAY FROM LONDON WHILE...>
<ENOUGH!>
<WHEN EXACTLY DID YOU PLAN TO INFORM ME THAT HOLMES' ASSISTANTS HAD BECOME INVOLVED?!>
<DID YOU REALLY THINK OUR AGENT WOULD LEAVE IT OUT OF HIS REPORT?>
<I WILL HOLD YOU ACCOUNTABLE!>
WHY WOULD I BOTHER YOU WITH SUCH DETAILS? I... I NEVER THOUGHT THOSE BRATS CONSTITUTED A THREAT TO THE OPERATION, AND...>
<AND TRIED TO COVER UP YOUR MISJUDGMENT! YOU HAVEN'T HEARD THE LAST OF THIS!>
<OUR PARIS OFFICE SENT ME A TELEGRAM THIS MORNING: SHER-LOCK HOLMES IS ON HIS WAY BACK... YOU HAVE 24 HOURS TO SETTLE THE MATTER--ONCE AND FOR ALL!>

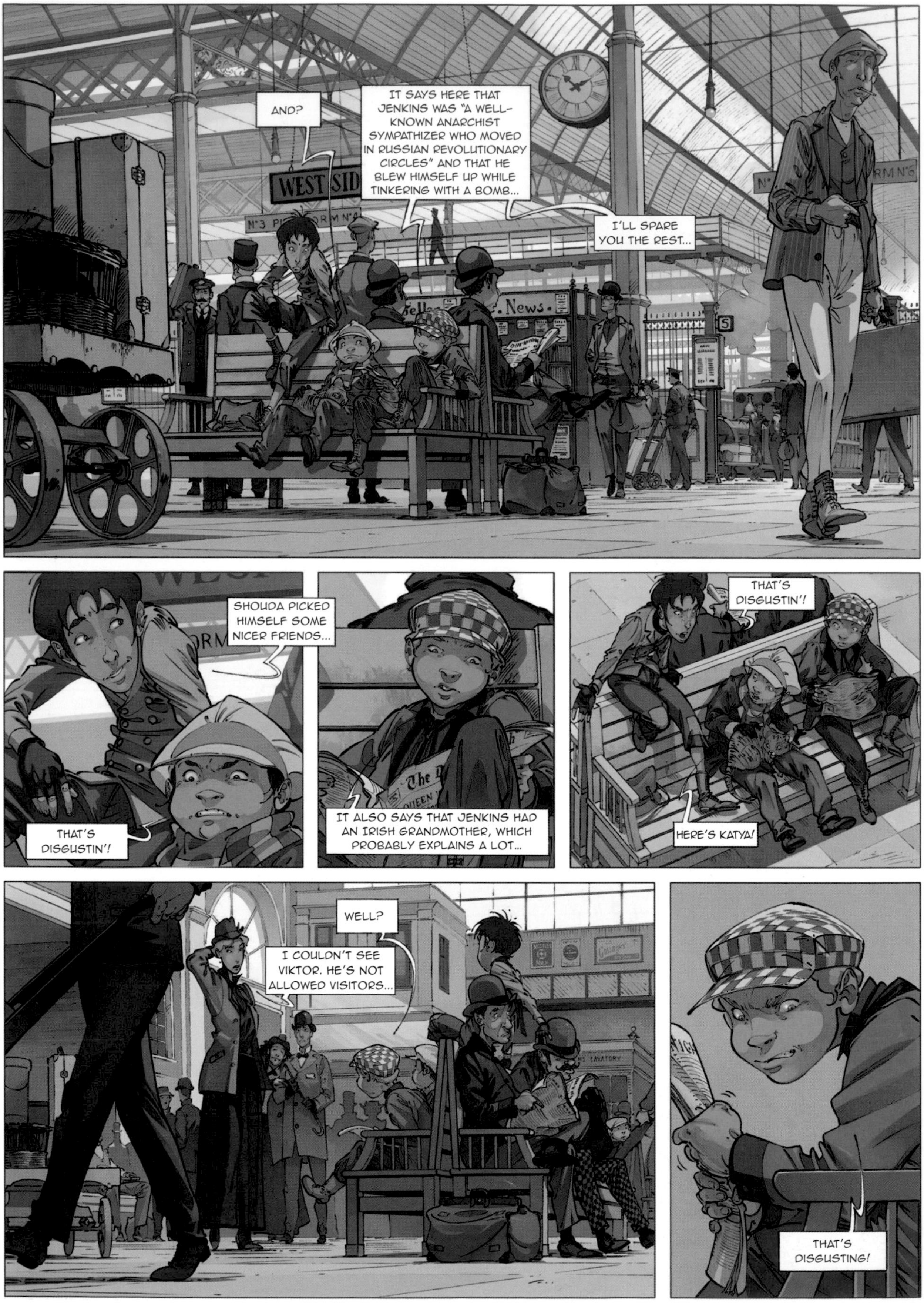

AND?
IT SAYS HERE THAT JENKINS WAS "A WELL-KNOWN ANARCHIST SYMPATHIZER WHO MOVED IN RUSSIAN REVOLUTIONARY CIRCLES" AND THAT HE BLEW HIMSELF UP WHILE TINKERING WITH A BOMB...
I'LL SPARE YOU THE REST...
SHOUDA PICKED HIMSELF SOME NICER FRIENDS...
THAT'S DISGUSTIN'!
IT ALSO SAYS THAT JENKINS HAD AN IRISH GRANDMOTHER, WHICH PROBABLY EXPLAINS A LOT...
THAT'S DISGUSTIN'!
HERE'S KATYA!
WELL?
I COULDN'T SEE VIKTOR. HE'S NOT ALLOWED VISITORS...
THAT'S DISGUSTING!

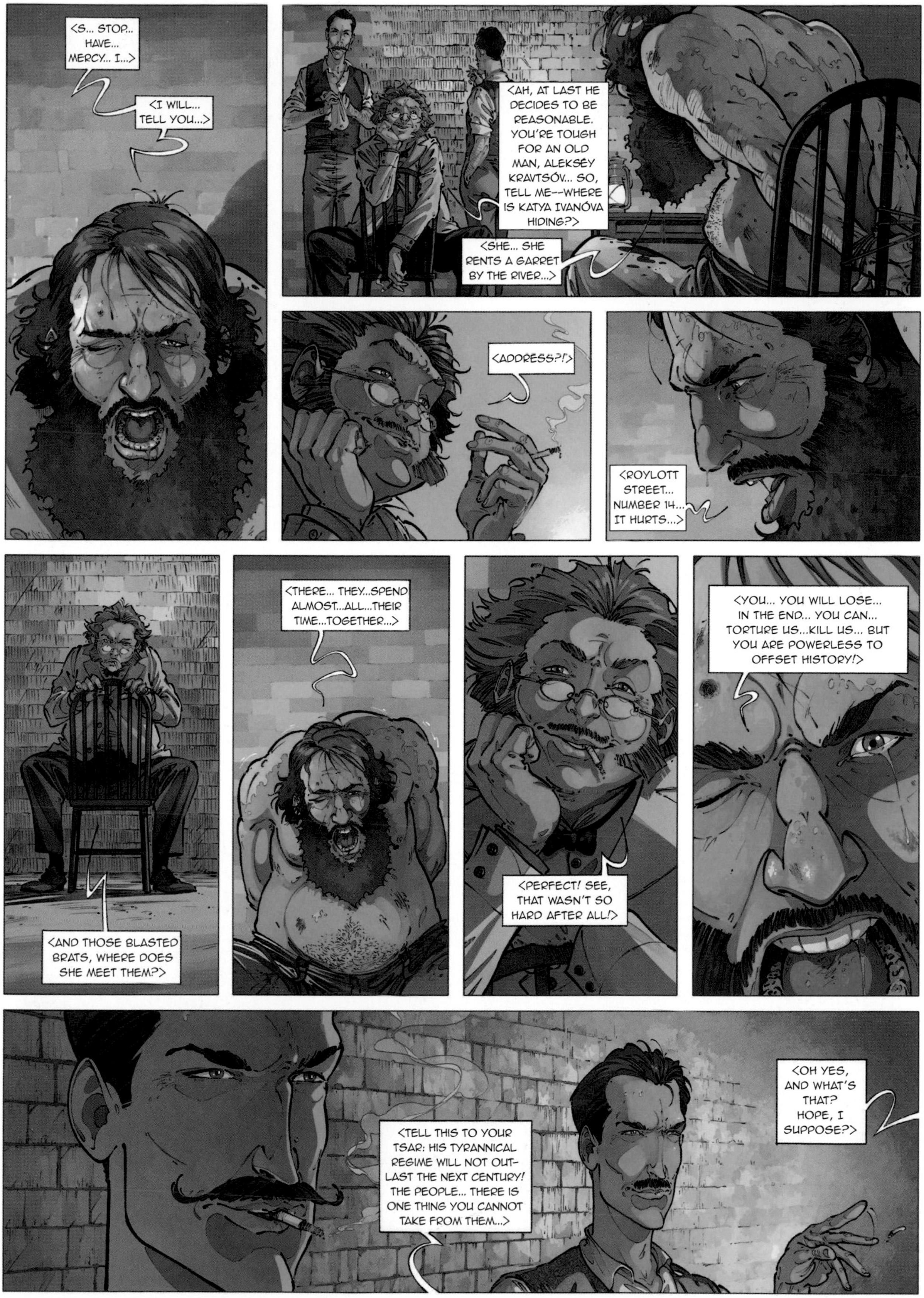

<S... STOP.. HAVE... MERCY... I...>
<I WILL... TELL YOU...>
<AH, AT LAST HE DECIDES TO BE REASONABLE. YOU'RE TOUGH FOR AN OLD MAN, ALEKSEY KRAVTSÓV... SO, TELL ME--WHERE IS KATYA IVANÓVA HIDING?>
<SHE... SHE RENTS A GARRET BY THE RIVER...>
<ADDRESS?!>
<ROYLOTT STREET... NUMBER 14... IT HURTS...>
<AND THOSE BLASTED BRATS, WHERE DOES SHE MEET THEM?>
<THERE... THEY...SPEND ALMOST...ALL...THEIR TIME...TOGETHER...>
<PERFECT! SEE, THAT WASN'T SO HARD AFTER ALL!>
<YOU... YOU WILL LOSE... IN THE END... YOU CAN... TORTURE US...KILL US... BUT YOU ARE POWERLESS TO OFFSET HISTORY!>
<TELL THIS TO YOUR TSAR: HIS TYRANNICAL REGIME WILL NOT OUT-LAST THE NEXT CENTURY! THE PEOPLE... THERE IS ONE THING YOU CANNOT TAKE FROM THEM...>
<OH YES, AND WHAT'S THAT? HOPE, I SUPPOSE?>

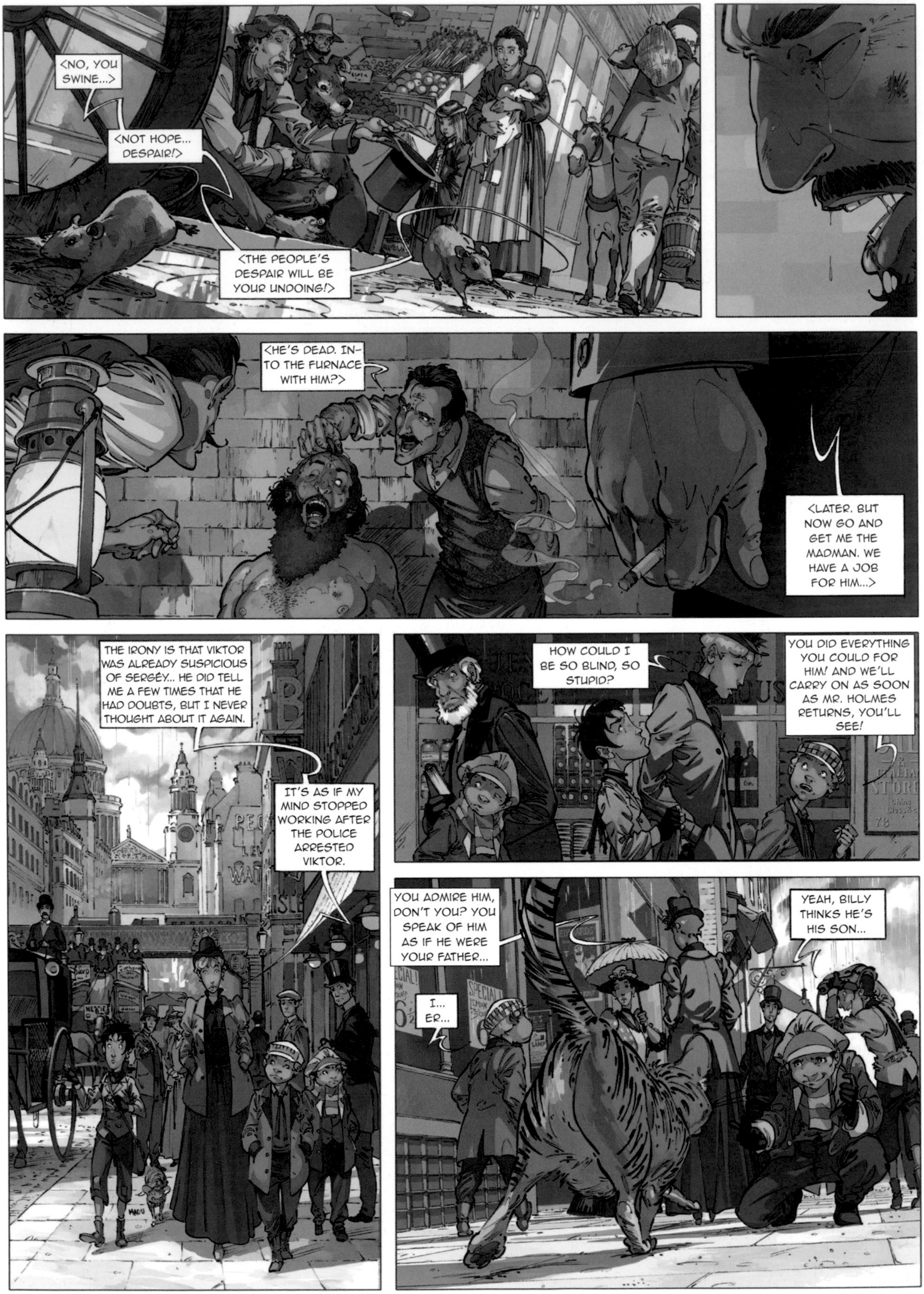

<NO, YOU SWINE...>
<NOT HOPE... DESPAIR!>
<THE PEOPLE'S DESPAIR WILL BE YOUR UNDOING!>
<HE'S DEAD. INTO THE FURNACE WITH HIM?>
<LATER. BUT NOW GO AND GET ME THE MADMAN. WE HAVE A JOB FOR HIM...>
THE IRONY IS THAT VIKTOR WAS ALREADY SUSPICIOUS OF SERGÉY... HE DID TELL ME A FEW TIMES THAT HE HAD DOUBTS, BUT I NEVER THOUGHT ABOUT IT AGAIN.
IT'S AS IF MY MIND STOPPED WORKING AFTER THE POLICE ARRESTED VIKTOR.
HOW COULD I BE SO BLIND, SO STUPID?
YOU DID EVERYTHING YOU COULD FOR HIM! AND WE'LL CARRY ON AS SOON AS MR. HOLMES RETURNS, YOU'LL SEE!
YOU ADMIRE HIM, DON'T YOU? YOU SPEAK OF HIM AS IF HE WERE YOUR FATHER...
I... ER...
YEAH, BILLY THINKS HE'S HIS SON...

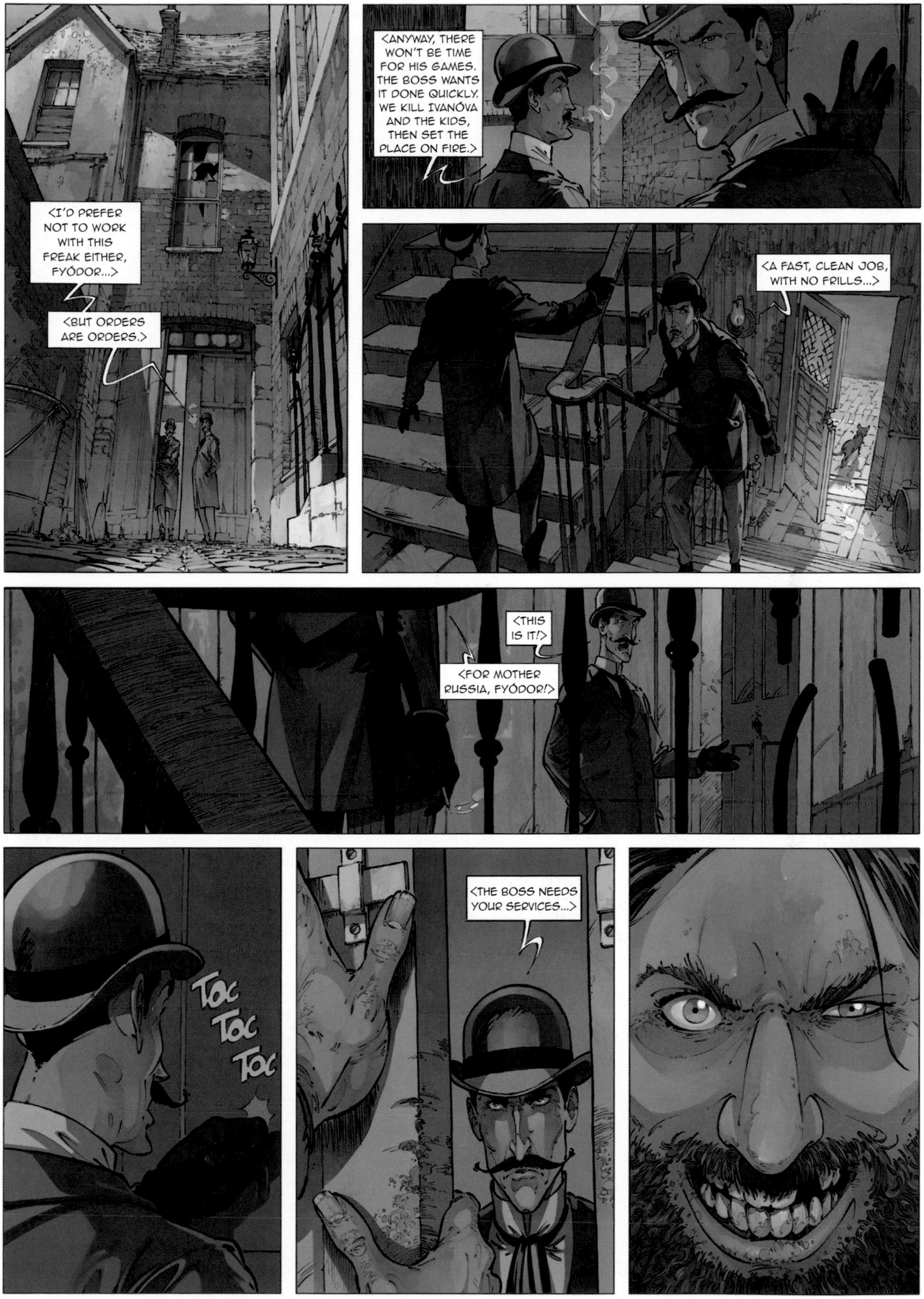

<I'D PREFER NOT TO WORK WITH THIS FREAK EITHER, FYÓDOR...>
<BUT ORDERS ARE ORDERS.>
<ANYWAY, THERE WON'T BE TIME FOR HIS GAMES. THE BOSS WANTS IT DONE QUICKLY. WE KILL IVANÓVA AND THE KIDS, THEN SET THE PLACE ON FIRE.>
<A FAST, CLEAN JOB, WITH NO FRILLS...>
<THIS IS IT!>
<FOR MOTHER RUSSIA, FYÓDOR!>
TOC
TOC
TOC
<THE BOSS NEEDS YOUR SERVICES...>

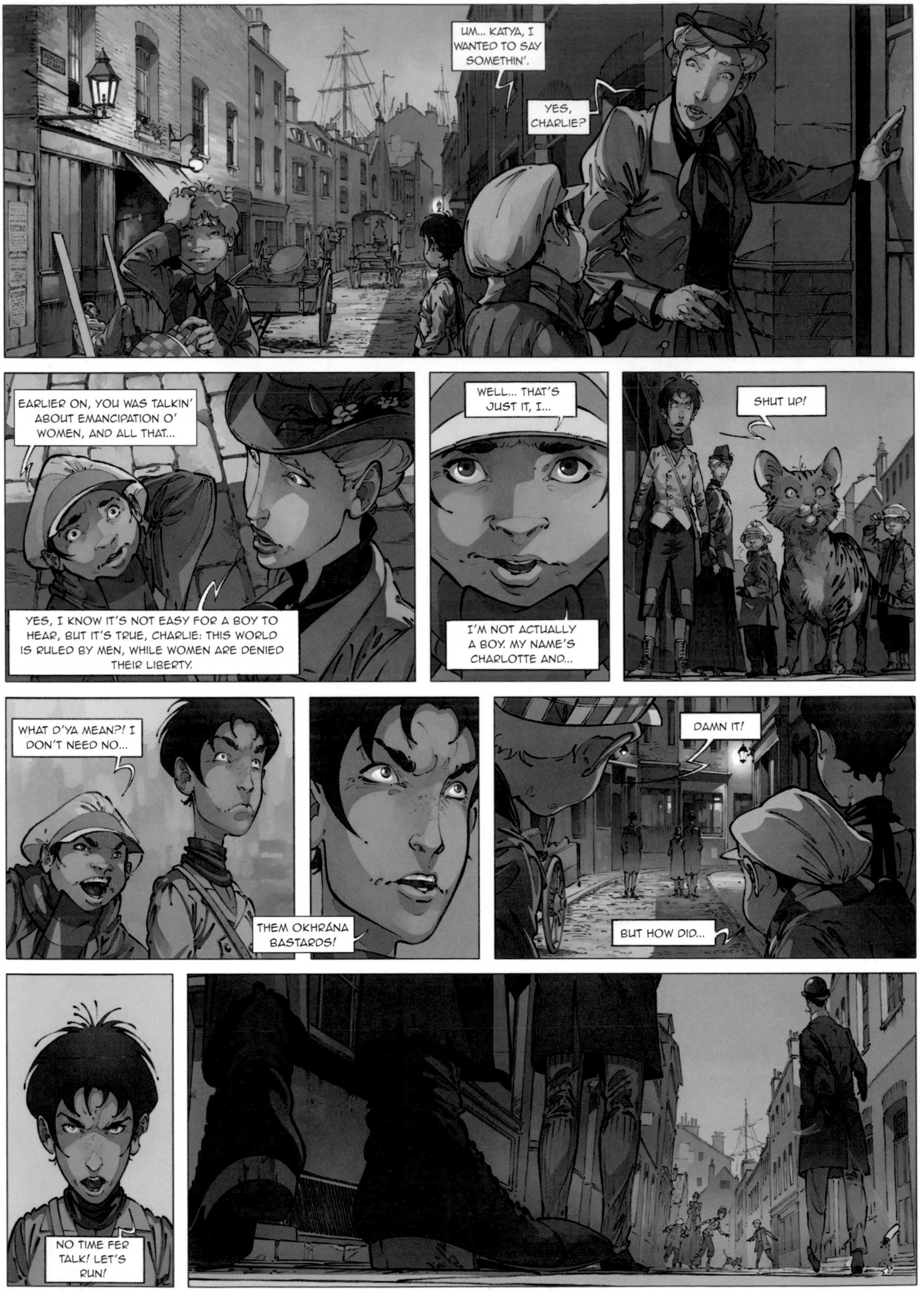
UM... KATYA, I WANTED TO SAY SOMETHIN'.
YES, CHARLIE?
EARLIER ON, YOU WAS TALKIN' ABOUT EMANCIPATION O' WOMEN, AND ALL THAT...
YES, I KNOW IT'S NOT EASY FOR A BOY TO HEAR, BUT IT'S TRUE, CHARLIE: THIS WORLD IS RULED BY MEN, WHILE WOMEN ARE DENIED THEIR LIBERTY.
WELL... THAT'S JUST IT, I...
I'M NOT ACTUALLY A BOY. MY NAME'S CHARLOTTE AND...
SHUT UP!
WHAT D'YA MEAN?! I DON'T NEED NO...
THEM OKHRÁNA BASTARDS!
DAMN IT!
BUT HOW DID...
NO TIME FER TALK! LET'S RUN!

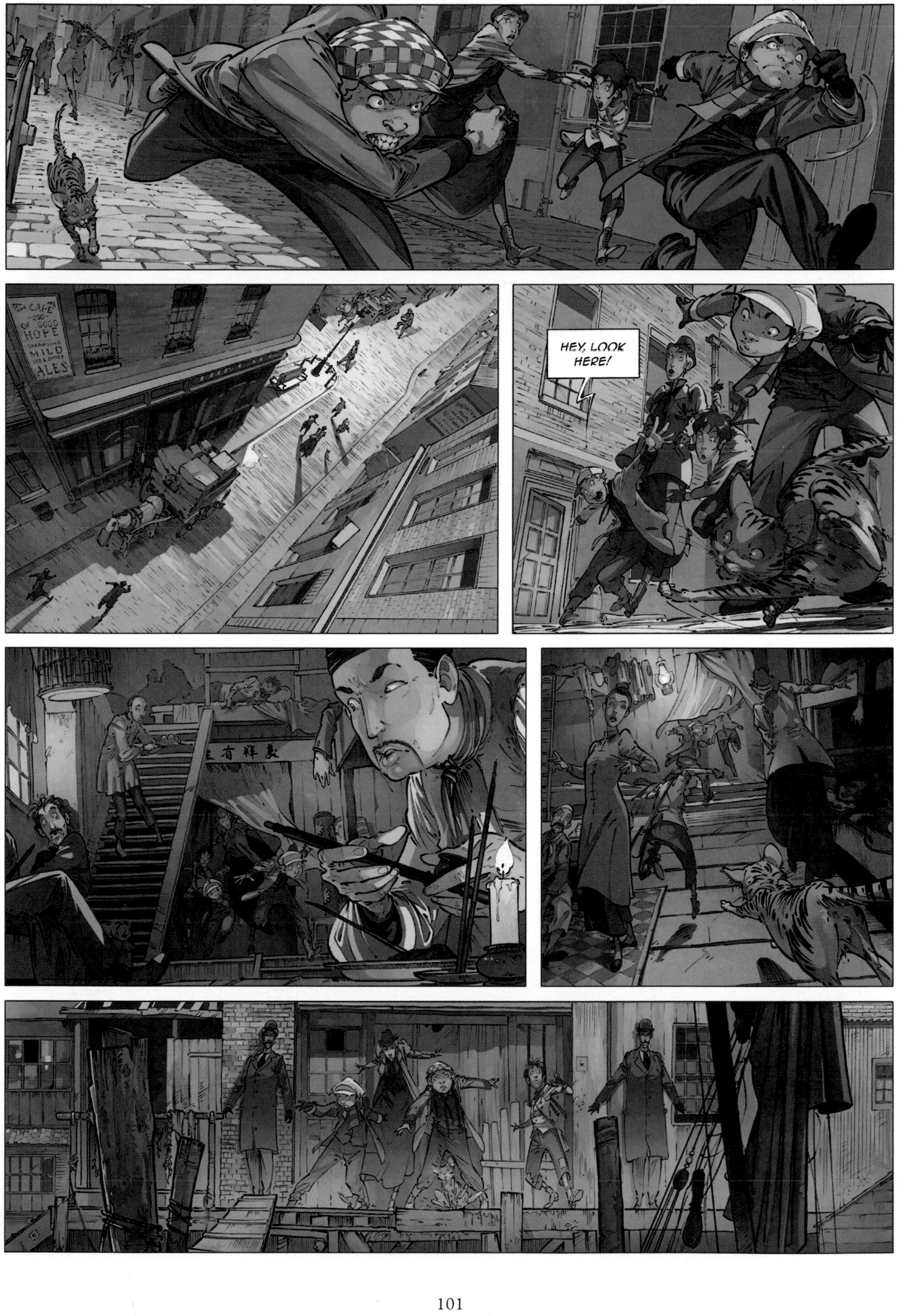
HEY, LOOK HERE!

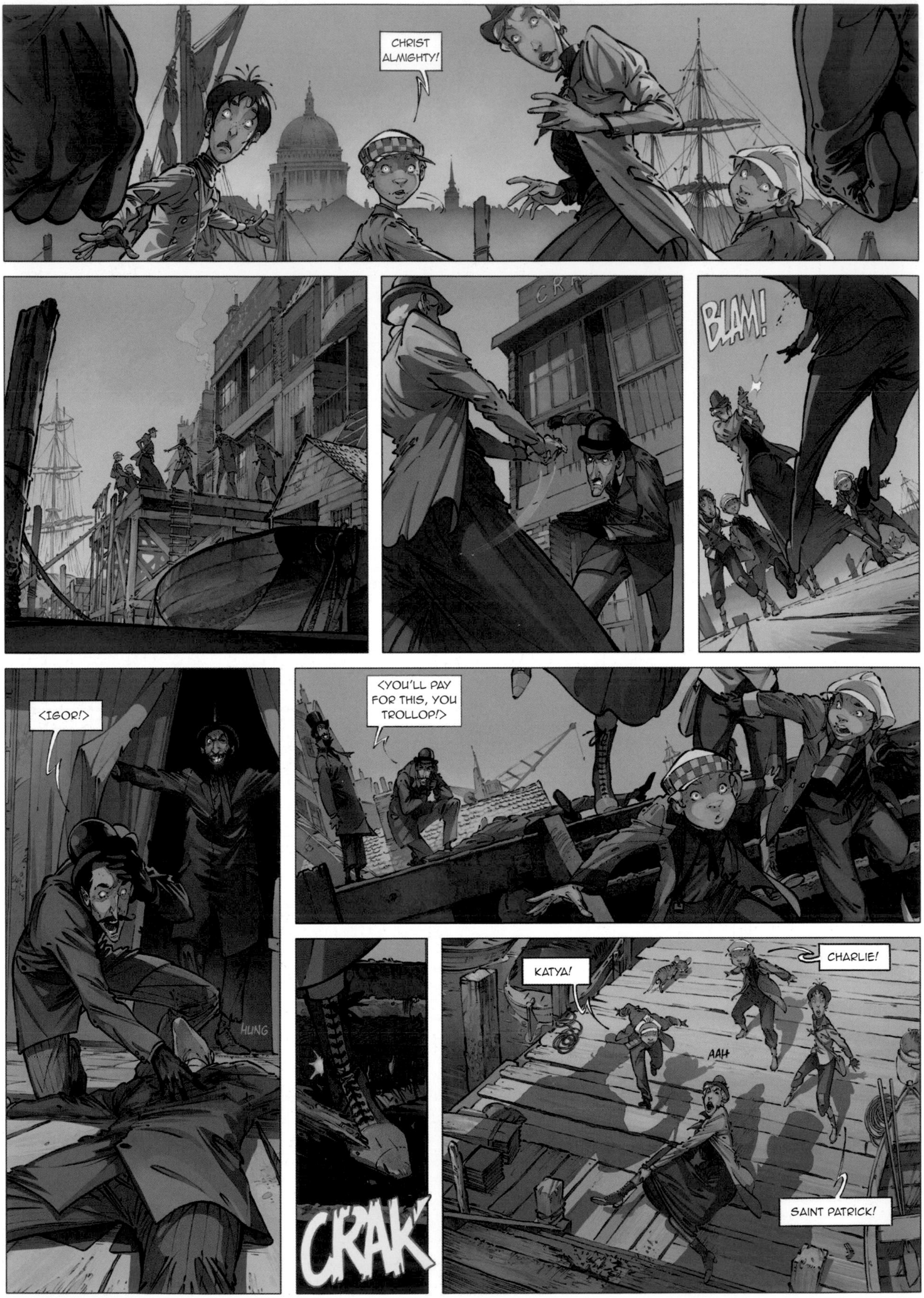
CHRIST ALMIGHTY!
BLAM!
<IGOR!>
HUNG
<YOU'LL PAY FOR THIS, YOU TROLLOP!>
CRAK
KATYA!
CHARLIE!
AAH
SAINT PATRICK!

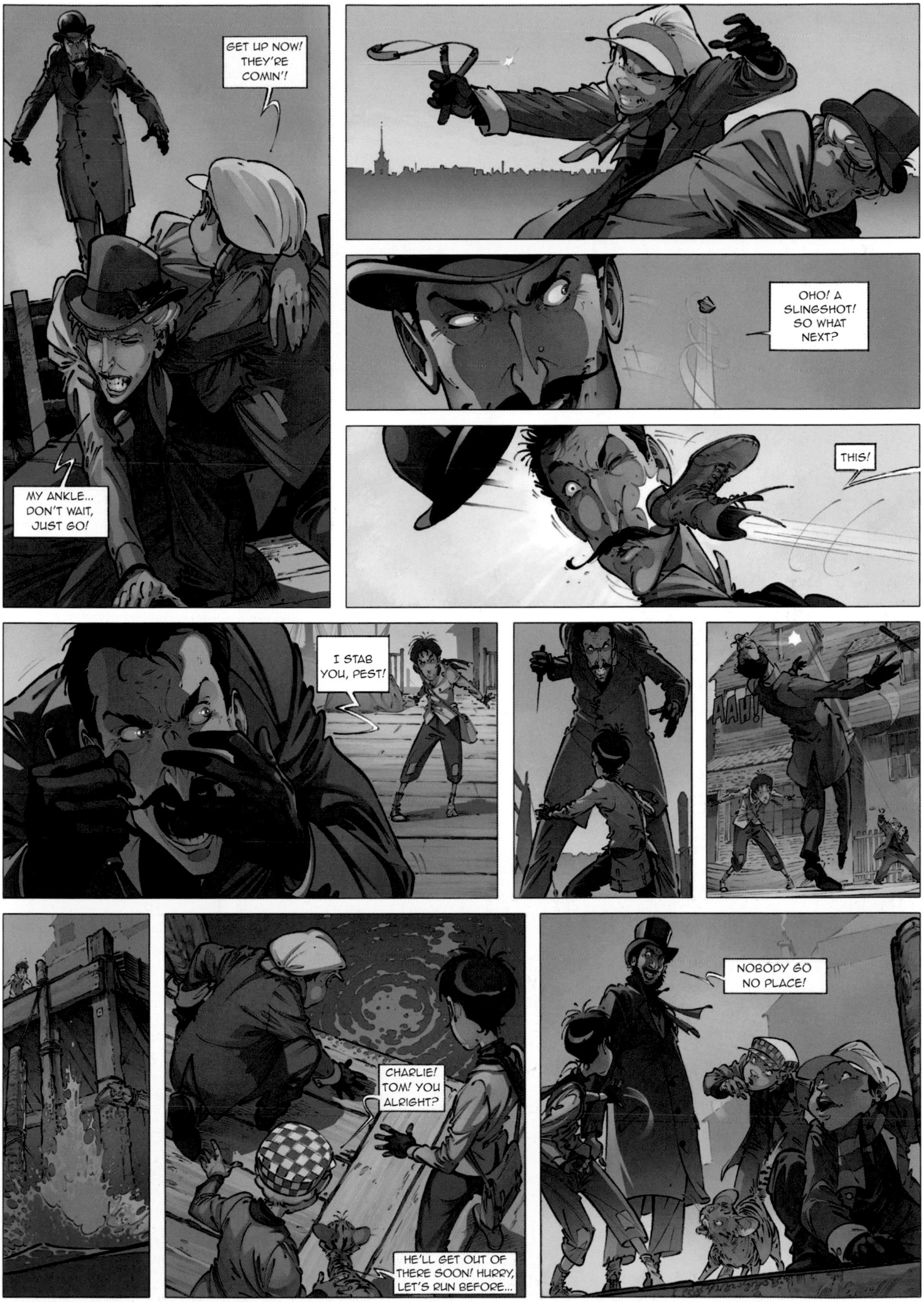
GET UP NOW! THEY'RE COMIN'!
MY ANKLE... DON'T WAIT, JUST GO!
OHO! A SLINGSHOT! SO WHAT NEXT?
THIS!
I STAB YOU, PEST!
AAH!
CHARLIE! TOM! YOU ALRIGHT?
HE'LL GET OUT OF THERE SOON! HURRY, LET'S RUN BEFORE...
NOBODY GO NO PLACE!

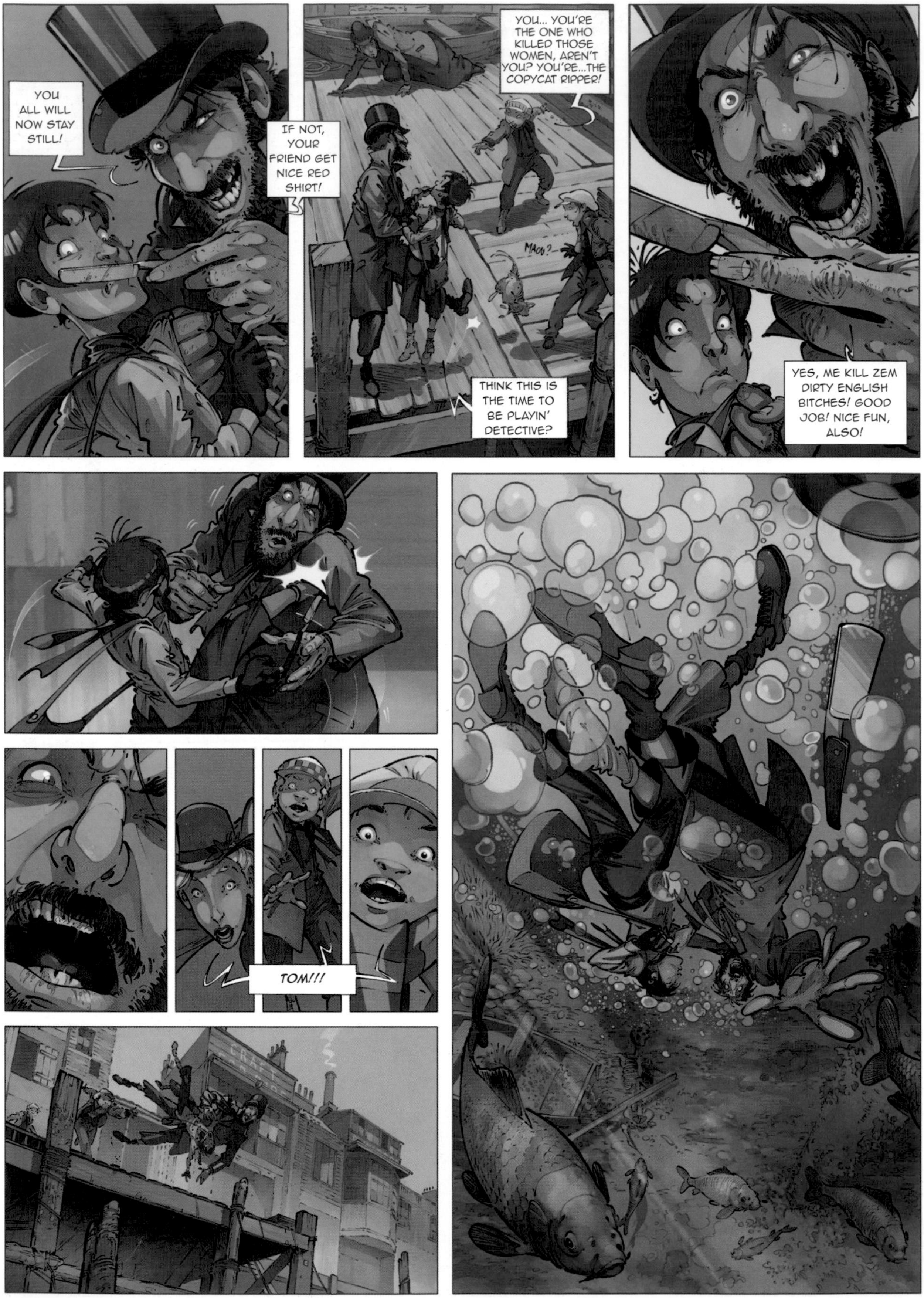
YOU ALL WILL NOW STAY STILL!
IF NOT, YOUR FRIEND GET NICE RED SHIRT!
YOU... YOU'RE THE ONE WHO KILLED THOSE WOMEN, AREN'T YOU? YOU'RE...THE COPYCAT RIPPER!
MAOU?
THINK THIS IS THE TIME TO BE PLAYIN' DETECTIVE?
YES, ME KILL ZEM DIRTY ENGLISH BITCHES! GOOD JOB! NICE FUN, ALSO!
TOM!!!

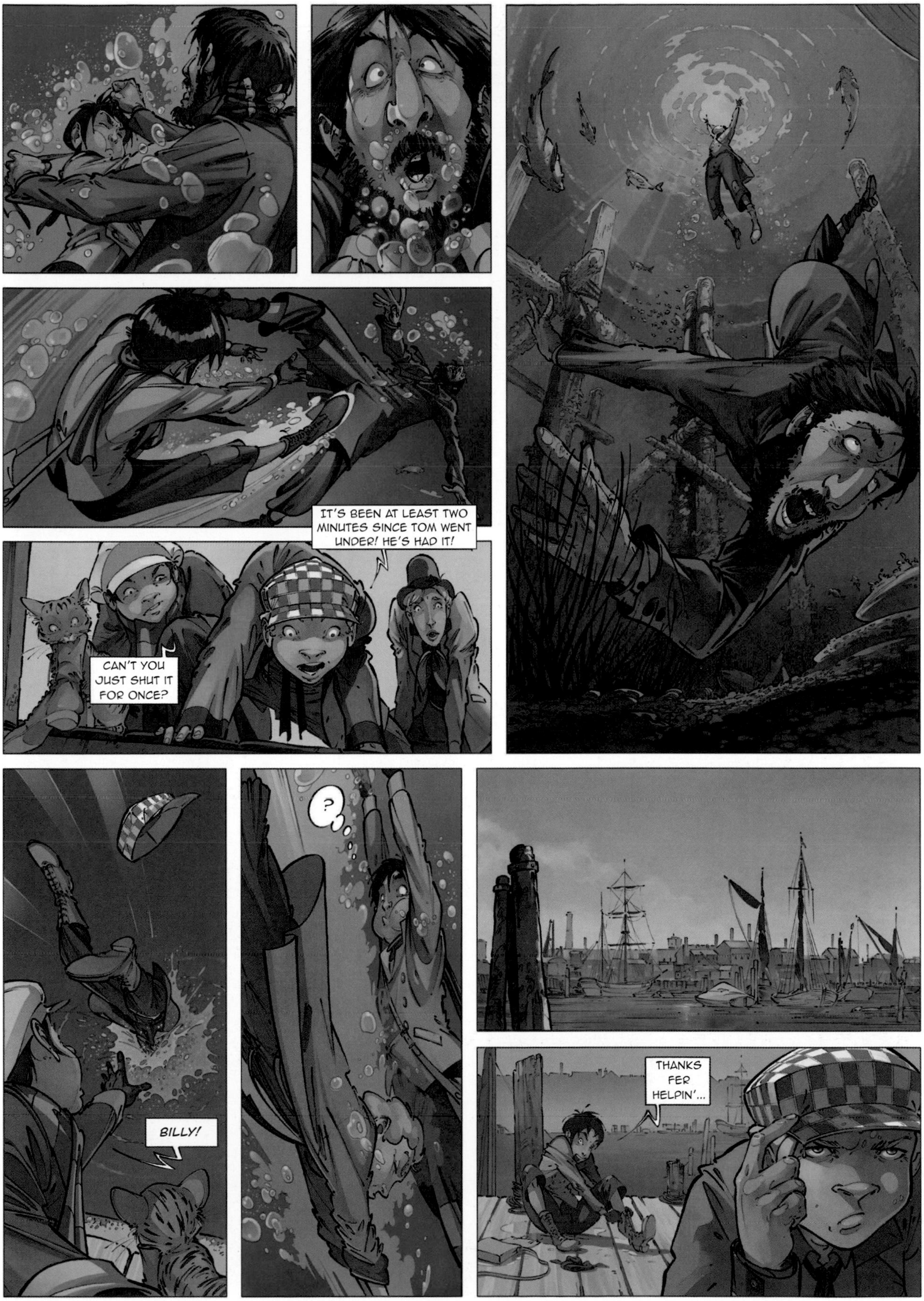
IT'S BEEN AT LEAST TWO MINUTES SINCE TOM WENT UNDER! HE'S HAD IT!
CAN'T YOU JUST SHUT IT FOR ONCE?
BILLY!
?
THANKS FER HELPIN'...

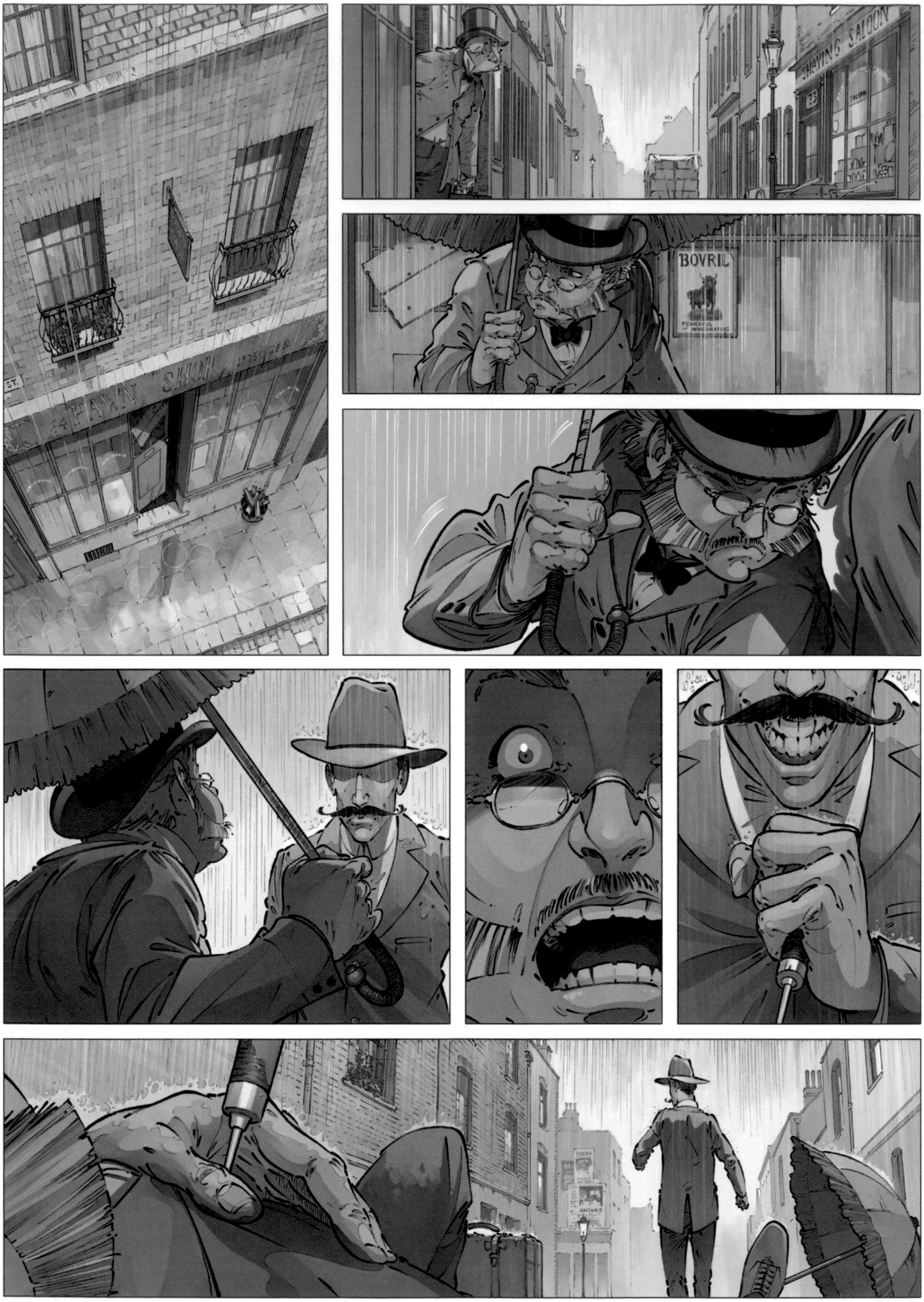
PAWN SHOP
SHAVING SALOON
BOVRIL
POWERFUL INVIGORATING
ANSWER

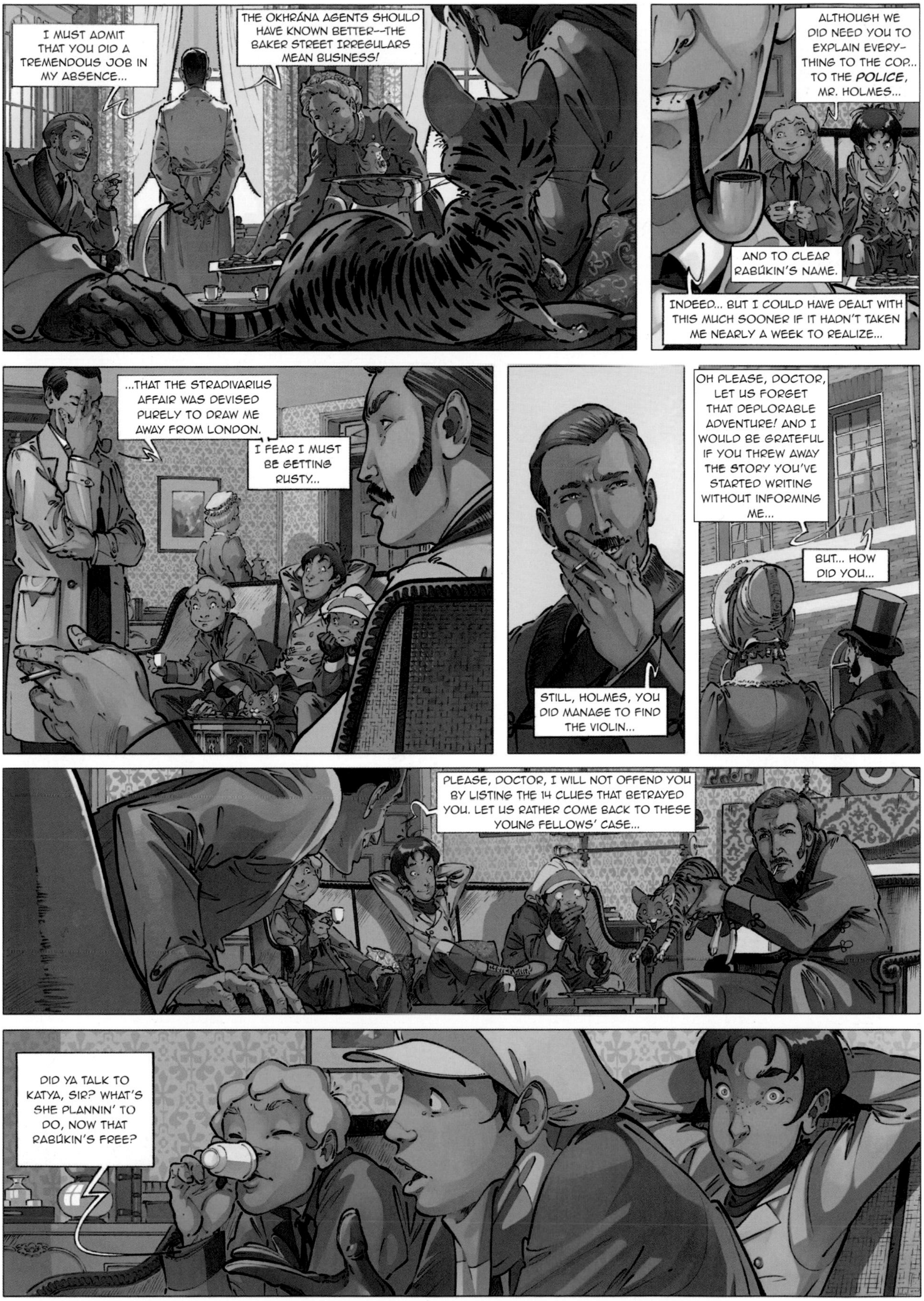
I MUST ADMIT THAT YOU DID A TREMENDOUS JOB IN MY ABSENCE...
THE OKHRÁNA AGENTS SHOULD HAVE KNOWN BETTER--THE BAKER STREET IRREGULARS MEAN BUSINESS!
ALTHOUGH WE DID NEED YOU TO EXPLAIN EVERY-THING TO THE COP... TO THE *POLICE*, MR. HOLMES...
AND TO CLEAR RABÚKIN'S NAME.
INDEED... BUT I COULD HAVE DEALT WITH THIS MUCH SOONER IF IT HADN'T TAKEN ME NEARLY A WEEK TO REALIZE...
...THAT THE STRADIVARIUS AFFAIR WAS DEVISED PURELY TO DRAW ME AWAY FROM LONDON.
I FEAR I MUST BE GETTING RUSTY...
STILL, HOLMES, YOU DID MANAGE TO FIND THE VIOLIN...
OH PLEASE, DOCTOR, LET US FORGET THAT DEPLORABLE ADVENTURE! AND I WOULD BE GRATEFUL IF YOU THREW AWAY THE STORY YOU'VE STARTED WRITING WITHOUT INFORMING ME...
BUT... HOW DID YOU...
PLEASE, DOCTOR, I WILL NOT OFFEND YOU BY LISTING THE 14 CLUES THAT BETRAYED YOU. LET US RATHER COME BACK TO THESE YOUNG FELLOWS' CASE...
DID YA TALK TO KATYA, SIR? WHAT'S SHE PLANNIN' TO DO, NOW THAT RABÚKIN'S FREE?

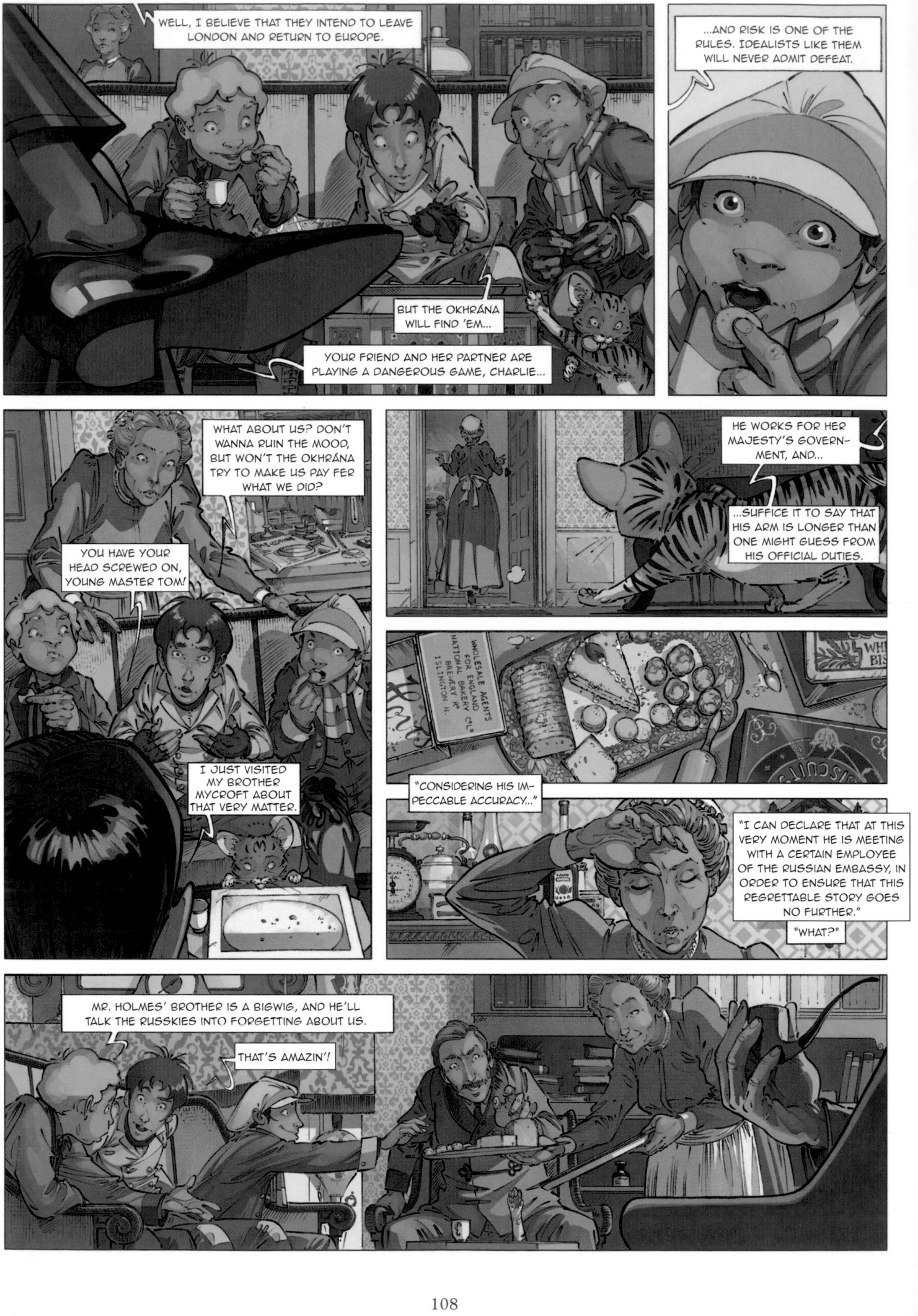
WELL, I BELIEVE THAT THEY INTEND TO LEAVE LONDON AND RETURN TO EUROPE.
BUT THE OKHRÁNA WILL FIND 'EM...
YOUR FRIEND AND HER PARTNER ARE PLAYING A DANGEROUS GAME, CHARLIE...
...AND RISK IS ONE OF THE RULES. IDEALISTS LIKE THEM WILL NEVER ADMIT DEFEAT.
WHAT ABOUT US? DON'T WANNA RUIN THE MOOD, BUT WON'T THE OKHRÁNA TRY TO MAKE US PAY FER WHAT WE DID?
YOU HAVE YOUR HEAD SCREWED ON, YOUNG MASTER TOM!
I JUST VISITED MY BROTHER MYCROFT ABOUT THAT VERY MATTER.
HE WORKS FOR HER MAJESTY'S GOVERN-MENT, AND...
...SUFFICE IT TO SAY THAT HIS ARM IS LONGER THAN ONE MIGHT GUESS FROM HIS OFFICIAL DUTIES.
WHOLESALE AGENTS FOR ENGLAND NATIONAL BAKERY CO. BREWERY Rd ISLINGTON N.
"CONSIDERING HIS IM-PECCABLE ACCURACY..."
"I CAN DECLARE THAT AT THIS VERY MOMENT HE IS MEETING WITH A CERTAIN EMPLOYEE OF THE RUSSIAN EMBASSY, IN ORDER TO ENSURE THAT THIS REGRETTABLE STORY GOES NO FURTHER."
"WHAT?"
MR. HOLMES' BROTHER IS A BIGWIG, AND HE'LL TALK THE RUSSKIES INTO FORGETTING ABOUT US.
THAT'S AMAZIN'!

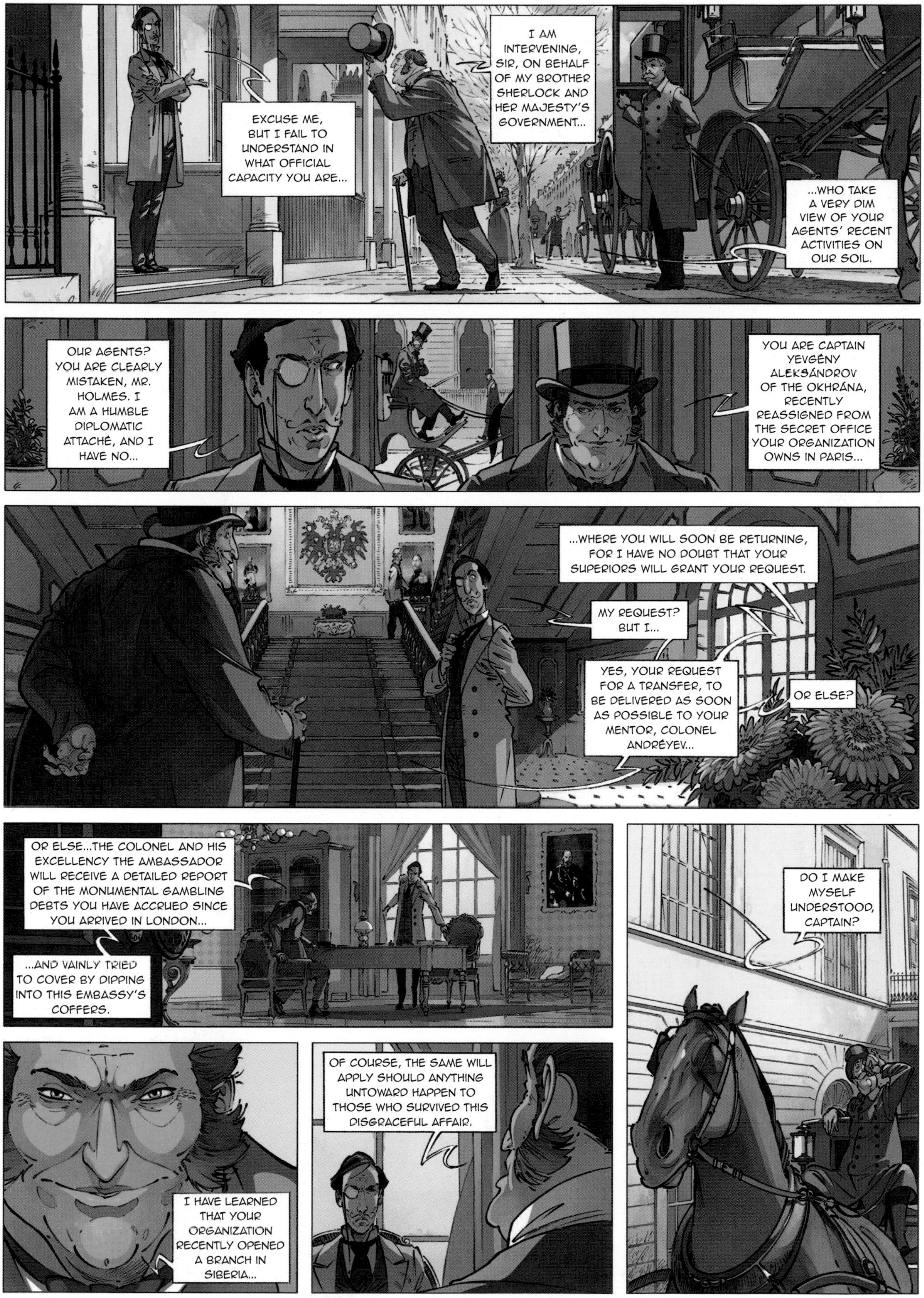
EXCUSE ME, BUT I FAIL TO UNDERSTAND IN WHAT OFFICIAL CAPACITY YOU ARE...
I AM INTERVENING, SIR, ON BEHALF OF MY BROTHER SHERLOCK AND HER MAJESTY'S GOVERNMENT...
...WHO TAKE A VERY DIM VIEW OF YOUR AGENTS' RECENT ACTIVITIES ON OUR SOIL.
OUR AGENTS? YOU ARE CLEARLY MISTAKEN, MR. HOLMES. I AM A HUMBLE DIPLOMATIC ATTACHÉ, AND I HAVE NO...
YOU ARE CAPTAIN YEVGÉNY ALEKSÁNDROV OF THE OKHRÁNA, RECENTLY REASSIGNED FROM THE SECRET OFFICE YOUR ORGANIZATION OWNS IN PARIS...
...WHERE YOU WILL SOON BE RETURNING, FOR I HAVE NO DOUBT THAT YOUR SUPERIORS WILL GRANT YOUR REQUEST.
MY REQUEST? BUT I...
YES, YOUR REQUEST FOR A TRANSFER, TO BE DELIVERED AS SOON AS POSSIBLE TO YOUR MENTOR, COLONEL ANDRÉYEV...
OR ELSE?
OR ELSE...THE COLONEL AND HIS EXCELLENCY THE AMBASSADOR WILL RECEIVE A DETAILED REPORT OF THE MONUMENTAL GAMBLING DEBTS YOU HAVE ACCRUED SINCE YOU ARRIVED IN LONDON...
...AND VAINLY TRIED TO COVER BY DIPPING INTO THIS EMBASSY'S COFFERS.
I HAVE LEARNED THAT YOUR ORGANIZATION RECENTLY OPENED A BRANCH IN SIBERIA...
OF COURSE, THE SAME WILL APPLY SHOULD ANYTHING UNTOWARD HAPPEN TO THOSE WHO SURVIVED THIS DISGRACEFUL AFFAIR.
DO I MAKE MYSELF UNDERSTOOD, CAPTAIN?

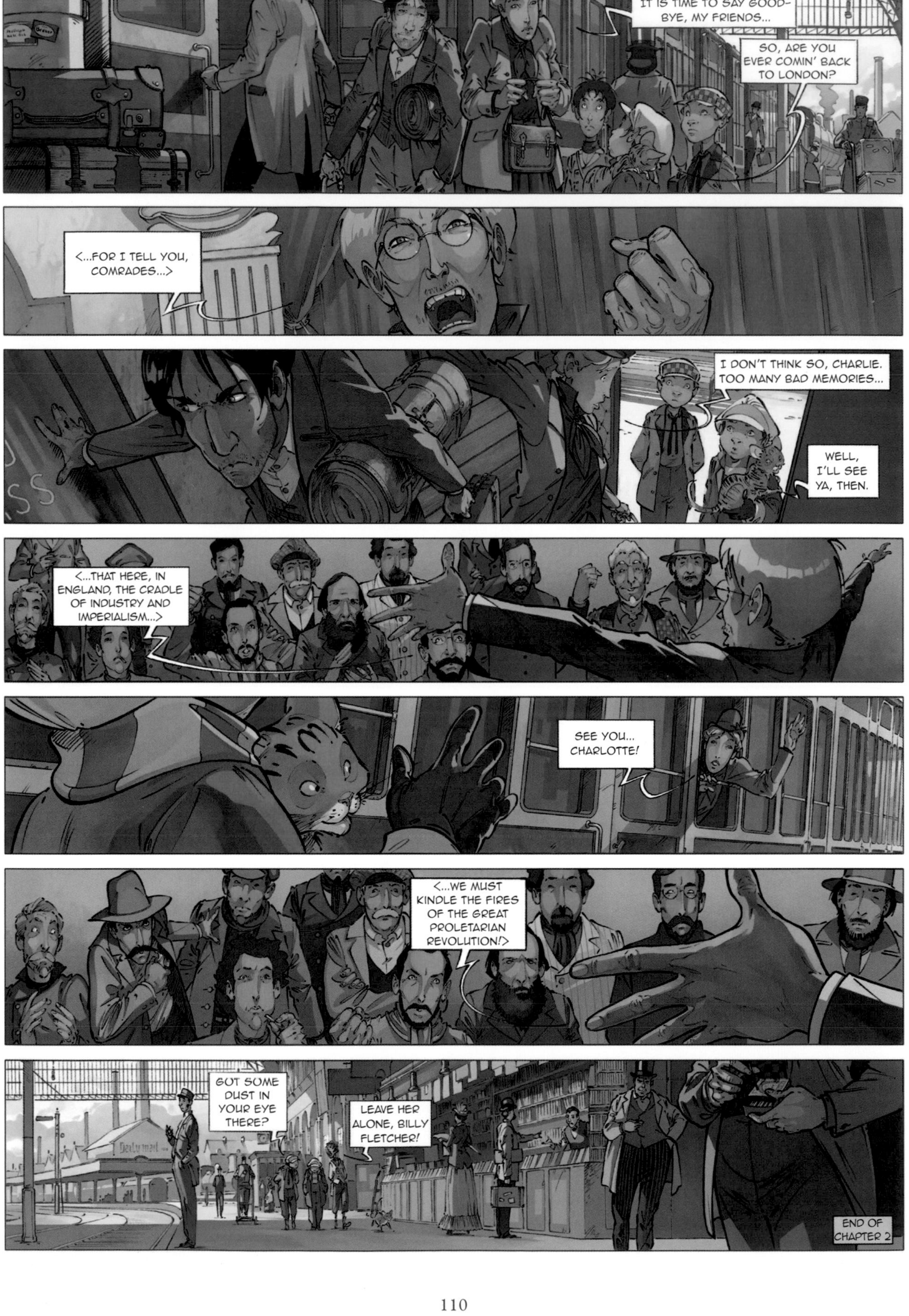
IT IS TIME TO SAY GOOD-BYE, MY FRIENDS...
SO, ARE YOU EVER COMIN' BACK TO LONDON?
<...FOR I TELL YOU, COMRADES...>
I DON'T THINK SO, CHARLIE. TOO MANY BAD MEMORIES...
WELL, I'LL SEE YA, THEN.
<...THAT HERE, IN ENGLAND, THE CRADLE OF INDUSTRY AND IMPERIALISM...>
SEE YOU... CHARLOTTE!
<...WE MUST KINDLE THE FIRES OF THE GREAT PROLETARIAN REVOLUTION!>
GOT SOME DUST IN YOUR EYE THERE?
LEAVE HER ALONE, BILLY FLETCHER!
END OF CHAPTER 2

www.insighteditions.com
PO Box 3088
San Rafael, CA 94912

Find us on Facebook:
www.facebook.com/InsightEditionsComics

Follow us on Twitter:
@InsightComics

Follow us on Instagram:
Insight_Comics

Original Title: Les Quatre de Baker Street vol. 1
Authors: J.B. Djian, Olivier Legrand, David Etien

Library of Congress Cataloging-in-Publication Data available.

ISBN: 978-1-60887-878-9

Publisher: Raoul Goff
Executive Editor: Vanessa Lopez
Senior Editor: Mark Irwin
Managing Editor: Alan Kaplan
Art Director: Chrissy Kwasnik
Production Editor: Elaine Ou
Production Manager: Alix Nicholaeff
Production Assistants: Pauline Kerkhove Sellin and Sylvester Vang

ROOTS of PEACE
REPLANTED PAPER

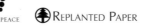

Insight Editions, in association with Roots of Peace, will plant two trees for each tree used in the manufacturing of this book. Roots of Peace is an internationally renowned humanitarian organization dedicated to eradicating land mines worldwide and converting war-torn lands into productive farms and wildlife habitats. Roots of Peace will plant two million fruit and nut trees in Afghanistan and provide farmers there with the skills and support necessary for sustainable land use.

Manufactured in China by Insight Editions

10 9 8 7 6 5 4 3 2 1